Hearts
& Homes

Hearts & Homes

How creative cooks
fed the soul and spirit
of America's Heartland, 1895-1939

Rae Katherine Eighmey

Published by Farm Progress Companies

Designed by Al Casciato
Edited by Destiny Justic Scott

Illustrations have come from issues of *Wallaces' Farmer*,
1895-1939. Material for the Time Lines was drawn from
issues of *Wallaces' Farmer* and from "Chronicle of the
20th Century," Clifton Daniel, editor in chief.
Copyright Chronicle Publications, Inc.,
Mount Kisco, New York, 1987.

Published by Farm Progress Companies
191 South Gary Avenue
Carol Stream, IL 60188
Telephone: (630) 690-5600
www.farmprogress.com

First Printing

New ideas, like young animals, are weak defenseless things.
But given a little food they grow amazingly
H.A. Wallace
October 15, 1926

For those who believe in progress and truth and work to promote both.

And always, for John.

A Brief Introduction to *Wallaces' Farmer*

The floor of my study is covered with copies from *Wallaces' Farmer.* An article praising sleeping porches here, economic analysis of farms practices in the 1920s there, Josh-Away jokes and "Country Air" opinions. Pieces on soil conservation, hybridization of corn, soybeans as a cash crop, mechanization, women on the farm, the role of the farm in national policy and much, much more still catch my eye. There is scarcely an issue of importance to the farm or the nation that was not carefully studied and written about in the pages of *Wallaces' Farmer.*

Through the first half of the 20th Century, *Wallaces' Farmer* was the singular product of three generations of dedicated, progressive agricultural journalists. Father, sons and grandsons primarily — Henry Wallace known as Uncle Henry, Henry C., John P. and Henry A. Uncle Henry's wife Nannie began writing a woman's column, "Hearts and Homes." Their daughters Josephine, Ruth and Harriet were frequent contributors to the homemaking and recipe columns over the years.

The masthead statement on every issue of *Wallaces' Farmer* says it all: "Good Farming Clear Thinking, Right Living."

Reading back issues is to discover the history of 20th Century Midwestern agriculture. Every trend, every concern, every opportunity for betterment was explored by *Wallaces'* editors. The articles were written with unfailing dedication to the improvement of farming practices, rural prosperity and farm life. As Uncle Henry's first editorial said, "The paper is dedicated to the farmer and its purpose is to voice his thoughts and feelings as well as his interests. Its supreme aim would be the advancement of agricultural interests of the west and especially the state of Iowa."

The Wallaces didn't limit their role to writing about farm practices and economics. They established programs to work for and benefit farmers. They established a fund to reward subscribers for the capture of thieves in the countryside. They set up a buying service to seek hard-to-find items of particular interest to farm wives. They established the Master Farmer and Master Farm Homemaker programs rewarding outstanding farmers and citizens. The Wallace family was active in national politics. Henry C. served as Secretary of Agriculture under President Coolidge. Henry A., his son, served not only as Secretary of Agriculture, but as Vice President in Franklin Roosevelt's administration. He also actively experimented in hybridization of corn, leading to better seed and practices for farmers.

The family of *Wallaces' Farmer* extends to readers who corresponded with each other through the pages of the paper. Questions were asked and answered, advice exchanged. This outreach was actively promoted by the Wallace family editors. This larger *Wallaces'* family made important contributions to the paper.

In the pages that follow I have tried to capture some of the important and small contributions of the Wallaces farmers to American agriculture. The pieces I've excerpted in this book are a small percentage of the enlightening pieces I've read during the past year. I could have written a book four times as long and still wished to find space for "one more article."

Uncle Henry called farming a science, a business and a life. He saw himself as a friendly, advice-giving uncle. As he said in his "Letters to Farm Folks," "(T)he biggest thing in life, whether in city or country, is to be just a fine human being, interested in all things that interest or should interest human beings."

I hope you find some of those things in this book.

Introduction

Hearts and Homes

The title Mrs. Wallace selected for her *Wallaces' Farmer* column is as meaningful now at the beginning of the 21st Century as it was at the beginning of the 20th Century.

She could not know in September 1895 of the changes that would come in farm and home life, the challenges of war, peace and economics and the courage each person would require not only to carry on, but to succeed. The bedrock values in this three-word title resonate today. We do not know what the next five, ten or thirty years will bring, but if we keep true to the hope instilled in the anonymous poem from which Nannie Wallace took her inspiration, we will be inspired, too:

"Hearts and homes, sweet word of pleasure,
Music breathing as ye fall.
Making each the other's treasure
Once divided losing all.
Homes, you may be high or lowly,
Hearts alone can make ye holy;
Be the dwelling ere so small,
Having love it boasteth all —
Hearts and homes."

In this past year I have learned much from my research in the fragile pages of *Wallaces' Farmer*. Recipes by the dozen presented rediscovered combinations, methods and flavors. Time flew as I read and marked recipes and articles for copying. Decades passed before my eyes in sepia-toned pages. Much more than a research project, I became absorbed as I witnessed discovery and struggle. The pages of *Wallaces' Farmer* are filled with the immediacy of progress.

But I always begin with the food. I've worked with thousands of recipes during the past decade, tested and tasted hundreds. I've learned a lot, enough to answer the questions that frequent my presentations:

"Why do you fuss with all those old recipes? They must be hard to make."

"Health food. I bet those recipes are full of fat. No one could have eaten healthfully back then."

"I'm sure those old recipes are interesting, but tastes have changed. We don't eat like they did back then."

Whether people are talking about recipes from the 1840s or the 1920s, they approach the recipes with skepticism. Sure, it is interesting to read through old cookbooks, they say, but no one in her right mind would want to cook from them. There must have been improvements in our cuisine in the past century. We simply must eat better now.

I disagree. It is hard to beat foods prepared with ingredients fresh from the farm. This collection of *Wallaces' Farmer* recipes from 1893 to 1939, and my earlier book "Prairie Kitchen" with recipes from 1841 to 1900, powerfully demonstrate how wrong our preconceptions are. Farm cooks were as concerned about efficiency and ease of preparation as we are today. Our tasks may be different, but they were certainly no less busy than we. Healthful cooking begins on the farm. Countless recipes and articles stress the importance of matching nutrition with the amount of work a person needs to do. Finally, the flavor combinations, whether complex in the early recipes or simple during the 20s and 30s, are delightfully different from what most of us prepare today. The food was good then, and it is great now. I know I am a better cook because I have worked with these recipes. I use them all the time, even when I'm not working on a cookbook.

Finding new ways of doing things from old friends; indeed this is how I think of the *Wallaces' Farmer* writers and editors. The subscribers, too, who sent in their best recipes or responded to contest requests or wrote letters to the editors. These good folks are friends as well. I feel as though I know Frank Wheery, whose winning entry to the Men's cooking contest is in chapter 17. Some women have more than one recipe included. I looked at the recipes first and only after testing them, paid attention to the name of the contributor. My hat is off to Mrs. R.E. Lucas of Holt, Nebraska and Mrs. Clive Butler of Audubon County, Missouri. The *Wallaces' Farmer* editors selected several of their recipes for publication, often paying them $1 for each one printed in the Cookery Corner. I have, however, modernized the recipes, rewriting ingredient lists and directions to include standard measurements, mixing and cooking instructions. Wherever possible I have adapted recipe directions to take advantage of microwaves and other appliances.

As wonderful as the recipes are, it is impossible to write only about the food. The history of these dynamic years informs our understanding of the recipes, and the cuisine helps us see the impact of history on farm families. I selected editorial material to cover the significant and interesting events of the first part of the 20th century. This is a personal selection. I hope what interested me will be of interest to you. In this book I have tried to let the voices of the past speak for themselves. So much happened during these years — World War I, The Depression, women's suffrage, electrification and mechanization on the farm, radio, telephone, and the automobile. It is important to read what the people on the farm and the *Wallaces'* editors thought at the time. We have organized this book to take advantage of this wealth of information. In addition to regular recipe chapters, with a little bit of history in them, there are chapters focused on events with a few recipes.

There are 11 Time Line pages placed throughout the book, covering the events during a presidential term of office. I found as I was working with this material my recollection of events was a bit shaky. It helped me to understand what was going on to have the historic highlights on a list. On those pages I've included quotations from *Wallaces' Farmer* to highlight the paper's impact on progress and political issues.

I hope you enjoy visiting the *Wallaces' Farmer* family as much as I have.

About the name. For the first 50 years of publication the name of the paper was spelled *Wallaces' Farmer*. The use of the plural possessive apostrophe indicating a publication very much a product of the Wallace family. I have used that spelling as appropriate for the time period covered.

RE This symbol appears next to comments I've written about some of the recipes, as well as with personal introductions to a few of the chapters. These editorial notes are varied and include more information about the recipe, cooking tips, comments on history, ways to use the recipe, and even an opinion or two.

Contents

■ **November 1895** Wallace family, Henry, Henry C. and John P. publish *Wallaces' Farmer* — *"The paper is dedicated to the farmer and its purpose would be to voice his thoughts and feelings as well as his interests and the voice would not be that of a corporation without conscience or soul but that of a living man responsible at once to public opinion and that higher law by which men are to be judged. Its supreme aim would be the advancement of agricultural interests of the west and especially the state of Iowa."*

■ *Wallaces'* realized from the first that no permanent or successful agriculture could be built up on corn growing alone; that there must be rotation of crops, the growing of grasses and cattle to eat the grass. Pioneer in calling attention to the value of the manure spreader, co-operative creameries, elevators, the value of the silo — in short, anything that made for real farm progress.

■ **November 1896** McKinley beats William Jennings Bryant, 271-176 electoral votes. McKinley's slogan: "Vote for McKinley and the Full Dinner Pail."

■ **March 1, 1897** *Wallaces' Farmer* editorial — *"Just now one of the most important lines of work is to educate farmers to the necessity of maintaining a first-class physical condition in their soils. We are talking much of the time to deaf ears. When we get farmers to realize this, they will see for themselves the necessity of supplying vegetable matter to maintain and increase the humus supply, and thus keep their soils well stored with nitrogen. They will see the necessity of rotation of crops."*

■ Spanish American War.

■ **April 30, 1900** Hawaii made territory of United States.

■ **October 30, 1900** Official United States Census reports population at 76 million in the 45 states (1 in 7 is foreign born).

■ **November 6, 1900** William McKinley reelected president, New York Governor Theodore Roosevelt elected vice-president. Their slogan: "Four More Years of a Full Dinner Pail" and "Let Well Enough Alone." Electoral votes 292-155.

CHAPTER 1

Threshers

Preparing and Serving a Dinner for Threshers
Farmer's Daughter July 31, 1905

Beef is the best and most convenient meat to serve. If you buy a pound for each man to be fed and two or three pounds extra you will always have enough meat and just a little extra.

Be sure to have your pickles ready and put aside for use, as threshers always enjoy them. Beets and cucumbers are both very nice.

Lay aside all "style" in serving, but give the men good, clean, wholesome food, and of the very best that your larder contains. Remember that you are serving your neighbors and that they are working hard.

Threshing is the ideal topic for the first chapter of "Hearts and Homes." No activity reflects more powerfully the changes in farming practices and the related effects on home life during these years than bringing in the harvest.

The editors of Wallaces' Farmer *were progressively analytical regarding mechanization of farm labor. Results of field trials were reported. Farmers were interviewed to provide economic comparisons of one method to another.*

It is hard to imagine today what it must have been like to bring in a crop with a harvesting machine such as the room-sized thresher in the Smithsonian Institution, requiring a team of 40 horses to pull it through the field to cut and thresh. Old time Thresher's Reunions held around the Midwest help us to experience steam power and gasoline engine improvements.

However we get the human in the words of the women, and some men, who wrote into "The Hearts and Homes" columns describing the menus, serving style and preparations for feeding the work crews. As one writer suggested, "As soon as the seeds are sown, the farm wives begin planning their harvest menus."
As much as is written about the hard work for the men in the field, preparing a meal that would, as the writers were concerned with, provide all the nutrition necessary for their work was just as hard for the women.

Rochester Cake

3 eggs, separated
2 cups sugar
2/3 cup butter
1 cup milk
3 cups flour, sift before measuring
2 teaspoons baking powder
To half the mixture add
   1 tablespoon molasses
   1 cup chopped raisins
   1 tablespoon each cloves, cinnamon, nutmeg

Preheat the oven to 350 degrees F. Beat the egg whites until they form stiff peaks and set them aside. Cream the butter and sugar. Add the egg yolks and beat well. Add the baking powder and half the flour, then the milk, and finally the remaining flour. Mix well after each addition. Gently fold in the beaten egg whites. Grease and flour four 8-inch cake pans. Pour half the batter into two of the pans. Stir the molasses, raisins and spices into the remaining half of the batter and pour into the two remaining cake pans. Bake until the layers are firm to the touch, 20 to 25 minutes. Cool in the pans for 5 to 10 minutes and finish cooling on wire racks. Frost between layers with a vanilla buttercream frosting (see recipe in Cakes chapter).

Sweet Relish

1 peck of ripe green tomatoes
6 sweet green or red peppers
6 onions
2 cups chopped celery
1/2 cup salt
2 tablespoons cinnamon
2 tablespoons white mustard seed
6 cups vinegar
3 cups brown sugar, firmly packed
1/2 cup grated horseradish

Chop all the vegetables. Mix with the salt and allow to stand at least 4 hours, or overnight, in a very cool place, or refrigerate. Drain off the accumulated juices and rinse to remove excess salt. Combine the vinegar and brown sugar in a very large pot. Bring to a boil, add the cinnamon and mustard seed. Add the vegetables and return to a boil, reduce the heat and simmer for 15 minutes. Stir in the horseradish. Seal in sterilized jars and process according to manufacturer's guidelines, or store in the refrigerator.

Threshing Meals

To Hearts and Homes

In my neighborhood, which is "somewhere in Iowa," the farmers say that as soon as seed oats are sown, their wives begin worrying as to what they shall cook for the threshers. While that is not quite true, yet, as my garden grows, I begin wondering what will be there at threshing time — will I have plenty of ripe tomatoes, etc.?

I have been a farmer's wife for the past nine years and in that time have cooked for many men — carpenters, harvest hands, and on down the list. I like to serve a good meal; but, to keep cooking from becoming monotonous I aim to avoid temptation of serving too many dishes at one meal, so I may have a change for the next.

I have learned that some men in our neighborhood like one form of food and some another. I am sending what I think a good menu for our neighborhood as regards the number of dishes:

Meats – *roast beef, cold sliced meat*
Vegetables – *mashed potatoes and brown gravy, peas, corn, sliced tomatoes, salad, pickles*
Spreads – *jams, jelly, butter*
Bread – *wheat and rye or graham*
Dessert – *pie, cake and fruit*
Beverage – *coffee (hot), cold tea*

Meals for Threshers

In establishing the amount needed for a crew of men, for safety, the amount should be increased one-fourth. Remember in preparing meals that variety increases consumption. More ounces of meat, potatoes, peas, beans, beets, pie and sauce will be required than if the variety was limited to meat, potatoes, beets and pie. In planning the meal for threshers, two vegetables, one pickle or salad, and one meat is an abundance with dessert. If cabbage salad or cold slaw is served and beets were on the menu we would serve the beets as a vegetable and not as a pickle or salad. Use more vegetables if vegetables are plentiful, as they save meat. Don't give a choice of meats or desserts.

A harvest hand will not know he is being stinted if he is given all he can eat of a few dishes. If he is given small helpings of many dishes — tho he has all he can eat — he will feel as if he were not well fed. Then, too, men will take a portion of everything passed and more is left on the plates where too much of a variety is offered. The best way to practice the gospel of the clean plate is to supply food which fills and satisfies without creating an abnormal appetite by serving tidbits which tickle the palate but have little food value. Ice cream is a luxury but also a wholesome food. If cream and ice are abundant it may cost no more than pie, but pie a la mode would be extravagant.

An item in an exchange claimed that the Kansas farmers were giving up pie. Our experience is that the average man feels better fed after eating a meal which finishes up with pie than after eating a pudding. Pudding usually requires a sauce; we doubt there is any saving in money by substituting pudding for pie and we would serve pie. Threshers deserve that much humoring. Two desserts are unnecessary and in this year too wasteful.

Pork Cottage Pie

2 eggs, separated
6 potatoes
2 carrots, cut in 1/2-inch chunks
2 turnips, cut in 1/2-inch chunks
2 tablespoons butter
2 tablespoons flour
1 cup milk
1 onion, cut up fine
3 cups cooked, chopped pork

Cook the potatoes and mash them. Set aside to cool to lukewarm. Cook the carrots and turnips and drain well.

Make a white sauce by melting the butter in a 2- to 3-quart saucepan. Stir in the flour and cook until bubbly. Add the milk and lightly beaten egg yolks. Cook, stirring constantly until the sauce is thickened. Add the onion, vegetables and chopped pork.

In a large grease-free bowl, whip the egg whites until stiff. Fold in the mashed potatoes.

Preheat the oven to 350 degrees F. Lightly grease a deep 9-inch square pan. Put half the potato mixture in the bottom, pour in the pork mixture and top with the remaining mashed potatoes. Bake until the top is a rich golden brown, about a half hour.

Whole Wheat Raisin Nut Bread

Mrs. Clive Butler, Audubon County, Missouri

3 eggs, separated
2 cups whole wheat flour
2 teaspoons baking powder
1/2 cup butter
1 cup brown sugar, firmly packed
1 cup honey
1 teaspoon vanilla
2/3 cup milk
1 cup walnuts
3/4 cup raisins

Preheat the oven to 350 degrees F. Beat the egg whites until stiff and set aside. Combine the whole wheat flour and baking powder and sift 4 or 5 times to assure a light loaf of bread. In a large mixing bowl, cream the butter and sugar. Stir in the honey, vanilla and egg yolks. Add half the flour mixture, then the milk and finally the remaining flour, beating well after each addition. Stir in the walnuts and raisins and finally gently fold in the beaten egg whites. Pour the batter into two large (1 1/2-pound) loaf pans or two 1-pound loaf pans and a mini-loaf pan. Bake until the center is firm and the bread is just beginning to pull away from the sides, about 50 minutes.

Threshing Time

"One who learned how"

I will give my menu that I used last year and then tell of my preparations. In defense of the menu in case some food expert should happen to read this and raise their hands in holy horror of such a conglomeration as this menu appears to be, I wish to state that in cooking for some twenty-odd men perhaps some relish tomatoes and despise corn and vice versa. Therefore we can not sit down and figure out a threshers' meal according to the amount of calories to be eaten during the day, but must try to fix the dishes that will be palatable to all. So on with the menu:

Bread   Butter

Roast beef   Potatoes   Gravy

Noodles   Baked beans   Cabbage salad

Sliced tomatoes   Sliced cucumbers   Scalloped corn

Apple pie   Cheese   Custard pie   Fruit cake

The roast beef was prepared in the winter. I roasted the meat in the oven while cold packing meat for summer use. I then packed it in fruit jars, putting a piece of suet on top and processed it from one-half to an hour's time. Four or five quarts was sufficient for a threshing meal. I just emptied it from the jars into a roaster and let it cook thru, making gravy from the stock that melted from the meat.

The noodles I made several days before, letting them dry thoroughly and then packing them in an air-tight can. The noodles on threshing day were cooked in broth that I had canned in the winter when canning meat. The beans I baked two weeks before threshing time one day while I was ironing and when they were done, sealed them up in jars, processed for a few minutes and set away.

It is the little details that get so on our nerves when we are in a rush. The bread was baked the day before. The apple pie was made the day before and the crust rolled and fitted for the custard pie which I filled the next morning. The fruit cake I made the first of July and had it stored away in some big round marshmallow tins.

The day before threshing I swept and cleaned the house and in the evening peeled a bucket of potatoes. In the morning I get together my array of jars and combine in the manner and way in which the contents belong. I had a dishpan of good hot suds and soon had all the fruit jars washed and presto, my dinner was prepared without one bit of nervousness to hinder in the preparation.

Cooking for Threshers

Cooking for threshers means work. Whether or not this is congenial work depends upon the point of view of the farmer's wife. The meal that is cooked in a spirit of rebellion tho it be ever so elaborate, will not taste as good as that prepared with the attitude of getting ready a "good tuck in" for a lot of hungry boys.

More than one farmer has lost a good hand because his wife skimped at the table. A good meat for threshers is beef. A dish which is always sure to please is round steak cut thick and prepared like **Swiss steak.** Have the meat cut an inch or more thick. With the rolling pin pound flour, salt and pepper into it — as much flour as it will take. Then brown on both sides in hot fat, being careful not to burn. Put in a little boiling water, cover tightly and let simmer on top of the stove or in the oven for two hours. Make plenty of good milk gravy to eat with this. Serve with hot mashed potatoes, one side dish of vegetables. Good bread and butter with a spread of some kind. Threshers are tired, sugar and sweets act as a stimulant and are absorbed by the system quicker than other food elements.

However, no farmer's wife needs suggestions as to what to cook for threshers; as we have said before, give them a full meal, and a hearty welcome if the threshers' dinner is to be a real success.

Tomato Catsup

1 6 pound can tomato puree
1 1/3 cup sugar
2/3 cup vinegar
1 teaspoon celery seed
1/2 teaspoon dry mustard
1/2 teaspoon cayenne pepper
1/4 teaspoon cinnamon
1 medium onion, minced

Combine all ingredients in a large sauce pan. Cook over low heat until the mixture is thickened, stirring frequently. Pour into sterilized jars and keep refrigerated.

October 5, 1928
Patchwork Thoughts

I see that the law is being tested in regard to whether women have to give their ages and birth dates at the polls. It seems that there are several hundred women here in Iowa who are objecting to having to tell what they regard as a sacred secret and also, as someone has said, what the beauty parlors hide.

Keeping the Corn Huskers Fit

"Gee, mother, things never tasted so good!"
And mother smiles as she places on the table a huge volcano of steaming mashed potatoes with its crater of butter streaming over and down the sides. There's ham and eggs, too, and pudding and jam and steaming coffee, for she knows that a few things but plenty of each of them is the cooking rule to follow in keeping her cornhusker fit.

Beef stew to serve four or five very hungry persons
4 strips bacon
6 medium sized onions, peeled and cut in chunks
2 1/2 pounds round or chuck steak, cut in one-inch pieces
1/4 cup flour
3 cups boiling water
6 medium sized carrots
5 white turnips
8 rather small potatoes
1 teaspoon salt, optional
1 teaspoon pepper
1 to 2 teaspoon paprika
2 tablespoons catsup, homemade preferred
2 sprigs parsley

Chop up the bacon into small pieces and put it in a large kettle over low to medium heat. Cook, stirring, until the fat has been rendered out. Remove the crispy bacon bits and set aside. Add the onions to the hot bacon drippings and cook over medium heat until they are golden brown.

Shake the meat chunks in the flour until they are well coated. Brown the meat in the bacon fat until it is seared on all sides. Stir frequently to keep from sticking.

Add the boiling water, cover and turn down the heat and simmer for an hour. While the meat is cooking, peel the remaining vegetables and cut into 1-inch chunks. Add the carrots and turnips to the beef mixture, and simmer for another hour. After the second hour, add the potatoes and seasonings. Continue to simmer until the potatoes are done, another 20 to 30 minutes. Garnish with chopped parsley.

There are a lot of good things to be made from the porker that is usually butchered during cornhusking. **Sausage with cabbage** is one of those. Boil several cabbage leaves in salted water until tender, but not soft enough to fall apart. Make small balls of fresh pork shoulder and sear them quickly in hot fat. Grease deep muffin pans and place in each a sausage ball rolled up in a cabbage leaf. Squeeze a few drops of lemon juice over each and bake 20 minutes in a slow oven. Homemade catsup or tomato sauce is poured over just before serving.

Cherry Custard Pie

Ruth Jacobs

Pastry for a one-crust 8- or 9-inch pie
2 cups lightly packed cherries, 2 regular sized cans (about 15 ounces), drained
1 cup sugar
2 tablespoons flour

For the custard:
1 egg
2 tablespoons sugar
1/2 cup heavy cream

Preheat the oven to 425 degrees F. Line the pie plate with the pastry. Combine the cherries, sugar and flour and mix well. Put cherry mixture into the pie crust and bake at 425 for 15 minutes. Then lower the heat and bake at 350 until the filling is almost "set," about 35 more minutes. Make the custard by combining the egg, sugar and cream and mixing very well. Pour the custard over the top of the pie, spreading to cover the pie in a thin layer. Return the pie to the oven until the custard is set, about 10 minutes.

Corn a la Southern

Mrs. R.D. Freeman, Sac County, Iowa

This makes a splendid picnic thresher or just plain supper dish

2 cups corn, cut from the cob, or canned
1 teaspoon salt
1 teaspoon sugar
2 tablespoons minced green pepper
1/4 teaspoon paprika
2 eggs
1 1/2 cups milk
1/2 cup cracker crumbs
2 tablespoons butter

Preheat the oven to 300 degrees F. Combine all ingredients and pour into a well greased casserole. Place this in a large pan and pour hot water around the casserole until the level is half way up the side. Bake until the custard is set, about 25 minutes.

1901·1904

■ **January 22, 1901** Queen Victoria dies, Edward VII crowned King.

■ **January 10, 1901** Rich Texas oilfield Spindletop is struck.

■ **February 15, 1901** Carrie Nation continues her campaign against alcoholic beverages by smashing kegs of beer in Topeka, Kansas bars.

■ **May 11, 1901** Morristown, New Jersey drivers fined for exceeding 8 mile per hour limit going 30 mph in auto race.

■ **August 9, 1901** Oklahoma territory opened to settlers. 6500 homesteaders stake their claims.

■ **September 14, 1901** President McKinley assassinated. Theodore Roosevelt takes oath of office — "I wish to say it shall be my aim to continue absolutely the policy of President McKinley for the peace and prosperity and the honor of our beloved country."

■ **March 9, 1902** American Automobile Association formed to benefit nation's 23,000 car owners.

■ **June 28, 1902** United States to pay $40 million for Panama Canal.

■ **June 19, 1902** President Roosevelt signs irrigation bill to allow sales of public lands to underwrite dam construction in the west. Eastern and Midwestern farmers charge act will increase the amount of agricultural goods when they are already oversupplied.

■ **July 23, 1903** Henry Ford Motor Company sells its first automobile — Model A.

■ **August 21, 1903** First transcontinental auto race ends. Winners took 51 days averaging 80 miles per day.

■ **October 13, 1903** First baseball World Series played. Boston beat Pittsburgh.

■ **December 17, 1903** Wright brothers fly heavier than air plane at Kitty Hawk, North Carolina.

■ 1903 Motion picture "The Great Train Robbery" plays in theaters for five cents' admission.

■ **October 27, 1904** New York city subway opens.

■ **November 8, 1904** Theodore Roosevelt elected president, electoral votes 336-140. Election slogans "Three Cheers for the rough rider" and "We Want Teddy for Four More Years."

■ **December 1904** United States admits 1 million immigrants in 1904. Half are from Italy and Austria-Hungary.

CHAPTER 2

Breads

Champion Bread Bakers' Don'ts
January 9, 1932 Grace M. Ellis

Don't use poor fat, flour or sweetening. A teaspoon of strong
molasses has ruined many a loaf.

Don't guess at measurements unless long and successful
experience has proved your eye to be as accurate as a cup.

Don't use too much flour. A sticky dough makes better
bread than a too stiff one.

Don't begrudge 25 cents for a thermometer to check
the dough temperature unless your finger knows
82 degrees F. when it feels it.

Don't allow the dough to more than double its bulk
unless you want really sour bread.

Don't set pans of rising dough on a warming oven.
This practice has given many a light loaf a heavy bottom.

Don't forget that bread, like babies, will always act the
same if treated the same.

Don't depend upon Lady Luck to give good bread.
She doesn't exist. Yeast, not luck, is the soul of the dough.

Some Recipes from Scotland

Hatie Wallace Ashby

As Mrs. Ashby says, "The oat meal used in these cakes is as fine as granulated sugar." To make them successfully you can process regular oatmeal in a food processor until it is finely ground. The unusual combination of ginger and caraway makes for a very interesting and hearty cake-like bread.

Oat Cake

1 cup finely ground oatmeal
3 tablespoons soft butter
3 tablespoons boiling water

Put the oatmeal into a medium-sized bowl. Add the butter and boiling water. Stir the water around the butter until it is melted, then mix with the rest of the oatmeal. Form the mixture into a ball and roll out quite thin. Originally this would have been baked on a board in front of the fire. You can bake it in the oven, or on foil on the grill. If you are baking, preheat the oven to 350 degrees F. Place the cake on a lightly greased cookie sheet. Bake until light brown, about 15 minutes. On the grill, place the cake on a lightly greased piece of foil and put this over the cooler part of the fire. Watch it carefully.

Parkins

3 1/3 cups finely ground oatmeal
1/2 cup butter
2/3 cup molasses
2/3 cup honey
1 tablespoon ginger
1 tablespoon caraway seed
1/2 teaspoon baking soda
1/4 cup milk

A food processor works well to combine the ingredients in this recipe.
Preheat the oven to 325 degrees F. Cut the butter into the oatmeal until it looks like cornmeal. Stir in the molasses and honey. Add the ginger, caraway seeds and baking soda. Stir in the milk. Pour the mixture into a lightly greased 9-inch square pan. Bake until the center is firm and the cake has begun to shrink away from the sides, about 35 to 40 minutes. Slice into thin pieces when cool.

January 4, 1907

Aunt Charlotte's Recipe for Berry Muffins

This recipe is from an advertisement for Hunts Perfect Baking Powder Company. The ad offered "this and 100 other recipes" to be sent free. If they were as good as this one, they certainly were worth the one-cent stamp.

3/4 cup sugar
2 2/3 cups flour
2 teaspoons baking powder
3/4 cup soft butter
1 1/2 cups milk
1 egg
1 cup blueberries or other berries

Preheat the oven to 350 degrees F. Combine the sugar, flour and baking powder. Cut the butter into the flour until it looks like corn meal. Add the egg and milk. Stir until almost blended and add the berries. Spoon the batter into well greased muffin pans and bake until the muffins are golden brown, about 35 minutes. Makes 12 regular-sized muffins.

October 30, 1908

Winesops

This makes a very large quantity, but they keep well in a cool place and can be frozen. Once you try them, you will be happy to have so many on hand. The name originates from the practice of "sopping" them in wine. But they are dandy just as they are.

1 cup butter
1 1/2 cups brown sugar, firmly packed
1 cup molasses
3 eggs
1/2 teaspoon cinnamon
1/2 teaspoon cloves
1/2 teaspoon allspice
1 teaspoon baking soda
3 1/2 cups flour
1 cup milk
1 cup currants

Preheat the oven to 350 degrees F. Cream the butter and sugar. Stir in the molasses and eggs, mixing well. Combine the dry ingredients and add half to the creamed mixture. Stir in the milk and then the rest of the dry ingredients, mixing well after each addition. Stir in the currants. Spray gem pans with non-stick spray and fill two-thirds full. Bake until firm in the center, about 20 minutes. This makes about 8 dozen miniature muffin size cakes.

Potato Scones

2 cups mashed or riced potatoes, cooled
2 cups flour
2 tablespoons butter
2 teaspoons baking powder
1/2 cup milk, more or less

R E *These are sturdy scones. They have a hearty flavor and would make a very good base for creamed dishes. You do need to use real mashed potatoes, instant will not work.*

Preheat the oven to 425 degrees F. Mix the flour and baking powder. Cut the butter into the mixture until it looks like corn meal. Knead in the mashed potatoes. Add the milk gradually, the amount you will need depends upon how moist the mashed potatoes are. Knead the dough and pat out to 1-inch thick. Cut in squares, place on a lightly greased cookie sheet and bake until the tops are just light brown, 15 to 20 minutes.

November 15, 1895
Iowa's New Sensation

Iowa's "beautiful land" so famed in verse and song, so noted
for all that is good and true, has now another claim to historical
reminiscence. Tradition has long taught that only "the early
bird catches the worm." Alas! For the worm; and alas! For those
early awake on the morning of Oct. 30, 1895 — or those
awakened by the shock of Iowa's earthquake. I am glad
to have been one of the sound sleepers on that day, yet I have
trophies of the terrible shaking up in the ruins of five
China plates and what is more valued and precious,
a quaint old sugar bowl, an heirloom in the family,
over one hundred years old, which the jar of the
earthquake threw from the upper shelf on the side-board
onto the plates beneath, thus breaking them and both lovely
handles off from the ancient sugar bowl.

Health Bread

2 cups Old Fashioned oatmeal
4 cups warm water
2 packages instant rapid rise yeast
2 tablespoons sugar
1 cup milk
2 teaspoons molasses
6 cups whole wheat flour, or more
1 cup bread flour

R&E *This health bread is typical of recipes for breads and other baked goods developed during World War I. Much of the white wheat flour, butter and eggs were reserved for soldiers serving in France and in the United States. Health and War bread and cake recipes are not seen much today, but they are still worth making. I've lightened the original mixture with one cup of bread flour. This is a large recipe. Keep extra loaves in the refrigerator or freezer. They make wonderful toast.*

Combine the warm water and oatmeal and follow the box directions for making oatmeal either in the microwave or on top of the stove. Set aside to cool until lukewarm.
Sprinkle the yeast and sugar on top of the oatmeal gruel and stir. Set aside until the mixture begins to rise. Pour the oatmeal mixture into a very large mixing bowl. Add the milk, molasses and 4 cups of the whole wheat flour and the cup of bread flour. Stir to mix. Begin kneading in the remaining flour until you have a smooth and elastic dough. Place the kneaded dough into a clean, lightly buttered bowl and butter the top. Set aside in a warm place to rise until doubled. Punch the dough down and divide into 5 loaves. You may bake these in greased 1-pound loaf pans or form into round or oblong loaves, like French bread, to be baked on lightly greased cookie sheets.

Allow the dough to rise until doubled. Preheat the oven to 350 degrees F. Bake until the loaves are firm, lightly browned on the bottom and sound hollow when tapped on top, about 25 to 35 minutes depending on the style of bread. If baked in loaf pans, remove the bread from the pan and tip on its side to cool on a rack.

Biscuits

2 cups flour
2 teaspoons baking powder
3 tablespoons fat
3/4 cup milk

Basic directions:
Preheat the oven to 425 degrees F. Combine the flour and baking powder in a medium sized mixing bowl. Cut in the butter until the mixture looks like cornmeal. Stir in the milk until just barely blended. Knead the dough by hand for a minute. Roll or pat out to 1-inch thickness. Cut with a well floured round cutter. Place on ungreased cookies sheets and bake until lightly browned, about 12 minutes.

RKE *This recipe opens a window into meal planning in the 1920s. This one recipe can be made three different ways — with meat, with a fruit filling or with peanut butter. Each of these reflects a specific type of food situation. The meat version, of course, gets the most from leftovers by turning a bit of meat and stock into another meal. The fruit suggested for "Sabbath Evening Tea" reminds us that Sunday dinner was the big meal of the week, and although we may not consider it to be such, the peanut butter version shows the emergence of convenience foods to add protein variety to the menu.*

Meat Filling

Combine 1 cup chopped meat with 1 cup of meat stock or gravy. Roll the dough out to 1/2- inch thickness. Cut into circles a bit larger than usual biscuit size. Butter one half of the circle, leaving the edges clean. Put a tablespoon of the meat filling on top of the butter and fold the remaining half over the filling, pressing the sides together firmly and bake as above.

Sabbath Evening Tea

Fill with a mixture of dried fruits such as apricots and raisins, a berry jam or the Fig Preserves on the following page.

Peanut Butter

Combine 2 tablespoons of peanut butter with the 3/4 cup milk and mix and bake as in the basic directions. You may want to melt the peanut butter in the microwave to make mixing a bit easier.

Fig Preserves

Cut package of dried figs in small pieces, removing the stems. Measure them and add an equal amount of sugar. Place the figs in a sauce pan and barely cover them with water. Add the sugar and simmer until the preserves are thick, stirring frequently.

Nut Bread

1 egg
1/2 cup sugar
1 cup milk
3 cups flour
4 teaspoons baking powder
1 cup nutmeats

Preheat the oven to 350 degrees F. Beat the egg and sugar together until light. Add the milk and mix well. Stir in the flour and baking powder. Lastly, stir in the nuts. Pour the batter into a greased loaf pan. Bake until the top is brown and the bread has begun to pull away from the sides, about 45 minutes.

October 1, 1897
Buying

For sixty years I have followed one method in gathering up the necessaries of the home. A pencil and a small blank book are kept always in sight and when wife thinks of anything that is needed she sets it down; when I think of anything at the hardware store or anywhere else that is needed, I set it down. Sometimes we have more than twenty articles down. In a busy time wife takes the money and butter and eggs if she has them, goes to town and brings home these things. I was never interested enough to know how much money she takes or how much she brings back. It is our plan to never buy anything except what is set down. It is a poor plan for anybody to go into a store and look about to see what they need, or to buy in very small quantities such things as are often needed such as thread, pins, needles, etc. This plan saves some worry and saves coming home having forgotten the most important thing. You may smile over my calico arrangements, but it is better to have too much than too little. We have good fuel in a dry shed that we have not been able to get to for six years. I wish everybody could say this.

— W.L.C., Kearney, Nebraska

Marmalade Biscuits

2 cups flour
1 tablespoon sugar
4 teaspoons baking powder
3 tablespoons butter (the original called for lard)
3/4 cup milk
1 egg, lightly beaten
1/3 cup orange marmalade

Preheat the oven to 350 degrees F. Mix the flour, sugar and baking powder. Cut in the butter until the mixture looks like cornmeal. Combine the milk, egg and marmalade. Stir into the flour mixture. You may need to add up to 1/4 cup more flour depending upon the texture of your marmalade. Quickly mix the dough. Form into loose balls in your hand and place on a well greased baking sheet. Bake until lightly browned, about 15 minutes. Made this way, the biscuits resemble scones. You can roll or pat the dough out and cut with a biscuit cutter if you prefer. Makes 2 dozen 1-inch biscuits.

October 2, 1931

Spoon Bread

2 cups corn meal
2 1/2 cups boiling water
2 tablespoons melted butter
2 eggs
1 1/2 cups buttermilk
1 teaspoon baking soda

Preheat the oven to 425 degrees F. In a medium saucepan, mix water and corn meal, bring to the boiling point, reduce heat and simmer for five minutes. Beat eggs well. Combine with the butter, buttermilk and baking soda. Stir into the corn meal. Beat well and pour into a well greased 9-inch square pan. Bake until golden brown and firm in the center, about 25 minutes. Serve with a spoon from the baking pan.

Coffee Cake

Mrs. Nordholm, Polk County, Iowa

1 package dry yeast
1/3 cup warm water
1 tablespoon sugar
1 small can evaporated milk, about 5 ounces
1/2 cup water, approximate
1 tablespoon very soft butter
3/4 cup sugar
2 egg yolks
1/2 teaspoon ground cardamom
4 to 5 cups bread flour

Enough topping for three braided coffee cake rings:
1/2 cup melted butter
1 cup brown sugar, firmly packed

RKE *The original recipe calls for kneading the dough for 30 minutes. This is a dough that requires a long kneading process. I prefer to make this bread in my food processor with the plastic blade and knead it in there for about 3 minutes. The smooth, elastic dough is wonderful to work with. You may, of course, make this by hand.*

Proof the yeast by combining it with the warm water and sugar. If it begins to bubble up and get frothy, it is good to use. Pour the evaporated milk into a glass measuring cup and add enough water to make 3/4 cup. Put 4 cups of flour in the bowl of the food processor, fitted with the plastic dough blade. Add the yeast mixture, butter, sugar, egg yolks and cardamom.

Begin processing and gradually add the milk and water mixture. Add enough remaining flour to make a dough that is not sticky. Knead in the processor until the dough ball is smooth and elastic. You may need to divide the dough into two parts to do this effectively. Place the dough in a well greased bowl, turn it over to grease the top, cover with plastic wrap and set aside in a warm place to rise until double. This could take up to two hours.

Punch the dough down. Form into coffee cakes as follows: Divide the dough into thirds. Divide each third into thirds. Roll each dough piece into a long thin tube, about 15 inches long. Pinch three of these tubes together at one end and braid them. Form the braid into a ring and place it in an 8-inch pie plate. Brush the top with melted butter and sprinkle with brown sugar. Allow the coffee cakes to rise until doubled, about a half hour. Preheat the oven to 350 degrees F. Place the coffee cakes in the oven and bake until golden brown and the loaves sound hollow when tapped, about 35 minutes.

April 5, 1929

*Small hangers on rods placed low enough
in the closet for children to reach them encourage
children to care for their clothes, teach them
habits of neatness and independence, and relieve
the busy housewife.*

Peanut Butter Bread

4 teaspoons baking powder
3 cups flour
1/2 cup sugar
2 cups milk
1 cup chopped dates
2/3 cup peanut butter

Preheat oven to 350 degrees F. Sift together the baking powder, flour and sugar. Combine the milk and dates into a microwaveable bowl and heat on medium power until the dates are softened, about 4 minutes. Stir in the peanut butter until smooth and add the dry ingredients. Stir quickly, until just blended. Batter will be stiff and lumpy. Divide mixture into six well greased mini-loaf pans. Bake until firm in the center and the bread has begun to pull away from the sides of the pans, about 30 minutes.

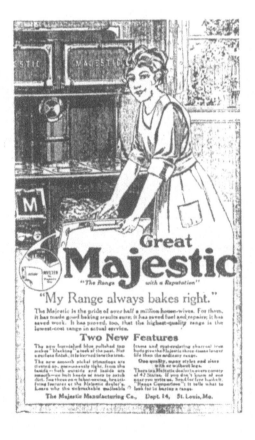

Carrot Bread

1 cup shredded carrots
1 cup brown sugar, firmly packed
1 teaspoon baking soda
1 cup boiling water
2 eggs, beaten
2 tablespoons melted butter
1 cup chopped walnuts
1 1/4 cups whole wheat flour
1 1/2 teaspoons baking powder

Preheat the oven to 350 degrees F. Combine the carrots, brown sugar and baking soda in a medium sized heat-proof bowl. Pour the boiling water over, stir quickly and set aside until the mixture cools. Add the remaining ingredients and stir until just blended. Pour batter into four well greased, mini-loaf pans and bake until the bread is firm in the center and just beginning to pull away from the sides of the pans, about 35 minutes.

October 23, 1925

There is something about crisp fall days
that always makes me want to put on a big
kitchen apron, build a roaring fire in the range
and turn out a full batch – 144 – of those utmost
of delicacies of sugar and spice – gingersnaps.
I remember that the recipe copied from
grandmother's cook book said, "these cookies
will last for six months if kept in a tight jar."
But aside from the times a can full was hidden
away on the top shelf and forgotten about,
I never actually knew any
to last this long.

Coffee Cinnamon Rolls

Mrs. R. E. Lucus, Holt County, Nebraska

> *2 packages instant dry yeast*
> *1/2 cup warm water*
> *2 tablespoons sugar*
> *1 cup coffee, cooled*
> *2 tablespoons melted shortening*
> *1 egg, lightly beaten*
> *1/4 cup sugar*
> *5 to 6 cups bread flour*
>
> **For the filling:**
> *1/3 cup soft butter*
> *3 tablespoons cinnamon*
> *1/2 cup sugar*

Proof the yeast by combining with the warm water and sugar and setting aside until it is foamy. Put 4 1/2 cups flour in a large mixing bowl. Stir in the sugar. Add the yeast mixture, coffee, shortening and egg. Mix well and begin adding additional flour until you have a dough that is not sticky. Knead until it is smooth and elastic. Put the dough in a well greased bowl, turning it so the top is greased. Cover and put in a warm place until it has doubled in bulk. Punch down and roll out until it is 1/2-inch thick, 5 inches wide and 24 inches long. Spread with softened butter. Combine the cinnamon and sugar and sprinkle over the dough. Roll up from the long side. Cut in 1-inch sections. Grease a baking pan and place the rolls cut side down. Allow to rise until doubled. Preheat the oven to 350 degrees F. Bake the rolls until they are light brown on top and sound hollow when tapped.

October 23, 1896
Cheerfulness

This is such a beautiful and interesting world notwithstanding the evil,
the misery and sorrow in it, that we should guard against despondency
and doleful sightings. Sympathy and help can be given in a cheerful heartfelt
manner that will inspire faith in humanity and hope for the future.
Let us look for the good, the benevolent, the heroic, rather than for the un-
lovely and dreary in life. A fine should be imposed on newspapers that steep
the mind with the horrors of suicides, murders, and accidents, the reading
of which becomes a mania that awakens dismal foreboding and
unfits for life's duties.

Cranberry Coffee Cake

For the bottom layer:
1 cup sugar
1 cup water
1 package fresh cranberries
1/8 teaspoon nutmeg

For the dough:
1 cup flour
3 tablespoons sugar
2 teaspoons baking powder
1/4 cup chilled butter
1 egg
2 tablespoons milk

For the topping:
1/4 teaspoon cinnamon
1 tablespoon sugar

Preheat the oven to 350 degrees F. Make the bottom layer. Combine the sugar and water in a heavy saucepan. Bring to boil, lower the heat and simmer for 10 minutes. Add the cranberries and cook until the berries are heated through. Stop cooking before they begin to pop. Set aside. Make the dough by combining the flour, sugar and baking powder. Cut in the butter as though you were making pie crust. Quickly stir in the beaten egg and milk. Put the cranberries for the bottom layer in a greased 9-inch cake pan. Take bits of dough, flatten them slightly between your fingers, place them on top of the cranberries until they are completely covered. Sprinkle with cinnamon and sugar. Bake until the dough is lightly browned and firm. Carefully turn the pan over onto a serving plate, leave the pan on top so the cranberries will settle on top of the coffee cake.

Cranberry Sauce Muffins

2 cups flour
2 teaspoons baking powder
2 tablespoons sugar
1 egg
1 cup milk
3 tablespoons melted butter
1/4 cup cranberry sauce, approximate

Preheat the oven to 350 degrees F. Sift together the flour, baking powder and sugar. Lightly beat the egg and add the milk and slightly cooled melted butter. Stir the liquid ingredients into the dry ingredients until just blended. You will only need about 10 strokes of the spoon. Spray 12 muffin cups with non-stick spray. Drop a tablespoon of the batter into each cup. Place a teaspoon of cranberry sauce in the center of each and top with another tablespoon of batter. Bake until lightly browned, about 20 to 25 minutes.

April 12, 1939

Pan Dressing for Pecan Rolls

Mrs. Benj. Nielsen, Hamilton County, Nebraska

I got this recipe from a better than good baker. It keeps well in the refrigerator.

1 cup brown sugar, firmly packed
4 tablespoons honey
4 teaspoons butter
4 tablespoons water
1/2 teaspoon maple flavoring
1 cup nutmeats

Blend all ingredients in a small sauce pan. Simmer over low heat until the sugar is dissolved. Put in the bottom of the baking pan when you are making pecan rolls and cover with the sliced pinwheels of dough. Bake according to bread dough recipe. Turn the pan upside down on a piece of foil so the dressing can settle on the rolls.

Pecan Rolls

Mrs. Karl Morath, Whiteside County, Illinois

1 cup milk
1/2 cup sugar
1/4 cup melted butter
1/4 cup warm water
1 package instant dry yeast
1 tablespoon sugar
3 eggs
5 to 6 cups bread flour

For the filling:
1/4 cup very soft butter
2/3 cup brown sugar, firmly packed

For the topping:
1/2 cup melted butter
3/4 cup brown sugar, firmly packed
2 ounces chopped pecans

Make the bread dough by scalding the milk and adding the sugar and butter. Set aside to cool to lukewarm. Dissolve the yeast in the warm water and add the tablespoon of sugar and set aside until the mixture is bubbly. In a large mixing bowl combine the milk and yeast mixtures. Stir in 2 cups of flour and the eggs. Begin adding the rest of the flour until you have a stiff, non-sticky dough. Knead until it is smooth and elastic. Put the dough into a well greased bowl, turning it to grease the top. Set aside in a warm place to rise until doubled. Roll the dough out into a rectangle about 1/2-inch thick, 6 inches wide and 24 inches long. Spread with the 1/4 cup soft butter and sprinkle with the brown sugar. Roll the dough into a long sausage shape and cut into 24 pieces. Pour the 1/2 cup melted butter in a baking pan 14 x 17 inches (approximately). Sprinkle with the brown sugar and pecans. Place the rolls cut side down and allow to rise until doubled. Preheat the oven to 350 degrees F. Bake the rolls until they are light brown on top and sound hollow when tapped. Cover the pan with heavy-duty foil, sealing the edges. Turn the pan upside down and let stand for about five minutes so all the topping will drop down onto the rolls.

August 29, 1931

There are a whole lot of middle western boys and girls
not going to college this fall simply because there isn't
money enough. Hope needn't die in the heart of those who
aren't going to college this year. There are thousands
of ways to grow without it. Sometimes stronger individuals
are developed outside the class room than in it.

Sunday Night Supper Bread

1/2 cup dried apricots, cut into small pieces and soaked in warm water for 1/2 hour
1 teaspoon baking soda
2 teaspoons baking powder
2 cups flour
1 tablespoon very soft butter
1/2 teaspoon vanilla
1 egg
Rind of one orange, grated
Juice from one orange, plus boiling water to make one cup
1/2 cup raisins
1/2 cup chopped nuts

Preheat the oven to 350 degrees F. Drain the apricots and pat dry. In a medium mixing bowl combine the baking soda, baking powder and flour. Stir in the butter, vanilla, egg, orange rind, apricots, raisins and chopped nuts. Quickly stir in the orange juice and boiling water. Stir until the batter is just mixed. Pour the batter into a greased and floured bread pan and bake until the bread is firm in the center, about 50 to 60 minutes.

Ham Muffins

Mrs. Charles Knox, Hardin County, Iowa

RKE *You may need to add a bit more milk to make a sfiff, but still loose batter. Some whole wheat flours absorb more liquid then others.*

1/4 cup melted butter
1 egg
1 cup milk
1/4 teaspoon salt
3 teaspoons baking powder
3/4 cup graham flour
1 tablespoon sugar
1 cup flour
3/4 cup minced ham

Preheat the oven to 350 degrees F. Mix together the melted butter, egg and milk. In a medium mixing bowl, combine the salt, baking powder, graham flour, sugar and regular flour. Add the liquid ingredients and ham and stir until just combined. Drop into well greased muffin tins and bake until the tops are golden and the muffins are firm, about 25 minutes.

Waffles

Waffles with honey or waffles with sorghum are "lickin' good for supper." The cook will not need to jump up and down during the meal to turn the waffle iron if she will bake them early and put them on the top rack in the oven with the door left open. Try adding a cup of drained canned corn to add to the waffle batter for a change and see how good they are.

Gingerbread Waffles

3 cups flour
1 1/2 teaspoons ginger
2 teaspoons baking powder
1/4 teaspoon salt
1 cup dark corn syrup
1 tablespoon butter
1/2 cup sour milk
1 egg

Combine the dry ingredients. In a small saucepan, heat corn syrup and butter until the butter is melted. In a measuring cup, add the egg to the milk and beat lightly. Stir the corn syrup into the dry ingredients followed by the milk mixture. Bake in a hot, well oiled waffle iron. Serve with whipped cream.

Waffles

Mrs. Joe Crenshaw, Boone County, Missouri

2 eggs
2 cups flour
2 cups milk
2 tablespoons sugar
2 teaspoons baking powder
1/4 cup melted butter

Separate the eggs. Beat the egg whites until stiff in a perfectly clean bowl and set aside. Mix the dry ingredients together and sift three times. Beat the egg yolks and add to the milk. Combine the milk mixture and the dry ingredients. Stir in the melted butter. Fold in the beaten egg whites. Bake in a hot waffle iron.

1905 · 1908

- **March 4, 1905** Teddy Roosevelt inaugurated for full term.

- **July 1905** World's first drive-in gas station opens in St. Louis.

- **April 19, 1906** Earthquake levels San Francisco.

- **June 30, 1906** Pure Food and Drug Act becomes law, prohibits mishandling or adulteration of all foods and drugs manufactured or shipped in the United States.

- **December 10, 1906** Nobel Peace Prize given to President Roosevelt for his role in ending the war between Japan and Russia.

- **December 31, 1907** American suffragettes opened their campaign for votes for women in New York.

- **February 11, 1908** Edison wins patent rights for motion picture projector.

- **June 18, 1908** Republicans nominate William Howard Taft for president.

- **August 12, 1908** First Model T to roll off Ford assembly line. Cost $850.

- **November 3, 1908** Taft defeats William Jennings Bryant for president, 321-162.

- Election turns on 4 P's – Prosperity, Progressivism, Prosecution of business and economic trusts and Personality.

CHAPTER 3
Soups

October 9, 1925

Once a day is none too often to serve soups. At least they ought to appear four or five times a week. Incidentally, a great number of left-overs such as scraps and trimmings of meat, poultry carcasses, necks and feet, left over vegetables and the outer leaves of celery and lettuce may be used. The heavier soups, those which are hearty enough for a whole meal, are better made from fresh materials, although it is often practical to utilize certain left-overs that are on hand.

April 20, 1917

Nourishing Soups Without Meat

Soups without meat are very nutritious containing both vegetables and milk — which have high food value. It is best to serve a clear soup at the beginning of a heavy dinner, but if the soup is to be the main part of the meal, always serve a thick cream soup or a puree of beans when the menu does not contain meat.

RKE *Many of the soup recipes in* Wallaces' Farmer *were simply purees of the cooked vegetables simmered with milk and perhaps thickened with butter and flour. These simple soups are quickly made. The only seasonings are salt and pepper. At first I thought they would be bland. However, the combination of ingredients makes for a subtle, delicious soup. You may add more spices or herbs if you like, but try it first with just the salt and pepper. I think you'll be surprised as I was.*

December 24, 1915

Vegetable Soup

4 tablespoons butter
1/2 cup diced carrots
1/2 cup diced turnips
1 cup diced potatoes
1/2 cup diced onion
1/2 cup chopped cabbage
1 tablespoon flour
3 cups tomato juice, or one large can (46-ounce) diced tomatoes
1 tablespoon celery seeds
1/2 teaspoon chopped parsley
1/4 teaspoon black pepper
Salt to taste
1 quart water

In a large frying pan, melt the butter and add the vegetables. Cook, stirring frequently, over medium heat until the vegetables begin to soften. Sprinkle with the flour and continue to cook and stir until the vegetables and flour turn golden. Add the tomato juice and stir to loosen any browned bits. Pour the mixture into a large stock pot or crock pot. Add the seasonings and water. Simmer until the vegetables are tender and the soup is done. If you are doing this on top of the stove, you can finish it up in about 15 to 20 more minutes. If you want to cook it in the crock pot all day, that's fine too.

Pea Vermicelli

4 cups fresh or frozen peas
1 quart milk
2 ounces vermicelli, broken into small pieces

Cook the peas until they are tender. While the peas are cooking, simmer the vermicelli pieces in the milk until they are tender. Puree the peas in a blender or food mill. Add the peas to the milk mixture and blend. Serve with small pieces of crisp buttered toast or croutons floating on top.

April 20, 1917

Peanut Soup

2 cups peanuts
1 slice onion
1 stalk celery
1 quart milk
2 tablespoons butter
2 tablespoons flour
Salt and pepper to taste

RKE *This recipe begins with raw peanuts. You can use unsalted roasted peanuts. However the cooking process can take quite a while until either type is tender enough to "pass through a sieve" as in the original directions. You may substitute 1/2 cup peanut butter for the 2 cups of nuts, and cook the onion and celery until tender.*

Put the peanuts, chopped onion and celery in a saucepan with a lid. Add just enough water to keep them from sticking, perhaps 1/4 to 1/2 cup depending upon the size of the pan. Cover and cook over very low heat until the peanuts are tender. Drain the water, reserving it. Puree the nuts and vegetables either by pressing them through a sieve or food mill or in the blender. Use the reserved cooking water as needed. In a larger sauce pan, melt the butter and stir in the flour. Cook until the mixture starts to bubble. Add the milk, stirring until the mixture thickens slightly. Whisk in the peanut puree and simmer, but do not let the soup come to a boil.

April 15, 1919

One thing the automobile has done for women is that it has made a costume suitable for driving the fashion. Long auto coat, the close-fitting hat, the veil to protect from wind and sun, are as suitable for the woman who drives to town on the seat of the spring wagon as for the woman who rolls along in her limousine.

The Point of View

A friend was chuckling over the difference a two years course in an agricultural college had wrought in his son.

"The year that boy went to college," he said, "my south field was awful thin. One day, Mr. Blank looked over the fence where John and I were plowing and offered me a heap of well-rotted manure from an old barn. John was taking a load of corn to town and I told him to hitch onto the old wagon and fetch a load of manure when he came home. Do you think he did it? Not he. I had to send the hired man because John was too tony to ride home on a load of manure."

"But last year," he smiled reminiscently, "after John had had a two year course in agriculture he came home from town with a wagon load of manure reaching up to the top of double side boards.

"I nudged his ma when he drove into the gate. 'What's that you've brought home with you?' I asked.

"The rascal just grinned at me. 'I've brought home a great load of humus,' he said."

Cream of Celery Soup

1 bunch celery, cleaned and chopped, about 4 cups
2 cups water
2 tablespoons flour
2 cups milk
3 tablespoons cream
1 teaspoon pepper

Clean the celery and remove the "strings." Cut into 1/2-inch slices. Place in a 2 1/2- to 3-quart saucepan. Add the water, bring to a boil, lower the heat and cover. Simmer until the celery is tender, about 30 minutes. Puree the celery and water in a food mill or blender. Return to the cooking pot, whisk in the flour and add the milk and cream. Cook until the soup is thickened, stirring frequently, about 10 minutes. Serve in bowls with bread browned in butter. Or you may use commercial croutons.

Some Good Cream Soups

On a cold day there is nothing that tastes any better than a bowl of smooth, delicate, rich cream soup. In fact, it is a meal in itself and a particularly fitting one for the short winter days when dinner appears to follow breakfast so closely, and something that can be fixed with little fuss is to be desired. For supper when the children are home from school and hungry as bears, cream soup will fill them, and at the same time, supply them with all of those things necessary to good health — proteins, carbohydrates, fats and the very important vitamins.

Cream of Carrot Soup

1 pound carrots
2 stalks celery
1 thin slice onion
2 tablespoons flour
2 tablespoons butter
2 cups milk

Peel and grate the carrots. Mince the celery and onion. Cook the vegetables in water just to cover until they are tender, about 15 minutes. Puree the vegetables until smooth. While the carrots are cooking, make a white sauce by blending the flour and butter in a medium saucepan. Cook until the mixture bubbles, and carefully add the milk. Cook, stirring, until the mixture thickens. Stir in the pureed vegetables and add salt and pepper to taste.

Cream of Beet Soup

Follow the above recipe, only use 1 pound of beets instead of the carrots.

Green Onion Soup

This is something to look forward to for early spring when the winter onions are in season. Serve with plenty of hot buttered toast.

20 green onions
3 medium sized white potatoes
1 1/2 cups cream
4 cups milk

Slice the onions into thin rings, using all of the white part and about 2 inches of the green. Peel and dice the potatoes. Put in a medium sized sauce pan and just barely cover with water. Simmer, covered, until the vegetables are tender. Add the cream and milk, slightly mashing the potatoes.

Some Good Cream Soups

Tomato Soup

Tomato soup combines a lot of good-for-you things in one dish. There is no danger from curdling if the soup is made this way.

> *1 quart of canned tomatoes*
> *   or a large can tomato puree*
> *1 onion*
> *3 stalks of celery*
>
> **To thicken the soup:**
> *2 tablespoons flour*
> *2 tablespoons butter*
> *1 tablespoon sugar*
> *Dash red pepper*
> *1 cup cream*
> *2 cups milk*

If using whole tomatoes, press them through a food mill to remove the seeds. Dice the onion and celery and simmer in a little water until tender. Drain and press them through the food mill or process in a blender or food processor. Add this puree to the tomato. Blend the flour and butter together in a medium sauce pan. Cook over medium heat until the mixture bubbles. Add the seasonings and the cream and milk, stirring until the mixture thickens. Stir this mixture into the tomato mixture and heat together 5 to 10 minutes.

Cabbage Soup

> *3 tablespoons butter*
> *2 tablespoons flour*
> *2 cups boiling water*
> *2 cups finely shredded cabbage*
> *2 more cups boiling water*
> *Sausage cakes*

Melt the butter in a large sauce pan, blend in the flour and then the boiling water. Stir until slightly thickened. Add the cabbage, cover and simmer until the cabbage is tender, about 30 minutes. Make small sausage cakes or meatballs and brown in a frying pan. Drain well. Add the sausage cakes to the soup and simmer for 20 minutes longer.

Carrot Soup

3 tablespoons butter
1/2 cup chopped onion
1 tablespoon flour
1 cup boiling water
2 cups diced carrots
1 cup thinly diced potatoes
1/4 cup minced ham
Boiling water to cover
1 cup cream
1 cup milk
1 teaspoon pepper

In a large soup pot, melt the butter and sauté the onion until golden. Add the flour and stir until it is lightly browned. Pour in the boiling water and cook, stirring until the mixture thickens. Add the vegetables and ham. Cover with more boiling water. Cover the pot and simmer until the vegetables are tender. Stir in the cream and milk. Season with pepper.

Vegetable and Cheese Soup

1/2 cup cabbage, finely shredded and chopped
1/2 cup diced carrots
1/2 cup diced potatoes
1 tablespoon minced onion
1 tablespoon minced green pepper
3 cups meat stock
1 teaspoon pepper
1/2 teaspoon paprika
1/2 teaspoon salt, optional
1/2 cup grated cheese

Combine the vegetables with the meat stock and simmer until they are tender. Add the seasonings and stir in the grated cheese just before serving.

July 31, 1925

Eat vegetables rather than so much meat during the hot days
of July and August and you will feel much better. Drinking plenty
of water, too, will add to the general comfort of this season.

*Life on the farm is an equal opportunity employer.
When the cows need milking it doesn't matter if it is the
farmer or his wife who gets the job done. Certainly the pages
of Wallaces' Farmer and earlier agricultural papers speak
of the importance of the contributions of all members of the
family to keep the farm on the road to success.*

*Beyond the farm gates, opportunities and responsibilities
for women were more limited. Perhaps the most visible
reflection of these struggles is that of the women's right
to vote. Western and Midwestern states lead the way. Women
were enfranchised in Wyoming in 1869. Colorado, Utah and
Idaho all gave women the right to vote before the
20th Century. In Iowa in 1916. But it wasn't until the
19th amendment to the Constitution was ratified in 1920 that
women all over the nation could vote in national elections.
The attitudes of women toward getting the vote made many
appearances in the pages of Wallaces' Farmer. One article
especially, speaks powerfully today. The writer urged
women to use their newly achieved right, reminding in a
country where "disenfranchisement is punishment for
a crime, it is a disgrace" that half of those eligible "choose
to disenfranchise themselves" by not voting.*

*This section also includes articles on women's attitudes
toward homework and homelife along with some recipes for
efficiently made dishes.*

CHAPTER 4

Woman's Life

Hearts and Homes

January 4, 1907

*Women should rest their nerves and bodies
by living in the open air and studying nature. Cut off the
extra cooking, live simply, take recreation. Enjoy life
to the fullest extent. Wear clothing suited to your work.
Rest and sleep, and cut off the extras that exhaust the
strength of the homemakers. The simple one is the one
for tired muscles and nerves.*

*The fashions for men seldom change. Men march
unfettered and proudly around in much the same garments
that their great-grandfathers wore a century ago; hence their
strength. Women might well learn some lessons from them.*

*The domestic science department in our schools, colleges
and universities will in a few years solve the question
of help. The dignity of labor should be everywhere upheld
and strengthened. We should simplify our lives where we can.
It is a profound truth that to lessen our meals is
to lengthen our lives and limitations of our wants
is better than extension of income.*

Mrs. Myrtle Lawrence, Crawford County, Iowa

It will soon be time to put up stoves, and to the sister who wished to know how to keep her stove black, I will tell her how I keep mine: I never polish a stove while hot. Clean all the dust and grease off with Gold Dust (advertised in *Wallaces' Farmer*). If the stove is red, rub it with a clean cloth, dampened with vinegar. After this, I blacken with Rising Sun Stove Polish, wet with cold coffee and a few drops of turpentine, which makes it polish very easy and without dust. I have a pasteboard box covered with black oil-cloth, lined with plain red calico, with the words "stove rag" cut in the oil cloth. In this box I keep a woolen rag, an old newspaper with which I wipe all the dust off my stove after putting in or taking up ashes. The box is tacked to the wainscoting just over the woodbox. If you clean your stove in this way I think you will receive many compliments as to appearance of your stove. I hope I haven't tired you.

September 20, 1895
When our Wives Vote

I'm going to the caucus, John:
So don't you go away,
But cook must come, for I suspect
We'll need her vote today.

Now, when you've made the beds, John
And dusted all the rooms.
Go out and do the marketing
But don't you buy meat at Vroom's!

Last caucus his wife bolted
And nearly spoiled my plan
By voting with the anti-snaps
To nominate a man!

Now, mind you put the kettle on
And baste the meat yourself,
And don't forget the baby, John —
His bottle's on the shelf!

The paregoric's on the stand.
Now, John, mind what I say!
Three drops in water every hour,
Come, cook! There, John, good day!

House Cleaning with Sense

To Hearts and Homes:

House cleaning days are here and the dust mop and dust pan are in evidence throughout the length and breadth of the land.

The way to be strong and do lots of work is never overdo, and after a couple of hours of hard work it pays to sit down, or better lie down, for a few minutes and let down the nerve tension. It is wonderful how much work a comparatively weak person can do if she knows how to husband and use her strength. Have the men folks move the heavy furniture out and beat the carpets and rugs. A little diplomacy will, in nearly every case, secure this help, but if the man can't or won't help, then you'd better hire some neighbor's boy for a couple of hours.

Don't ever start to clean house when you feel too tired to do anything else. That is when you'd better get out and dig in the flower beds for an hour or go see a jolly neighbor for a little visit, or take a drive in the fresh air — anything to get away from the grind of house work and forget yourself for a little while. If it takes two weeks to finish the house cleaning, or three weeks, or even four, which it wouldn't seem so bad if it is done a little at a time and without the horrors of the old time house cleaning where dinner was an hour late, the porch and hallways full of boxes, chairs, and bric-a-brac, with a place for everything and everything there while nobody knew just where, father hungry and cross, mother tired and wearing a cobweb on her ear and a patch of dust on her nose. The girls with the inexperience of youth and bubbling over with plans and ideas of re-arrangement looked upon it as a kind of lark at first but the small boy with something of his father's view of things thought it all a nuisance and "couldn't see the sense o' doing all this," especially when he was drafted to help and was hungry or wanted to play ball or marbles or together with his dog, enjoy himself in the thousand and one different ways peculiar to the farm boy.

May 28, 1909
House Cleaning Hints

Then there are some indispensable tools for house cleaning that you should no more do without than attempting to make garden without a hoe. A set of brushes with a long handle that is adjustable for cleaning windows, sweeping ceilings and walls saves much climbing and many steps. A step ladder, which any handy man can make, is a necessary for cleaning pantry and wardrobe shelves. Scouring powders, borax, and ammonia should be kept in readiness. A good timely beginning and plenty of things to work with will lighten the labor by half.

Housekeeping or Homemaking

Lucy B. White

To Hearts and Homes

A beautiful thing is a well kept house. There is no dust on the floor, furniture or walls; the windows shine clearly; the draperies are spick and span; the beds are in beautiful order, the cupboards and pantry are clean and inviting with every article in the proper place. The drawers are filled with clothing well mended, sorted and laundered. The housekeeper can put her hand upon anything she wishes in the dark. She has a system about her work that is never lightly disturbed. Each day has its allotted task that is rigidly adhered to, weather fair or foul. Her home is a delight to one fortunate enough to enter, especially if he desires to only look. The rooms are too good for use; you must do nothing that will bring in dirt, mar the paint or muss up things.

But what constitutes a home? Not merely four walls, we know, but a place where each member has particular rights and privileges that make it the most desirable spot on earth. Home is where mother is, anyway, be it a palace or a hovel. I am sure Abraham Lincoln loved his early home – that poor log shelter without door or window, stove or utensils, where poor Nancy Hanks ended her days.

I read not long ago: "Dust on furniture never hurt anyone, but getting dust off furniture and floors has been the death of many a woman." In my opinion the first duty of the homemaker is to provide a place where nothing is too good to use and enjoy, not worrying too much about appearances or display. Plan for all the sunshine and fresh air possible, sacrifice yourself if you must in times of sickness or other stress, but remember that the bread-winner and the children need you more than they do a spotless house.

In every home there is so much work to be done that only the love in the worker's heart can lift it above drudgery and if she allows this work to fill her life only a part of her powers will be employed. It takes brains to keep house, but the best and the brightest part of her mind will never be used that way. A woman may be a good housekeeper and yet be without influence in her little world. Homemaking on the contrary, is worthy of the best efforts of the highest mind.

In looking back, which people remember their mothers with most pleasure do you think – those whose mothers were always at work too busy with the day's duty so cumbered with much serving that they knew nothing beyond? I like to remember that my mother always loved good books and always found time to read and discuss them with her children. I believe in each mother's duty to spare herself time for at least a little reading each day, be it only one of the sweet old chapters and a glance at the daily paper that she may not lose a sense of life's perspective. It is easy to drop behind in the march to fall out of step with those with whom we perform life's journey and it is very hard to recover our place when once it is lost.

That *homemaker* who willingly strives day by day to honestly do her duty — the work of two women. Perhaps — unseen and unapplauded by the world, may never know how it seems to have a house in perfect order, but I feel sure that when this life is ended she will receive an extra shiny heavenly mansion, with perhaps an added star in her crown.

The Tools of Our Trade

Looking over the household department of a large department store with its bewildering array of pans and kettles of every size and shape, fruit pressers, potato peelers, egg beaters, cream whips, steamers and casseroles, jelly molds and pudding pans, we did not wonder at the delight the owner of a well equipped kitchen felt in camping in the woods with a skillet, a stew pan and a coffee pot as her sole tools.

The multiplicity of these things nowadays wears us out. The care of too many tools wearies us almost as much as the work. Kitchen aids allure us but unless we know they can stand the practical test of everyday use, unless they are easily cleaned, and put together, they may lose us more time than they save.

We have tried a good many in our own kitchen — a dish washing machine is in the attic because it takes about four gallons of water to wash the dishes of six people. In company with the dish washer is a collection of knives for cutting vegetables in fancy shapes, a slaw cutter and a number of egg beaters. Some of the latter discarded because they were too hard to clean, some because they wasted too much energy by wobbling, one because it was too small. For the farmer's wife a "hotel size" egg beater, heavy enough to have good running gears, is the best investment. A labor saver must be sufficiently useful to be good value, and it must not require too much time and care to keep in order. Cherry pitters, apple parers etc. — must do good work in less time than the same work can be done by hand to be profitable.

Small tools must be good and as few in number as we can get along with – they should be arranged near where they are to be used. For summer use over a one burner stove, a good steamer is a great labor savor. A steamer is easily abused. If it is to be a profitable investment it must be dried before putting away. In choosing a steamer, it is better to buy one that is equipped with a means of returning the steam as it condenses when it can be used again and will not soon boil dry. Few tools, but those that are good, are what the wise housekeeper chooses.

January 14, 1916

The Help Question

Most of us have known housekeepers who were overworked for lack of help in the kitchen. Women who, while protesting that they would be willing to pay the best of wages to a good girl, will yet refuse the help they might have had in the way of ready prepared foods, because the cost of the ready prepared is more than the cost of others. Prepared foods do cost more — they are worth more; but the added cost is, as a rule, less than the same preparation would cost in the home. Take a can of tomatoes, to prepare them for soup as they are prepared in the canned tomato soup would make the cost of canned tomatoes and canned tomato soup about equal. If the pancake flour on the market makes the kind of pancakes the family likes, this breakfast delicacy can be prepared quicker than cakes with flour, and by the unskilled labor, which is often an advantage to the housekeeper.

Ready-to-cook noodles are not as good as the old-fashioned egg noodles, but they are very good and when served with a rich broth the family may not be dissatisfied with their substitution.

The woman without help should not get a dried cod, because it is cheaper than the packages of boneless codfish. She can put in the time to better advantage by letting the factory furnish the help which bones and picks the fish to pieces. We called at a home one evening where an untidy mother with two wailing children had just finished putting up peaches at nine o'clock at night. She was very proud of the number of cans she had put up from two bushels of the fruit, but she was in bed all the next day with a sick headache and it seems to us her family would have been better off with dried peaches.

The mother who canned the peaches never has a minute to spare to give herself recreation. Her overwork costs her many a day of pain. The woman who can not afford to hire help in the house can afford help which is to be had by prepared foods and mechanical contrivances.

"Mother would simply have a fit if she knew I paid Matilda seven dollars for this week's work," a housekeeper said, referring to the help of a woman by the hour, "but I had reached my limit. It was either Matilda or the doctor, and Matlida was much more companion to me than the doctor would have been."

It would not be a bad idea if every house-keeper would ask herself this question, "Am I holding my own, or am I losing strength and efficiency day by day? What will become of me if I go on as I am going without help?"

April 20, 1917

Corn Soup

1 can corn, drained
2 quarts milk
3 tablespoons butter
1 cup mashed potatoes

In a large quart sauce pan combine the corn and milk. Whisk in the butter and potatoes. Cook over medium heat, stirring frequently, until the soup is smooth and heated through.

December 26, 1931

Chocolate Bread Pudding

1 cup stale (dry) bread crumbs
3 tablespoons cocoa powder
3/4 cup sugar
1/2 cup nuts or less
1 scant cup milk
Hot water

Preheat the oven to 325 degrees F. Combine the bread crumbs, cocoa, and sugar. Blend well with a whisk. Add the nuts and stir in the milk until the mixture is just blended. Lightly grease a small baking pan about 7 x 11 inches. Pour the batter into the pan and place this pan in a larger pan. Fill with hot water about halfway up the side of the pudding dish. Bake 20 minutes or until the pudding is set. This will be like a soft brownie. Serve warm with hard sauce or ice cream, or both.

Hard Sauce

1/4 cup very soft butter
1 cup confectioners sugar
1 teaspoon vanilla

Beat the butter and sugar together and stir in the vanilla.

In the Kitchen

The following suggestions are offered by Nellie E. Maxwell of the University of Wisconsin.

If you have a pine floor do not wear out your life scrubbing it. Cover it with a good linoleum which will cost about $1.25 a square foot. If varnished once or twice a year, it will last five or ten years with good care. If rugs are kept where standing, it will save the feet as well as the linoleum.

Corners are such hard places to keep clean, that carved brass corners may be tacked in them. These tips may be bought at any hardware store.

Save time in washing spoons by keeping old teaspoons in the soda and baking powder cans.

Shears in the kitchen may be great savers of time. Use them to trim lettuce, cut raisins and figs, dress chickens, prepare grapefruit and for many other uses that may be discovered daily by the thinking housewife.

Don't waste time scrubbing a sink with scouring powder, as kerosene will do the cleaning in half the time and will not hurt the enamel.

Vote Against Booze

On October 15th – next Monday – Iowa voters will have an opportunity to amend the state constitution and forever forbid the sale and manufacture of intoxicating liquors within the borders of the state.

The men and women on the Iowa farms should see to it that this amendment is adopted.

Vote YES on October 15th.

Now Let's Use It

When the men were voting on the paved roads question in Polk county, Iowa in late June in one community where four hundred men were eligible for the ballot, only ninety-eight votes were cast. Now that women are to have the ballot, let's do better than those men did.

We have the right to help choose the men who handle the money we vote in taxes, we have the right to know what candidates stand for and the platforms on which they stand. If good women will not vote, these things will be controlled by others. The element that always rallies all its forces when the question of morals comes up is the element opposed to the straight and narrow way.

At a meeting of the "vets" in California women were led by one of their members who, at the invitation of the chairman, mounted the speaker's stand and announced that she was "the first woman advocate of personal liberty in America." Stamping her foot and waving her handkerchief she said, "It will take a woman to put it across and you can bet your life I'll go to the devil if I don't do it."

Many of our women readers have never felt the need for suffrage; they have had the right kind of men folks to vote for them. But now that each woman is to have suffrage if she wants her man to still vote for her, she must cast a ballot by his side. The man who is on the opposite side had a voting wife — their two votes wipe one out and give one to carry.

If women believe that wars should cease, they should use their beliefs as rules for action.

A joke of long ago was that a man had all of his religion in his wife's name. Too many women have all of their convictions in their husband's name. Take the discussion relative to the modification of the Volstead Prohibition Enforcement Act, which is appearing as a political issue. At the meeting of farm representatives recently a speaker got a laugh by referring to the abbreviation "B.V.D." as "Before the Volstead Disaster."

If the Volstead act is modified to admit light wines and beer as non-intoxicants, these beverages may be sold in every schoolhouse cafeteria, at every place of refreshment, without restriction.

Women should realize the menace which threatens prohibition and should vote for men and women who are for strict enforcement of the Volestead Act.

The argument, "I don't believe in a law which can't be enforced," is no argument at all. Every law ever made by God or man is broken, but we don't remove the restriction. Of course the confirmed drinker will get drink, but we may hope to save the children from acquiring the taste for liquor.

There won't be a next war if the women use their power and get out their forces 100 percent at the polls.

The Covered Dish

He was a big, fat man whose "friends" were always urging him to sacrifice his personal wishes and run for office. At election time he was troubled about the woman vote: "It ain't right to put voting on the women," he fretted. "It just gives a woman one more thing to do when she's got all she ought to attend to now in looking after her family. Making women vote is like ordering from a covered dish, you never know what might be handed out to you."

If we accept the comparison we might stress the delightful mystery of a covered dish. The expectant diner wonders, "Is it new?" "Can I get the recipe?" just as the political leaders wondered, "Will the women go republican or democrat?" "Is there any rule which will tell us how to stir up the feminine political element into one body?"

Instead of giving women one more thing to do, the ballot helps women in their municipal housekeeping by giving them the help of organization, giving them a machine for getting municipal work done.

To some men the acceptance of women's part in politics may be like cultivating a taste for olives, but the appetite for it will come. The ballot came to women because men wanted and needed woman's help in the larger housekeeping which touches the family at every turn. The serving that is being handed out by women to all around the political table is a plea for educated citizenship, and the acceptance of the ballot.

Women are saying, "In a nation where disenfranchisement is a punishment for a crime, it is a disgrace that more than half of the women and men should so belittle their privilege of the participation in the government which belongs to them as to choose to disenfranchise themselves."

The covered dish is full of good things.

One Dish Dinner

Verena Myer Northey, Dickenson County, Iowa

Here is my favorite recipe for a one-dish dinner. Call it spinach loaf if you dare, or vegetable loaf if you "dassen't" do that. You can easily sense the psychology of putting the meat down first.

> *1 1/2 pounds hamburger*
> *1 quart carrots, ground*
> *1 onion, ground*
> *2 cups canned or frozen spinach, well drained*
> *4 eggs*
> *2 cups milk*
> *2 tablespoons flour*

Mix all the ingredients together. Mold into a loaf and place slices of bacon over the top. Bake in a slow oven for three hours.

Summer Company

"I could endure cheerfully the extra cooking, canning, poultry raising and gardening which summer brings," says a bright farm woman, "but I must say the summer guests floor me.

"In hot weather I long to spend Sundays quietly on our cool shaded lawn. Instead I must get up a big dinner for carloads of company from town. The plan of running away for a day's jaunt doesn't work out well in my case because I come home completely tired out."

You are not the only farm woman who suffers from summer guests, a chorus answered her. We all do and it is no joking matter.

I am a fellow sufferer. I have not entirely settled the problem to my satisfaction, but I believe I am on the right track at last and it may prove helpful to other tired women who long for rest and quiet after a week of strenuous work.

I decided to have the simplest of meal on Sunday and if company comes I explain that I am forced to get all the rest I can on Sunday but they are welcome to share our plain fare.

Circumstances of the season have a lot to do with our Sunday dinner. Sometimes we have bread and milk and a basket of cookies. We have been known to regale ourselves contentedly on popcorn, bowls of cold milk and apple pie when father elects to pop the corn. Sometimes a big pan of baked beans is prepared on Saturday and is eaten with bread and butter and fresh fruit. Again a dish such as escalloped potatoes, macaroni and cheese or rice and tomatoes is baked in the little oil stove oven on Sunday. Simple salads are liked.

Country Air

By a Farm Woman

To many a farm woman summer is merely a season of overpowering work and company. I confess I've seen summers when I felt I couldn't love anybody that drove a big car and liked chicken, thought it "wonderful to have your own cream," and had a two weeks' vacation. Those were the years when city friends from the security of their own lives said in a large and patronizing manner, "I'll tell you what you farmers need to do _____." It's different now. They look at us with the awesome admiration accorded stoicism and endurance and say, "And to think you farmers have been going through this for eight years. Why for us this past year has been so awful —," And so on and so on.

At family parties we've gone in for tray suppers and buffet dinners. And oh! the informality you can get by with! There is a nice patriarchal air about a long table and proper china surrounded by genial conversation. But a tray supper sets you off to snug little groups where you wisecrack with the gay, philosophize with the wise or just sit out under a tree with a favorite cousin or aunt and talk to suit yourselves.

But oh our cornfields! How beautiful they are! Innumerable radiating pairs of rows that, for a hilltop, look like plushy smocking on velvet cushions; deep healthy green chlorophyll beneath rough surfaces; sturdy, adolescent stalks tough and vibrant; shifting grace of pointed leaf; proud restless sea of blade and tassel — Iowa cornfield.

Swelling Family Incomes May 17, 1933

You can't keep farm women down. When income from hogs and corn goes down, they start piecing quilts and selling them. When live poultry prices slump, they eliminate the middleman by dressing and selling their own chickens. When they want some improvements in the house and cash is lacking, they trade eggs and butter to the carpenter and the hardwareman. Several women reported trading vegetables, canned meats, hams and eggs to the doctor and the hospital. In return, the hospital and doctor delivered a baby.

Our contest on swelling family incomes has brought in 300 entries. Dozens wound up with the sentence "I hope this will help others to get along."

One woman said very frankly, "I don't want to do this sort of work always. When prices of hogs and corn go up, I hope I can have more time to be with my family and enjoy life. However, right now it has been a godsend that I have been able to do some work that we get cash and goods for"
— From Mrs. Grace Comer of Black Hawk County

Baked Brown Bread

Mrs. J.A. Burroughs, Butler County, Iowa

The following is a recipe for brown bread which I have found very useful. It is quick and easy and is a change over the steamed variety.

1/2 cup molasses
1/2 cup brown sugar, firmly packed
2 tablespoons melted butter
1 well beaten egg
1 teaspoon baking soda
1 cup of sour milk or buttermilk
1/2 cup milk
1 cup white flour
3 cups graham (whole wheat) flour
1 cup raisins or currants

Preheat the oven to 350 degrees F. Combine the molasses, brown sugar and butter. Stir in the egg. Add the baking soda followed by the sour milk and regular milk. Mix well. Stir in the white flour and graham flour. Stir by hand until well blended. Stir in the raisins. Pour batter into two well greased standard loaf pans. Bake until the loaves are firm in the center, about 50 to 60 minutes. Turn out of pans and cool on a wire rack.

April 12, 1939

Sour Cream Fudge Cake

Mrs. E. T. Broadfoot, Adair County, Iowa

This is a recipe that can be put together quickly. In fact, I have often made it while my potatoes boiled for dinner. Using sour cream for shortening saves much time in creaming the butter. Why take the time to churn the cream when it is just as good for shortening before?

2 well beaten eggs
1 cup medium heavy sour cream
   made by combining 2 tablespoons vinegar with a scant cup of half and half
1 1/2 cups sugar
1/2 teaspoon salt
2 teaspoons baking soda
1/3 cup cocoa
2 cups flour
1 teaspoon vanilla

Preheat the oven to 350 degrees F. Grease and flour or spray with non-stick spray, 9 x 13 inch baking pan. Beat together the eggs and sour cream, gradually add the sugar while the mixer is running. Slowly stir in the salt, soda, cocoa and flour and mix until thoroughly combined. Stir in the vanilla. Pour the batter into the prepared pan and bake until the cake is firm in the center and slightly pulled away from the sides, about 50 minutes.

1909 · 1912

■ **February 21, 1909** Prohibition successfuly forces many saloons to close their doors, and states adopt local options outlawing liquor sales. Those in favor of sales state that the average working man spends only $12.50 of his annual income of $768.54 on liquor.

■ **March 4, 1909** Taft inaugurated in heavy winter storm.

■ **July 25, 1909** Louis Bleriot successfully flies airplane over English Channel.

■ **November 7, 1909** More than 2 million Americans now own stock.

■ **February 8, 1910** Boy Scouts of America incorporated.

■ **May 6, 1910** Edward VII dies.

■ **August 27, 1910** Edison demonstrates talking pictures.

■ 1910 Census shows 91.9 million Americans, 13 million foreign born.

■ **May 7, 1911** Thousands of women parade in New York City for the right to vote.

■ **June 23, 1911** King George V crowned.

■ **June 12, 1911** U.S. Constitutional amendment to elect Senators directly by popular vote passes, replaces election by each state legislature. Terms to be 6 years instead of 4.

■ **April 14, 1912** Titanic sinks.

■ **May 30, 1912** Second Indianapolis 500 race held, average speed 78.7 miles per hour.

■ **June 22, 1912** William Howard Taft nominated by Republicans.

■ **July 2, 1912** Wilson nominated by Democrats.

■ **August 5, 1912** Bull Moose party nominates former president Theodore Roosevelt.

■ **November 5, 1912** Wilson wins in three way race. 435 electoral votes for Democrat Wilson, 88 for T. Roosevelt on the Progressive Party ticket and 8 for Republican Taft. Wilson promises a vigorous effort in anti-trust legislation.

■ New Mexico enters Union as 47th state.

■ Arizona enters Union as 48th state.

CHAPTER 5

Beverages

"Soft Drinks"
To Hearts and Homes
W.T. Marrs M.D. July 30, 1909

All children who are in a normal state of health are always ready to drink something. The reasons are apparent for the body of the child is composed mainly of water. Water is a natural beverage for adults and doubly so for children. Lemonade and acidulated drinks, if not too sweet, are to be given to the young child, but the numerous sweet beverages sold on every side are to be discouraged. They are simply sweetened water with perhaps a little of the gaseous elements. Taken in moderation they may, for the time being, be harmless, but the worst feature about them is that they foster an abnormal thirst.

If these drinks are indulged in too freely, children think their thirst for them must be appeased on the slightest provocation. The habit is expensive and useless and it is a serious question whether this morbid thirst may not grow into a desire for something stronger with the passing of the years. The cupidity of the manufacturers of these summer drinks is only rivaled by that of the patent medicine promoters. The terms "wholesome," "nutritious," "tonic," etc. should deceive no one by creating the impression that they are of any benefit. There should be no excuse like these for indulging in them. It is like the pretext assigned by men for drinking beer in stating that "the water is bad."

Some of the so-called soft drinks have been found on analysis to contain deleterious products although the pure food authorities are working zealously to eliminate all such. Teach the children to drink pure water in as copious quantities as they may desire, but that it is better to spend their pennies for fruits, popcorn and peanuts.

Cool Summer Drinks

The country housekeeper, though far from carbonated waters and the alluring siphon bottle, can provide an attractive variety of cooling summer drinks as her city sister while a deep well and a cold cellar render ice unnecessary. Fruit in abundance should be always at hand during the season of fruits and a canned supply may be stored up for winter use. Mint grows, or may be induced to grow, in any damp, cool place, while fresh wintergreen, sassafras and black birch bark contain possibilities unapproached by the root beer of the city drug store.

R&E *Simple syrup forms the basis for many of these delightful beverages. Make a **simple syrup** by boiling together for five minutes:*

> *1 cup sugar*
> *1 cup water*

Mint Punch

> *2 cups bruised mint leaves, packed*
> *2 cups boiling water*
> *1 cup grape juice*
> *1 cup strawberry juice, or similar fruit juice*
> *1/3 cup simple syrup*

Pour the boiling water over the mint leaves and allow to cool. Drain and combine the juice with the other ingredients and chill. Serve over ice.

Indian Punch

> *1 recipe simple syrup*

Add the juice and grated rind of:
2 oranges
2 lemons

Set aside to cool then add:
2 cups cold tea
1 cup fruit juice
Water to make 2 quarts.

Serve over ice.

Iced Coffee

> *1 quart strong coffee, chilled*

Add to it:
1 cup orange syrup, made by simmering together for 10 minutes:
> *1 cup sugar*
> *1 cup orange juice*

Serve in glasses with one tablespoon ice and topped with one tablespoon of whipped cream.

Summer Punches

Rhubarb Tea

4 cups cold tea
4 cups sweetened rhubarb juice
1 lemon

R E These easy to make summer punches take full advantage of fresh from the garden produce. I continue to cut my rhubarb right until frost. The later stalks are not as tart and need less sugar. You can freeze the rhubarb juice and serve this all year.

Make rhubarb juice by slicing enough rhubarb to make 2 quarts. Add 1 to 2 cups sugar, depending on the tartness of the rhubarb. Stir and let stand, covered, in a cool place over-night. In the morning cook over low heat until the rhubarb turns into sauce. Strain through a jelly bag or layers of cheesecloth. Chill and combine with the tea and lemon.

Summer Punch

2 cups grape juice
4 cups cold tea
2 cups ginger ale

Mix the grape juice and tea. Add the ginger ale just before serving.

Love Potion Beverage

1 quart milk
1 stick cinnamon
2 teaspoons instant coffee
2 squares sweet chocolate, melted in 1/2 cup boiling
    water
1/2 teaspoon vanilla

R E This beverage is similar to a spiced cocoa recipe popular in the 1880s and to several cake recipes of that era. It combines cinnamon, coffee and cocoa into a delightfully grown-up winter drink.

Simmer the milk with cinnamon for ten minutes. Remove the cinnamon stick, stir in the instant coffee, melted chocolate and vanilla. Pour into cups and top with whipped cream.

Rhubarb Punch

Mrs. J. W. Carter

> *2 quarts diced rhubarb*
> *2 quarts water*
> *3 cups sugar*
> *3 oranges*
> *3 lemons*
> *2 quarts seltzer*
> *1 quart orange or lemon water ice, you can use a water sherbet*

Combine the rhubarb, water and sugar in large pot. Simmer until the rhubarb is very soft. Strain the liquid through a jelly bag or layers of cheesecloth. Grate the rind from the oranges and lemons and squeeze the juice. Combine the juice and the rinds with the cooled rhubarb and put in the refrigerator to chill. To serve: Put the rhubarb juice in a large punch bowl, add the seltzer and stir in the fruit ice or sherbet.

August 15, 1936

Honey Blossom Drink

To each glass of chilled milk allow 3 tablespoons honey and two drops lemon extract. Shake thoroughly before serving. Sprinkle with nutmeg.

July 21, 1934

Fruit Milk

Cold milk, served plain, has no equal for refreshment. There are some people, however, who do not care for milk in this manner. For them we recommend Fruit Milk: Beat well with an egg beater, 2 to 3 tablespoons fruit juice, adding 1 or 2 tablespoons of sugar or honey if necessary. Add 1 cup of milk and serve ice cold.

July 2, 1909
Let Us Have a Sane Fourth

*It would be interesting to know just how many patriots
perished by death or disease in the war of the Revolution and how
many young patriots have perished in the insane attempts
to commemorate their heroic deeds. We would not be surprised
to learn that more boys and girls have gone to an untimely death
through our foolish methods of celebrating the Fourth than ever
perished in the war for the establishment of the greatest republic
on the face of the earth.*

*Is it not about time that parents put a stop to this unutterable
foolishness? If we would celebrate the Fourth in the same way in
which our forefathers celebrated it there would be no such fearful
holocaust of the young. They were satisfied to get together on the
Fourth and listen to a discussion of the problems that confronted
them and to hear about the heroic and successful efforts to achieve
liberty. They did not have any cannon crackers nor toy pistols nor
did they make bedlam of the Fourth of July.*

*If the farmers will simply say to their boys: All the little
old-fashioned crackers you want, provided you keep away from
the barns and stables; no toy pistols; no cannon crackers; no gas
pipe cannons; none of this foolishness. Children are sensible if
handled right by sensible people and it is not a difficult matter to
teach boys and girls the higher meaning of the Fourth of July, and
show them how they must aim to become good citizens if
the liberties for which their ancestors bled and died are to
remain the heritage of their posterity. Let us have a sane
Fourth of July for once, at least.*

1913 - 1917

■ **March 4, 1913** Wilson inaugurated.

■ **May 8, 1913** Income tax passes Congress. Up to 6 percent tax on income $500,000. Married man earning $5,000 a year pays $10.

■ **October 7, 1913** Henry Ford starts up first assembly line.

■ **October 10, 1913** Panama Canal opened.

■ **January 1, 1914** Henry Ford pays workers $5 a day.

■ **June 28, 1914** Archduke Ferdnand of Austria-Hungary assassinated.

■ **August 31, 1914** 8 nations engaged in World War I in Europe.

■ **January 1, 1915** *Wallaces' Farmer* editorial — War or Peace?
". . . . Does anyone suppose that the nations of Europe would have gone to war had the common people been consulted? This war was forced upon them. It is time for the people of the United States should set an example to the people of the world and demonstrate that the strength of a nation does not lie in its armies nor its navies, but in adherence to the fundamental principles of righteousness and to true democracy."

■ **January 28, 1915** Rockefeller Foundation takes food to Belgium.

■ **May 12, 1915** Lusitania ocean liner sunk by the Germans.

■ **August 31, 1916** Ford Motor announces a price rollback $250 for a touring car. Claims it would reverse the exodus of farmers from country to the cities.

■ **November 11, 1916** Wilson re-elected in close race 272-259. Ran on the slogan "He Kept Us Out of War."

■ **November 7, 1916** Jeanette Rankin elected Congresswoman from Montana. First woman elected to Congress.

■ **December 15, 1916** 700,000 French and German soldiers die in battle of Verdun.

■ **December 22, 1916** *Wallaces' Farmer* Article — "Agriculture gets all the attention it needs until a civilization enters into the wealth period. The factory system which has been preparing the way for the wealth period which we are just entering pulls into the cities millions of farmers. Finally three-fourths of the people live in the cities. The bulk of these people have not the remotest perception of the danger of their situation. . . . The high cost of living is ever tending to bring attention of the nation to the necessity of people living on the land. . . . Strange as it may seem as a matter of immediate prosperity it is to our interests to let the cities continue unchecked; it means more mouths to feed and consequently higher prices for farm products. But the final outcome of the mad whirl is insanity."*

CHAPTER 6

Vegetables

Rounding Out
the Midwinter Menu

Midwinter always brings a menu problem, doesn't it?
It's not at all difficult to plan menus with fresh vegetables
during the summer and fall months, but winter months,
with their fresh meats and only a stored supply of fresh
and canned vegetables, present difficulties. Our daily
menus are so apt to become a habit. Try serving vegetable
combination salads with your next fresh meat menu.
Incidentally, one of the best of the fresh winter vegetables
is the lowly cabbage. However, overcooked cabbage has
no place on the menu.

Cabbage, beans, corn and carrots, with the occasional sweet potato, make up the majority of recipes in the vegetable section. This reflects the vegetable dishes presented in Wallaces' Farmer *during these years. I didn't really take note of the limited selection as I was paging through the issues, but once I began testing and organizing, I quickly discovered we were eating a lot of those four sturdy vegetables.*

That is the key. Certainly tomatoes were seen as the variety vegetable as they were put up as sauce, juice and catsup, but these four were among the most reliable to grow and easiest to store. In days when farm wives were limited at first by availability, later by economics, new ways to fix these standbys were important to share with others in similar straits. As the Wallaces' *editor wrote about cabbage, "Luckily we don't have to depend upon city markets for this staple. A greater problem lies in inducing our family to eat it as freely as desirable."*

Old Fashioned Boiled dressing for Lettuce

RÆ If you don't own a double boiler, you can put a heat-proof mixing bowl on top of a sauce pan of simmering water. The rim of the bowl should be secured by the top of the sauce pan so the bowl does not go completely inside the pan.

3 egg yolks
1 teaspoon pepper
1 teaspoon salt, optional
1 tablespoon sugar
1 teaspoon dry mustard
1/2 cup vinegar

Combine all ingredients and whisk until well blended. Cook over moderate heat in a double boiler until the dressing is thickened. Good cold on lettuce and hot on cabbage.

Use a variation of this dressing to make potato salad, as well as nut salad and salmon salad in the following chapter.

Potato Salad

10 medium sized red potatoes, cooked and diced
1 onion, minced
4 hard boiled eggs, chopped

Combine the vegetables and blend with the dressing while the potatoes are still warm.

Dressing
3 egg yolks
1 teaspoon pepper
1 teaspoon salt, optional
1 tablespoon sugar
1 teaspoon dry mustard
3 tablespoons butter
1 teaspoon celery seed
1/2 cup vinegar
3/4 cup half and half, approximately

Combine all ingredients except the half and half and whisk until well blended. Cook over moderate heat in a double boiler until the dressing is thickened. Let cool to lukewarm and thin with the cream.

Baked Beans Vegetarian

Which I think even a dyspeptic can eat.

> *3 regular sized cans small red beans, about 15 ounces each*
> *1/2 onion, minced*
> *2 tablespoons molasses*
> *2 tablespoons brown sugar, firmly packed*
> *3/4 cup half and half*

Preheat the oven to 325 degrees F. Drain the beans and rinse off. Put the beans, onion, molasses and brown sugar into a bean pot or other covered casserole dish. Cover with water. Bake 3 to 4 hours until beans are soft. An hour before the beans are finished, mash about a cup of them and combine with the cream. Return to the bean pot and stir well. Continue to cook until the beans are the desired consistency.

October 14, 1921

Creole Sauce

> *2 cups tomato sauce*
> *1/2 cup green peppers, chopped*
> *1 1/2 teaspoons parsley, minced*
> *2 tablespoons onion, chopped*
> *1 tablespoon sugar*
> *2 tablespoons butter*
> *4 tablespoons ham or bacon, minced*
> *1 bay leaf*
> *1 tablespoon celery seed*
> *Salt and pepper to taste*

Combine all ingredients in a medium sized sauce pan. Simmer, stirring frequently, until thickened. Serve over meats or seafood.

October 5, 1928
Patchwork thoughts

I see that the law is being tested in regard
to whether women have to give their ages and
birth dates at the polls. It seems that there are several
hundred women here in Iowa who are objecting
to having to tell what they regard as a sacred
secret and also, as someone has said, what
the beauty parlors hide.

Entertaining the Thanksgiving Company

Candied Fried Sweet Potatoes

Sweet potatoes
Butter
Brown sugar

Bake sweet potatoes with skin on until half done. Peel and slice. Melt butter in a frying pan. Brown the potatoes until crisp and slightly browned. Remove to a flat baking pan, and top with brown sugar. Pour water into frying pan and pour over the potatoes.

Thanksgiving Fruit Salad

Peeled orange slices
Coconut
Grape halves

For the Dressing:
1/4 cup sugar
1 teaspoon celery seed
1/8 teaspoon paprika
1 egg
1 teaspoon butter
Milk to make 1/2 cup
1 cup vinegar

Combine the sugar, celery seed and paprika in the jar of a blender. Put the egg in a glass measuring cup, add the very soft butter and enough milk to make 1/2 cup. Heat the vinegar in a microwave or on the stove. With the blender running, add the egg and milk mixture and then very gradually add the hot vinegar. Return to sauce pan and cook over low heat, stirring constantly until the dressing is thick.

To serve the salad: Mix the dressing with the cut up oranges and grapes and coconut. Spoon this mixture over lettuce leaves.

Christmas Dinner

Spiced Apples with Cranberry Filling

Apples
Sugar
Water
Red Hots cinnamon candies

Pare firm Jonathan apples, cut in half and core them. Make a sugar syrup of 2 parts sugar, 1 part water with a few red hot candies added for color and flavor. Cook the syrup over medium heat until the sugar and candies are melted. Add the apples and simmer very gently until the apples are tender and the syrup has taken on a jelly-like consistency. Chill the apples in the syrup.

For the Filling:
1 package fresh cranberries, about 12 ounces
Sugar
1 tablespoon lemon juice

Process or grind the cranberries until about 1/16-inch in diameter. Measure and combine with an equal amount of sugar in a heavy sauce pan. Add the lemon juice. Cook over very low heat until the sugar is dissolved and the mixture has thickened.

To serve: Put the apples on a serving platter or on lettuce on individual salad plates. Fill the center with the cranberry and spoon the remaining syrup over the top.

Mint Glazed Carrots and Peas

1 pound carrots, peeled and cut into 1/4 inch slices
1/4 cup butter
1/4 cup sugar
1 tablespoon mint jelly, or more to taste
1 can tender young peas (or 1 box frozen peas, thawed)

Boil the carrots until just tender and drain. In a large frying pan with a cover, melt the butter and add the carrot slices. Sprinkle in the sugar and stir to coat the carrots. Cover and simmer until the sugar is melted, about 5 minutes, stirring occasionally. Stir in the mint jelly, coating the carrots evenly. Add the drained or thawed peas and heat through.

Stuffed Bermuda Onions

Peel large Bermuda onions and simmer until just barely tender, about 45 minutes.

Cool to lukewarm. Cut a slice off the top and scoop out the center, reserving he cooked onion for another purpose.

Filling for 6 onions:
3/4 cup English walnuts
3/4 cup dry bread crumbs
1/3 cup melted butter
Salt
Pepper
Parsley, minced

Preheat the oven to 350 degrees F. Place onions in muffin cups or in a dripping pan and pour a little hot water around them. Bake for 30 minutes, basting occasionally with butter of bacon drippings. Serve on a platter surrounded by White Sauce.

Basic White Sauce

R*E* *This Basic White Sauce has appeared in several recipes in* Wallaces' Farmer *over the years.*

2 tablespoons butter
2 tablespoons flour
1 cup milk or cream
Salt and pepper to taste
1/8 teaspoon nutmeg

Melt the butter in a small sauce pan. Add the flour and cook over medium heat until the mixture begins to bubble. Slowly add the milk, stirring constantly to prevent lumps. Add the seasonings and continue cooking until the sauce is thickened.

May 14, 1928

The fireless cooker — how could we get along without it — homemade tho it is. It saves us many a moment of careful watching. A dish of pork and beans put into the cooker after breakfast with a pan or rice pudding — the old fashioned kind where uncooked rice, milk and flavoring are put together — are deliciously cooked by noon

Cabbage Salad Plus

So long as the cabbage comes up from the cellar crisp and juicy, we can hardly indulge too freely in cabbage salad.

Cabbage forms the country housewife's standby winter salad. Doctors tell us that we should eat raw cabbage every day during the "cabbage season." Not only does it furnish our diet with valuable vitamins and minerals but it induces mastication which promotes digestion and the preservation of teeth.

Luckily we do not have to depend upon the city market for this salad staple, but can store a generous supply in our own cellar. A greater problem lies in inducing our family to eat it as freely as is desirable.

Apple and onion in any desired quantity combined with the cabbage makes a welcome variety.

Tomatoes, olives and celery, used either separately or in combination, add a new and delicious flavor to the cabbage.

When lettuce is scarce or unattainable try using shredded cabbage in its place as a foundation for salad combinations. This is excellent when making a fish or meat salad such as shrimp, salmon, bacon or chicken.

At a hearty winter dinner have you ever tried substituting the salad for dessert? For this purpose add nuts and raisins, prunes or figs to the usual cabbage salad. The addition of a sliced orange and a few pimentos make a cabbage salad fit for a king. Pineapple or grapefruit may be used in the same way.

In fact, there is no need of allowing the family to become weary of this good winter standby.

Carrot Custard

2 cups cooked carrot pulp
2 eggs
1 teaspoon onion juice
1/4 cup cream

Preheat the oven to 350 degrees F. It will take about one pound of carrots to make the two cups of pulp. Cook them until quite tender, drain and process in a food processor, blender or food mill. If they are still hot, stir in the cream and onion juice. Beat the eggs and stir some of the hot mixture into them, to raise their temperature gradually so they won't turn into scrambled eggs when you add them to the carrots. Butter four 1-cup custard dishes or ramekins. If you like, you may coat them with fine buttered bread crumbs. Divide the carrot mixture among them. Place the dishes in a pan of hot water so that the water comes half way up the sides of the dishes. Bake until the carrot custard is firm in the center, about 40 to 50 minutes. Serve in the dishes, or carefully unmold.

Bean Salad

Mrs. Harry Barker, Chickasaw County, Iowa

> *2 cups cooked green beans*
> *1 cup shredded raw cabbage*
> *1 small onion, chopped fine*
> *5 tablespoons grated sharp cheddar cheese*
> *1/2 teaspoon black pepper*
> *1/2 cup chopped olives or 1 chopped green pepper*
> *1/2 cup mayonnaise*

Combine all ingredients and chill.

Dutch Cabbage

> *6 cups finely shredded cabbage, about one small head*
> *1 cup water*
> *1 cup sour cream*
> *1/2 cup crisp bacon*
> *Salt to taste*
> *Dash paprika*

Cook the cabbage in the water until just tender. Do not drain. Stir in the remaining ingredients and serve warm.

Tasty Potato Salad

Mrs. H.C.R., Jones County, Iowa

> *6 medium potatoes, boiled and diced*
> *4 hard boiled eggs, chopped*
> *6 small cucumber pickles, about 1/4 cup diced*
> *1 onion, diced*
> *1/4 cup diced celery*
> *1 tablespoon diced green pepper*
> *1 to 2 cups mayonnaise*
> *Salt and pepper to taste*

> **For garnish:**
> *1/2 cup nuts, chopped*
> *1 beet, cooked and diced*

Combine all the salad ingredients. Chill for at least 2 hours before serving. Garnish with the nuts and beet.

Spiced String Beans

2 pounds fresh green beans, cooked
2 or 3 small onions, sliced thin
1 cup vinegar
2 tablespoons butter
1/4 teaspoon mace
1/4 teaspoon cloves

Mix the vegetables in a heat-proof, non-metallic bowl. Combine the vinegar, butter, mace and cloves in a small sauce pan and bring to a boil. Pour over the vegetables and mix well. Let stand at room temperature for an hour before serving. You can make this ahead and store in the refrigerator. Warm slightly before serving, as it is best at room temperature.

May 3, 1930

Spring Salad

Mrs. J. Carter, Iroquois County, Illinois

2 - 4 green onions, thinly sliced
12 radishes, thinly sliced
6 new potatoes, cooked, chilled and thinly sliced
1 head loose-leaf lettuce, such as Boston
4 hard-boiled eggs, sliced

For the dressing:
1 tablespoon vinegar
1/4 cup vegetable oil
1/4 teaspoon pepper
Salt to taste

Carefully mix the sliced onions, radishes and potatoes. Make the dressing by whisking the ingredients together. Toss vegetables with the dressing and set aside for at least 15 minutes and up to 4 hours, if refrigerated. Arrange the torn lettuce leaves in a salad bowl or on individual plates. Place the dressed vegetables on top and garnish with hard-boiled eggs.

Bean Salad

Martha Van Gorp, Marion County, Iowa

1 can kidney beans, drained
1/4 cup celery
2 hard boiled eggs, chopped
1/4 cup chopped nut meats
2 tablespoons chopped pickles
2 tablespoons pimento
2 teaspoons chopped onion
1/2 cup mayonnaise

Combine all ingredients and chill for at least an hour before serving.

Scalloped Cabbage

Mrs. Era L. Shore, Lucas County, Iowa

4 cups shredded cabbage,
from one medium-sized head

For the sauce:
2 tablespoons butter
2 tablespoons flour
2 cups milk
1 cup bread crumbs

RKE *This was a recipe that I was not looking forward to testing. While I like cabbage, I just couldn't imagine it creamed. Well, I was wrong. This is really a very nice recipe. The key is to just simmer the shredded cabbage until it is tender. This makes a mild, slightly crispy vegetable that goes very well with a cream sauce. If you don't tell the kids what it is, they'll eat it right up.*

Cook cabbage until tender about, 15 minutes. Melt the butter, blend in the flour and slowly add the milk. Cook until thick, stirring constantly. Mix with the cabbage and pour into an oiled baking dish, cover with crumbs and bake in a hot oven until the crumbs are brown.

March 23, 1923
Brer Rabbit is Toothsome Food
Rabbits are a valuable source of food, and because they multiply rapidly, are comparatively cheap.

Sweet Potato Nut Loaf

Mrs. Chauncy James, Adair County, Iowa

> *6 sweet potatoes, cooked and cooled*
> *1/2 cup milk*
> *1/2 cup sugar*
> *1 tablespoon butter*
> *2/3 cup nuts, pecans are good*
> *12 marshmallows*

Preheat the oven to 350 degrees F. Mash together the sweet potatoes, milk, sugar and butter. Stir in the nuts. Form into a loaf and top with the marshmallows. Bake until heated through and the marshmallows are lightly browned, about 20 to 30 minutes.

Sweet Potatoes — Southern Style

V.K., Kissouth County, Iowa

> *4 medium sized sweet potatoes*
> *1/2 to 3/4 cup brown sugar, firmly packed*
> *4 tablespoons butter*
> *1 tablespoon molasses*

Boil the sweet potatoes until just tender. Peel and slice into 1/2 inch thick slices. Preheat the oven to 350 degrees F. Arrange the slices in a buttered baking dish. Pat brown sugar on top, about 1/4 inch thick. Melt the butter and molasses together. Drizzle over the potatoes and bake until glazed, about 20 minutes. Baste often.

Baked Onions with Corn Custard

6 to 8 sweet white onions
1 small can corn, about 10 ounces
2 eggs, well beaten
1 tablespoon melted butter
1 tablespoon cream
1/2 cup grated cheddar cheese,or any other kind you prefer

Carefully cut off the top and a small slice from the bottom of the onions and remove outer peels. With a small knife or sharp spoon, scoop out the center of the onion, leaving a layer at the bottom. Cook the onions in barely boiling water until tender, about 20 minutes. Carefully lift them out. Preheat the oven to 350 degrees F.

To make the corn custard: Drain the canned corn. Mix the kernels with the eggs, butter and cream. Fill the onions with this corn custard and place in a lightly greased baking dish. Cook until the custard is almost set, about 20 to 25 minutes depending on the size of your onions. Sprinkle with grated cheese and return to the oven to melt the cheese.

Note: You may wish to wrap each onion in foil to keep the filling from leaking out of the bottom of the onions. Left over custard is delicious simply baked by itself. Put into a lightly greased baking dish and place that dish in a pan of hot water before putting into the oven.

Louisiana Baked Beans

Marie Wylie, DeKalb County, Missouri

This is a wonderful recipe and has been in the family for years. My grandmother in Arkansas gave it to me. It is good when you are butchering and have fresh pork. It will serve ten persons.

1 large onion
3 cans of small red beans, about 50 ounces
1/3 cup molasses
1/3 cup dark brown sugar, firmly packed
3/4 cup catsup
3/4 cup boiling water

Preheat the oven to 325 degrees F. Drain the beans and rinse well. Combine all ingredients and put in a bean pot or large casserole. Cover and bake until the liquid is absorbed by the beans, 2 to 3 hours depending on the kind of beans you have. Stir from time to time near the end to keep from burning.

Dressing for Fruit Salad

2 eggs, well beaten
1/4 cup vinegar
1/2 cup commercial sour cream
1/2 cup half and half
2 tablespoons sugar
1/4 teaspoon dry mustard
1/4 teaspoon paprika

Combine all ingredients in the top of a double boiler and cook over simmering water until thick. Cool, stirring frequently to prevent a skin from forming. Store in a tightly sealed jar in the refrigerator.

June 28, 1939

All in One Salad

2 cups cooked string beans
3 tomatoes, diced
2 cups diced cooked potatoes
1 cup diced cooked chicken
3 hard cooked eggs, sliced
1/2 cup mustard pickles
1 sliced onion
1 teaspoon salt, optional
1 teaspoon pepper
1 cup mayonnaise

Mix together lightly, chill and serve on a bed of crisp lettuce. Serves 6.

March 12, 1938
If you have been one of those who talk about how dangerous auto driving has become since "these wild high school kids have started to drive cars," the report of John Hattery, chief of the Iowa highway patrol will come as a shock. Hattery says that of the sixty known drivers involved in fifty-three fatal accidents in 1937, only five were under twenty-one. The average age was thirty-seven years.

Cabbage in Cream Sauce

Mrs. Paul Lacy, Morgan County, Illinois

When new cabbage is boiled until just tender and served the way mother prepares it with a rich cream sauce, thick with crisp bacon squares, it's something different in the way of a cheap and delicious vegetable dish.

> 1 medium head of cabbage
> 2 teaspoons salt, optional
> 3 quarts boiling water

> **For the sauce:**
> 6 strips bacon
> 2 cups milk
> 2 tablespoon bacon fat
> 2 tablespoons flour
> 1 teaspoon pepper

Trim and cut the cabbage into eight sections, and plunge them into boiling water. Cook without covering 8 to 10 minutes. Drain and pour the white sauce over it.

To make the white sauce:
Cook the bacon until it is crisp. Drain and reserve 2 tablespoons of the fat, and combine it with the flour in a small saucepan. Cook, stirring, until it bubbles, then gradually stir in the milk. Cook, stirring, until the sauce is thick. Gently combine the sauce with the cooked cabbage and garnish with reserved bacon bits.

CHAPTER 7

Lunch Box

Country Schools
October 9, 1925

*According to 1924 statistics . . . . there are in Iowa
9,647 little schools, one or two-room schools and 388
consolidated schools. So the little schools outnumber the
consolidated twenty-five times. Once in a while some
pessimistic person tries to tell us that there aren't any good
schools among the small one and two-room schools, that,
at the best, they are rather terrible places — old,
inadequately equipped and poorly taught. Harking back
close to twenty years we recall that the little white
school house where we attended for eight years wasn't all
that it should have been. The building was forty some years
old then, its foundation gone except for props here and
there. And it was cobwebby and dirty and mouse-ridden,
tho it never seemed bad at the time.
In extremely cold weather we sat around the big drum
stove all day, for the windows and doors leaked air so
seriously that it was impossible to warm the extremities
of the room. At that, everybody who went to school
there had a lot of fun and it wasn't such
a bad place. It couldn't have been since our
memories are mostly pleasant.*

The School Lunch

Mrs. W. H.

Why not abolish the old dinner bucket and substitute a roomy basket which has a close-fitting cover? The cover should be left off when not in use. The basket should be scalded and washed in soap suds and then sunned and aired so it will be fresh the next day.

Whole wheat, rye, or graham bread should be used. The highly spiced sausages that have such a pleasant taste are ruinous for children and should be omitted from the lunch. Better give them a fresh egg boiled just enough to set the white.

The use of uncooked fruit should be encouraged instead of cake and pie that we thought we had to have in the old days. When cake is to be used, wholesome ginger bread or some brittle cookies are best. Pies have no place in the dinner basket scheme, as they often become soggy by carrying. Oranges are nice just as they are, but a good substitute would be glazed oranges which are easily made.

Glazed Oranges:
Peel the oranges, remove all the white from them and separate into sections. Remove the seeds carefully, then dip each piece in clear candy syrup. Lay on a dish and sift powdered sugar over them. Set in a cool place until hard. These made in the evening will be ready for the lunch in the morning.

Eggless Cake

1/2 cup butter
1 1/2 cups sugar
1 cup sour milk
3 cups flour
1 teaspoon baking soda
1 teaspoon nutmeg
1 cup golden raisins

Preheat the oven to 350 degrees F. If you don't have sour milk, add the vinegar to 7/8 cup milk and let stand for about 5 minutes. Cream the butter and sugar. Stir in the baking soda, nutmeg and 1 cup of the flour. Add the sour milk and mix well. Stir in the remaining flour and raisins. Divide the batter between two 9-inch greased and floured round cake pans. Bake until a toothpick inserted in the center comes out clean, about 40 minutes. Serve with frosting or applesauce.

The Lunch Bucket

I believe every child would do better work if he could have a hot lunch instead of a bite from a dinner pail each noon. Whenever it can be arranged, hot cocoa should be served the children with their lunch. The children could take turns bringing cream for the cocoa. The teacher could buy the cocoa and sugar and each child who is able assessed so much per term to cover the cost.

As to the contents of the bucket. Let it be a surprise if possible. Wrap each article in waxed paper (enough can be bought for ten to fifteen cents to last for some time). Buy an aluminum salt shaker for ten cents. A glass or two with a screw top for the same price and plain white paper napkins also a small jar with a screw top for the butter. So many handy little dishes with lids can be found at the stores now that the child can carry almost anything he fancies.

Lunch Bucket Leak

RKE *World War I had its impact all across daily life. Not even school lunches were immune from scrutiny by those responsible for assuring there would be enough food to feed the citizens of Europe, our soldiers and our own people.*

When our children went to country school they were instructed to bring home food they did not eat. Often they wanted to carry their lunch in a newspaper or paper lunch sack like some other children did, and have no bucket to bring home. "There are dogs around the schoolhouse that will eat up the scraps so they won't be wasted," my small boy urged one day in vain. Sometimes we would see bread and butter by the roadside that children had thrown away.

We had forgotten about this waste until the other day we met the janitor of a suburban school carrying home a bucket half filled with food scrap. On the top was a fat sandwich of home baked bread and meat. "The children get in a hurry to play and lots of them will throw out almost their whole lunch. The teacher makes them put every-thing in the waste bucket. I usually get more than this to take home to my chickens."

We are so sure of the waste in this direction — waste which is unwarranted and which no parent can afford to overlook if her children are guilty — that we wish to ask the parents of the school children to investigate. The appetite of a child is capricious. He should always be well fed, but he should bring home what he does not eat on those days when he has too much. There is a shortage of food, and will be until another season — perhaps longer. There is food enough for all if we do not waste it. Lunch-bucket leaks will be stopped once the children have their attention called to the need of their cooperation.

— Harriet Wallace Ashby
Chairman Iowa Agricultural Committee,
National League for Women's Service

For the College Thanksgiving Box

The boy or girl away at college expects a box for Thanksgiving. Yes, we know they will have Thanksgiving dinners at college with extras — probably more than they would have at home. We know that packing a box is a nuisance.

R&E College Thanksgiving vacations were different in the 1920s. Few students ventured home. Instead they stayed on campus. This article illuminates campus life and its relation to home. Imagine sending laundry home, or shipping roast chicken to campus, even if the distance was "less than six hours."

A box at college is the insignia of having folks at home who care. It may arrive when every other student is getting a box and the place is surfeited with food. We can recall one case where a boy was the envied of all the other boys because "his mother never returned his laundry without putting some eats in," — the mail is full these days of the parcel post packages sending and returning college laundry. The things that should go in should be food that will keep. No roast chicken if the distance is more than six hours.

Brown bread with raisins is good without butter and it keeps well. To make it extra good, add a cup of chopped dates and walnuts.

The boys will like **Eccles Cakes** as a substitute for pie. To make these cut out three-inch circles from rich pastry rolled to quarter inch thickness. Allow two for each cake.

Filling:
3/4 cup chopped seedless raisins
2 tablespoons chopped citron
2 tablespoons melted butter
1 tablespoon grated orange peel
1/4 cup brown sugar, firmly packed
3 tablespoons honey

Preheat the oven to 400 degress F. Spread the filling in the center of the circle to within 1/2 inch of the edge. Top with second circle. Moisten edges with cold water and press them firmly together with a fork. Roll lightly with a rolling pin to make as flat as possible. Prick tops with a fork to allow steam to escape. Bake at 400 degrees F. for 10 minutes, then reduce heat to 350 degrees F., and bake for 15 to 20 minutes more, or until browned.

For another **Choice Pastry:** Line patty pans with rich crust. Drop into the center a spoonful of cake batter and ice.

Nut Crisps are delicious
1 cup powdered sugar
1 tablespoon butter
2 eggs
2 1/2 cups rolled oats
2 teaspoons baking powder
Vanilla

Bake in a slow oven.

School Lunches

A lady who had returned home from a tuberculosis sanitarium was commenting on her changed attitude toward food. "They impress it on you so strongly that food is the cure for tuberculosis that I would be afraid to neglect my milk each day, and I will not let a child leave the house until he has taken his glass of milk, soft-boiled egg, and toast or cereal for breakfast with fresh fruit or a dish of prunes. I take as much pains with balancing the school lunches of the children as I would take in putting together the materials for a cake. I am making boys and girls with the food I give them, I dare not be careless."

It is too bad to learn what to do through tuberculosis. Many mothers need to learn the importance of good food for breakfast and good food for luncheon for the growing child. The no-breakfast habit is a bad one which girls especially form.

The hot lunch is the thing for every rural school, but if thru the indifference of teachers or parents, a hot lunch is not provided, there is no more important chore for school mornings than putting up the right kind of lunch.

April 14, 1916
The Child's Curiosity

There is, I think, no surer or better way to satisfy a child's curiosity than offer to explore with him and instead of merely answering questions to help him find out. In this way you teach him by your very companionship and without one word that would lead him to think he is being taught the habit of satisfying his own curiosity.

For children old enough to use them there should be a few good reference books. Care should be taken to teach them the use of these books. Not by precept, but by example. The child who sees his parents turning to some book of authority for the disputed answer to a question will take a certain pride in consulting the books himself.

His book shelf should have on it a few good books on the natural sciences. A good book on astronomy, on geology, on botany, on natural history, on chemistry, a good book of maps, one or two histories, these are worth their weight in gold to him, When, with your help, he has learned as a tiny fellow to take a pride in trying to satisfy his own curiosity these books will answer many questions for him.
June 16, 1916

Lunch Box Suggestions

The noon meal is the most important meal of the whole day to the child who is growing and it is unfortunate that children of school age do not have more general opportunities for warm food, eaten deliberately and with a rest period for a short while afterward.

Pickles in judicious quantity may be added to the older child's luncheon, also bananas which are best omitted from the six to eight-year olds' box. Ginger cakes, fruit-filled cookies and all such toothsome foods may be included in the healthy child's basket. Not too many however, of any of these for the youngest.

We naturally think of sandwiches when we think of packing a school lunch box — or any other lunch box for that matter. Here are a few suggestions that may prove helpful.

Chopped Meat
Run cooked meat though a food chopper. Season well, adding a little celery and moisten with melted butter.

Tomato and Egg Filling
2 tablespoons butter
1/4 cup tomatoes
1/4 cup minced onion
3 eggs, lightly beaten
2 tablespoons milk
1/8 teaspoon pepper
1/8 teaspoon celery salt

Peanut Butter
Combine peanut butter with chopped lettuce or chopped parsley and spread between bread slices.

Baked croquettes
1 cup white sauce, see recipe on page 15 of Vegetable chapter
1 cup finely chopped cooked chicken or pork
1/4 cup dry bread crumbs
2 eggs, well beaten
1 cup additional dry bread crumbs

Non-stick food spray

Preheat the oven to 350 degrees F. Combine the white sauce, meat and bread crumbs. Stir in the well beaten eggs. Chill the mixture for 30 minutes, or work with damp fingers. Form the mixture into balls, about 1 1/2 inches in diameter. Press the top to make a pyramid shape. Roll in the additional bread crumbs. Place on a lightly greased cookie sheet and press slightly to form a flat bottom. Spray with non-stick spray. Bake until the croquettes are golden, about 20 minutes.

When the School Bell Rings

The secret of the empty lunch box, according to nearly 150 lunch box letters, is careful planning that results in a well balanced menu for the school child and planning of that menu in such a way as it tempts the child's appetite.

Raisin Crunch

1 cup boiling water
1 cup seedless raisins
1/2 cup molasses
1/2 cup butter
1 teaspoon salt
1/2 cup brown sugar, firmly packed
1/4 cup water

Pour boiling water over the raisins and let stand until plumped, about 10 minutes. Drain well. Boil together the molasses, sugar, butter and 1/4 cup water to hard crack on a candy thermometer, 290 degrees F., stirring constantly. Remove from heat, add raisins and pour in a thin layer in a buttered pan. Break into pieces when set and store in an air-tight container.

January 1, 1926
Waggish diner menu: Chicken Croquettes? I say waiter,
what part of a chicken is the croquette?
Waiter: The part that's left over from the day before, sir.

December 24, 1930

Whole Wheat Date Cookies

R E *If you use the dates that come diced and sugared, you should plump them in boiling water for 10 minutes before putting them into the cookies.*

1/3 cup shortening
1 cup brown sugar, firmly packed
1 egg
1 cup white flour
3 teaspoons baking powder
1/4 teaspoon baking soda
1 cup whole wheat flour
1/3 cup sour milk
1 teaspoon vanilla
1 cup dates, chopped

Preheat the oven to 350 degrees F. Cream the shortening and sugar. Stir in the egg. Add the white flour, baking powder, baking soda and mix well. Stir in the sour milk, followed by the whole wheat flour. Add the vanilla and softened dates. Drop by teaspoons on lightly greased cookie sheets. Flatten slightly with your fingers. Bake until the cookies just start to brown, about 10 to 20 minutes.

September 19, 1931

Chocolate sandwiches

These are nice for a school lunch dessert, if you have a protein sandwich.

2 squares baking chocolate, melted
1 cup powdered sugar
1/2 cup nuts, chopped
1/2 cup raisins, chopped
3 tablespoons thick cream

Cook 5 minutes, cool slightly. Spread on slices of whole wheat bread.

School Lunch Bugaboo

"Dear Me," sighs tired mother. "Here's September again with that school lunch bugaboo tucked under its arm. If only it would have waited until I got a little school sewing done and the fall canning out of the way!"

If tired mother gives her youngsters the required quart of milk, two fruits, two vegetables besides potatoes and bread and hot cereal everyday no wonder she thinks of the lunch box as a bugaboo.

One of the fruits may be served for breakfast, the second fruit may be served in the lunch box, that leaves the required two vegetables if one is to meet the school child's food requirements for the day. One of these may be included in the school lunch in

R\E *This article provides an interesting perspective on nutritional guidelines and food preferences. I was surprised at the emphasis on providing vegetables as the main content of the evening meal as a way to round out the child's nutritional needs. The suggestions for varying peanut butter are evidently precursors to today's universal PB&J.*

the form of a sandwich spread as long as the vegetables can be used raw. Later on they may be taken in soups or as possibilities of warmed up dishes if there are facilities for taking such food at the school house. A second vegetable may be served for supper in the evening. I think it isn't a bad plan to make suppers as nearly as possible a vegetable meal since that is the one type of food the school child does not seem to get during the daily menu.

Peanut Butter Suggestions

It's nice to keep on the school lunch emergency shelf a jar of peanut butter. Don't make the mistake however of letting peanut butter sandwiches become a daily occurrence. The children look forward to the little daily surprises that are the result of different

menus. When you use the peanut butter spread add some drained canned cherries about half and half. Blend it with the peanut butter and spread on thickly sliced bread. The peanut butter is delicious mixed with fresh chopped vegetable or you'll find it nice with chopped bacon added to the spread.

August 29, 1931

There are a whole lot of middle western boys and girls not going to college this Fall simply because there isn't enough money. Hope needn't die in the heart of those who aren't going to college this year. There are thousands of ways to grow without it. Sometimes stronger individuals are developed outside the classroom than in it.

Little Recipes for Little Cooks by Betty

Chicken and Noodles

Here is a good recipe for a hot dish. Mother will be using it for her parties, too.

1 cup small flat noodles, uncooked
1 1/2 cups cold cooked chicken, cut fine
1 tablespoon pimento, chopped fine
1 cup canned peas, drained
1 cup thin white sauce or chicken gravy

For the white sauce:
1 tablespoon flour
1 tablespoon butter
1 cup milk

Melt the butter in a small sauce pan. Stir in the flour and cook until it bubbles. Add the milk and cook, stirring until the sauce is thick.

For the topping:
1/4 cup dry bread crumbs
2 tablespoons melted butter

To make the dish:
Preheat the oven to 350 degrees F. Layer the noodles, chicken, pimento, and peas in a baking dish. Repeat the layers. Pour the white sauce over the layers and top with buttered bread crumbs. Pour white sauce over. Mix the bread crumbs and butter and sprinkle over the casserole. Bake until bubbly and browned on top, about 1 hour.

RKE *In the early 1930s Wallaces' Farmer ran a series of columns featuring young Miss Betty Dahlberg. Readers were encouraged to send in for a binder to keep the columns organized. The lessons covered all types of cooking and it is hard to fathom having such a young child, she appears to be around age 8, to be doing so much cooking on top of the stove and baking in the oven. Some of the recipes are fairly sophisticated, others such as the directions for Animal Sandwiches are more fun.*

Animal Sandwiches

First I bake a nice loaf of brown bread. I like to bake it in a pound baking powder can so as to have nice round slices for my sandwiches. I cut thin slices and spread them with soft butter and then with sandwich filling, like cheese spread. Finely chopped walnuts mixed with salad dressing are fine too. When I have a sandwich made, I take one of the fancy animal cookie cutters I have and cut out an animal from the top slice of my brown sandwich. I cut carefully so as not to cut the lower slice at all. I used a lion cutter so there is a lion shaped hole in the top of my brown sandwich. I put the brown sandwiches to one side and make a nice white sandwich from some of the white bread. Then I cut a lion from the top of the white sandwich.

Now comes the fun! I put the little brown lion I had cut into the hole in the top of the white sandwich and the white lion into the hole in the brown sandwich.

I made a lot of sandwiches using different cutters till I had a big platter of sandwiches that looked like a zoo or circus — rabbits, ducks, horses, chicks. etc.

Rewarding Your Child with a School Lunch

The smoothest and reddest apples should go into the child's lunch box. When picking grapes for jelly, leave a few bunches on the vines, covering them with small paper sacks, tied tightly around the stems. Thus, safely protected from the birds, they will ripen to a deep purple and will make a nice surprise in the lunch box after the other grapes have been gone for a long while. It is the unusual things that please the child. Secretly, he likes to be envied just a tiny bit by his schoolmates who will be quick to notice his nice lunches.

Nice lunches as a reward for performing small tasks after school is a matter of more merit than might be evident at first thought. When the school bell first rings, mother takes upon herself many of the small tasks the children have been doing through the vacation. September days are often uncomfortably warm, and mother feels the children should be free after being released from school and does not insist that they do their usual chores.

However it would not seem best to have the child learn to associate school with idleness in this way. Fall days are extremely busy ones for mother, and these little tasks, well performed by the children, lighten her load considerably. It is not imposing on any child to insist that he continue to help at home in these small ways.

Frosted Spice Cookies

Mrs. Paul Lacey, Morgan County, Illinois

> *1/2 cup butter*
> *1 1/2 cups brown sugar, firmly packed*
> *2 eggs*
> *1 teaspoon vanilla*
> *1 teaspoon cinnamon*
> *1/2 teaspoon cloves*
> *1/2 teaspoon nutmeg*
> *1 teaspoon baking soda*
> *4 cups flour*
> *1/3 cup buttermilk or sour milk (you may need a couple of tablespoons more)*
> *1/2 cup nuts*

Preheat the oven to 350 degrees F. Cream the butter and sugar and stir in the eggs and vanilla. Add the spices and baking soda with half the flour. Stir in the buttermilk and then the remaining flour. Mix well after each addition. You will have a fairly stiff dough to drop onto greased cookie sheets. If the dough is too stiff, add one or two tablespoons more milk. Stir in the nuts. Drop by teaspoons on a greased cookie sheet and flatten slightly with dampened fingers. Bake until cookie is firm, about 10 minutes. Cool on a rack and frost. Yield 10 dozen.

Frosting for Spice Cookies
> *1 cup golden raisins*
> *3 cups confectioners sugar*
> *6 tablespoons melted butter*
> *6 tablespoons hot coffee*
> *2 teaspoons vanilla*

Chop the raisins by combining them with the confectioner's sugar in a food processor and pulse until the raisins are chopped. Put the butter and coffee in a mixing bowl. Add the sugar and raisins along with the vanilla. Stir until smooth. Spread on cookies. Add more coffee if needed to keep at the proper consistency.

May 10, 1918
View of the Farmer's Wife

*I take great pride in my garden and in the fresh
and canned fruits berries and vegetables with which I
supply my table both winter and summer.*

*Our nine-room house contains toilet, bath, hot
and cold water, furnace, etc. with complete laundry
equipment and churn operated by a gasoline engine in the
basement with a larger engine in the engine house
for sawing wood and grinding feed. Electric light lines are
being put up here also so we will soon have electric lights.
We have an automobile and go where we please. Our farm
consists of 395 acres, and we never have any trouble
keeping a hired man as long as we want him.
We also keep a horse for him (sometimes two), do his
washing, and he has as good a room and bed as anyone in
the house, is treated like one of the family, gets the highest
wages going and as good food and as well cooked as at
any restaurant in town, and plenty of it.*

*We are not living in a famine stricken land, not
in the dark ages, but in the enlightened twentieth century
and in the prosperous United States.*
—A Contented Iowa Farmer's Wife

■ **January 1, 1917** Report says United States wages and prices are up in record business profits. Unemployment non-existent.

■ **March 16, 1917** Czar Nicholas abdicates.

■ **April 6, 1917** Congress votes to enter the first World War.

■ **May 18, 1917** Selective service act signed into law. Draft seeks 500,000 men for military service.

■ **June 27, 1917** First American troops land in France.

■ **July 4, 1918** President Wilson outlines plan for peace after war, including a League of Nations for enforcing peaceful measures.

■ **July 16, 1918** Czar and family killed by Bolsheviks.

■ **October 31, 1918** 80,000 Spanish influenza deaths reported in the United States. 10 million die worldwide.

■ **November 11, 1918** World War I Armistice signed.

■ **November 22, 1918** *Wallaces' Farmer* article: November 11, "*Everyone and his family were out celebrating. The only ones who looked wearied were the overseas soldiers surrounded by an admiring crowd of people anxious to make heroes of them, and the soldiers from Camp Dodge who didn't get over in time to take a hand. We can't do the day justice. Think of the joy that should be displayed on the biggest day of the history of the world and know that it was so displayed.*"

■ **April 27, 1919** Statistics released show 203,523 miles of highway in the United States.

■ **August 14, 1919** Food prices soar due to profiteering and rampant inflation at end of War.

■ **August 15, 1919** *Wallaces' Farmer* article. "Words! Words! Words! *The incapacity of our national leaders to reason intelligently on our fundamental food problem is, to put it mildly, distressing. There is but one wise course for the government to pursue, namely to stop meddling with the prices. All food control acts should be repealed forth with. If this is done, we shall gradually work our way out of the trouble we are in and the world will be fed not on words, but on an ample supply of food.*"

■ Projected Corn yield for 1919 in bushels per acre: Iowa 36, Illinois 32.2, Indiana 33.6, Ohio 39.6, Missouri 24.4, Nebraska 21.3, Kansas 13.6.

■ **January 16, 1920** Prohibition takes effect at midnight.

■ **July 29, 1920** Urban population exceeds rural.

■ **August 26, 1920** 9th Amendment to the constitution ratified.

■ **November 2, 1920** Harding and Coolidge defeat Cox and F.D. Roosevelt, Electoral votes 404-127.

CHAPTER 8

World War 1

Notes about food
April 20, 1917

Food is going to be the deciding factor in the World War. Food is the thing that Iowa women can give her soldier boys. Food and labor are going to be scarce unless women step into the breach. In doing so, there is room for just as heroic work on their part as among their brothers who face machine gun fire. Learn to save and preserve the food raised. A clean and empty garbage can will be the sign of true Americanism from now on.

— Governor Harding of Iowa

By the Way

With the present war conditions, the shortage of food, the uncertainty of the season's crops, the suffering over the world and the assumption that on the United States will devolve the duty of feeding a large share of the world, one of the highest tasks in the country is the farm woman's work in the home. If a farmer's wife has ever felt that in her a potential genius was swallowed up by housekeeping; if she has begrudged the time given to cooking, to sewing, to washing little faces and hands and has felt that these humble have destroyed an artist or a poet, let her now find a joy in the little, tedious things of the home which today total one of the biggest openings for service. Let her look upon herself as a needed agent of her country, one whose strength and enthusiasm must be conserved for her country's sake. Her patriotic duty will be to keep herself "fit," to simplify the work that can be simplified, to leave undone the things that can go undone.

The French army has won for itself the admiration of the civilized world, and the French soldier is taught that the smallest thing and the most useless thing a man can do for his country is needlessly to give up his life. Next to getting killed, the smallest thing is needlessly to get wounded. The greatest thing he can do is to neither get killed nor wounded, but to keep on fighting so long as his country has need of his services.

This is the lesson the farm housewife should learn this year, when so much depends upon the farmer — and the farmer's health and good spirits depend upon the commissary department.

Canadian War Cake

2 cups brown sugar, firmly packed
2 cups hot water
4 tablespoons lard (I use butter)
1 teaspoon ground cinnamon
1 teaspoon ground cloves
1 cup raisins
3 cups sifted flour
2 teaspoons baking soda

Combine the brown sugar, water, lard (or butter), cinnamon, cloves and raisins in a 2-quart pot. Bring to a boil, stirring frequently and boil 5 minutes. Set aside to cool. Preheat the oven to 325 degrees F. Stir the sifted flour and baking soda into the raisin mixture. Pour the batter into 2 large loaf pans, or 6 mini-loaves. Bake until the center is firm and the cakes are just beginning to pull away from the sides of the pan, 50 minutes for the small loaves and 60 to 70 minutes for the larger ones.

Varieties of Bread

Why not put variety in meals thru the use of more types of bread? To be sure, flour is three times as high as it used to be, but other foods have risen in proportion. Meat, as high as it is, is really as cheap a food as we are getting, but we dare not use too much meat.

Let's try the Irish tea of three or four different kinds of bread with butter or jam and see if the members of the family do not feel well fed. If we want to add corn meal to the white flour we can use the Iowa State College recipe for **Corn and Wheat Bread** which calls for 2 and 2/3 cups corn meal, 3 1/2 cups cold water, two cakes compressed yeast, 2 cups lukewarm water, 3 tablespoons sugar, 1 1/2 tablespoons salt, 2 1/4 cups white flour, 2 1/4 tablespoons shortening. Stir the corn meal into the cold water, bring to the boiling point and cook in the double boiler for ten minutes. Cool. Dissolve the yeast in the warm water and add the corn meal mush. Sift the sugar and one cup of the flour together and stir into the yeast and corn meal mixture. Beat thoroughly, let rise then beat again. Stir in the melted shortening and the remaining flour. Knead until smooth and elastic. Let rise until double. Mold into four loaves and let rise again. Bake in moderate oven.

One of our good housekeepers writes us that she adds scalded oatmeal to her bread sponge.

Whole Wheat Bread

In the following recipe, oatmeal may be used as a substitute for half the wheat flour.

2 packages instant dry yeast, dissolved in warm water
1/2 cup water
2 tablespoons brown sugar, firmly packed
3 cups milk
2 tablespoons shortening or butter
2 tablespoons molasses
4 cups graham flour
3 1/2 cups bread flour

Proof the yeast by combining with the warm water and brown sugar. Scald the milk and cool, stir in the shortening and molasses. Put the milk and yeast mixtures into a large mixing bowl. Begin adding the flours, kneading in the last two cups. Knead until you have a smooth and elastic dough. Put in a lightly greased bowl, grease the top and cover with a dampened cloth. Put in a warm place to rise until double. Punch down and form into loaves, allow to rise again until double. Preheat the oven to 350 degress F. Bake until the loaves are browned and sound hollow when tapped, about 35 minutes. Cool outside of the pans on a wire rack.

Raisin Bread Variation

Follow directions above; when bread is ready to make into loaves take a pint of the raised dough and add:
1/2 cup shortening
3 eggs, well beaten
1/2 cup seeded raisins
1 teaspoon cinnamon
Enough bread flour to make stiff dough

Coffee Cake

Instead of making one baking of white bread only, try varying the loaves by the addition of graham flour, raisins, prunes or dates. These fruit additions have a food value which we should not ignore.

1 cup scalded milk
1/3 cup shortening
1/4 cup sugar
1 package instant yeast
1/4 cup warm water
1 egg
4-5 cups flour
1/2 cup raisins

For the topping:
1 egg
3 tablespoons melted butter
1/3 cup sugar
1 teaspoon cinnamon
3 tablespoons flour

Cover and let rise overnight. In the morning knead well, turn out on a floured board and roll into a half inch sheet. Put in a shallow pan, brush with beaten egg and spread with a mixture of 3 tablespoons melted shortening, 1/3 cup sugar and 1 teaspoon cinnamon. When the sugar is partially melted sift on 3 tablespoons flour. Put in a warm place until double and bake in a moderate oven.

For the Soldiers

Mothers whose sons are to be in camp will find small jars of jam very acceptable to the boys. The word which comes back from other camps is that the men long for mail. In canning fruit and making jams and jellies get some glasses with tight-fitting lids and remember the boys. Cakes, cookies, home-made candies, gum and good reading matter will all be welcome. A durable wrist watch or a good fountain pen or ink pencil are most welcome gifts.

The Wheatless Meal

"How can we have a wheatless meal when even for corn bread we require some flour?" is a question asked when women meet together.

The object of the wheatless meal is to enable us to ship more wheat to our allies. If we substitute corn meal, barley or rye for seven meals a week, we are fulfilling our pledge. We can also keep our pledge by substituting half corn meal, barley or rye for fourteen meals.

Eating bread of any kind with potatoes is thought an extravagance by some people, and heavy as well.

We should eat more corn meal because corn meal does not ship as well as wheat and we already like corn meal dishes. The allies are not accustomed to eating corn; to ask them to change their daily habits at this crisis would be unwise.

Radical changes to the food of men can have an upsetting effect. And in addition, men who are given a radical change of ration are apt to feel resentful. We should be increasingly thankful that the war into which we have entered is not being fought on our own soil. Surely we can have a wheatless meal each day — two of them if the government so orders — and send more wheat to our allies.

Food Salvage

An article reported up to 80 percent of the food shipped into New York was rejected because a small portion of it was spoiled.

We have been urged to save the wheat, to eat the crusts, to throw out nothing. As one suffragist put it, we believe that "flour should be followed farther than the trail across the kitchen floor." Farm wives may well inform themselves about the stages the wheat and other farm produce go thru after they leave the farmer's hand. In one freight depot in Des Moines there is no rat-proof room for storing grains, flour, etc. We received a consignment of flour from an

adjacent mill and every bag of it was cut by mice or rats. The man who put it on the barrow for us said that over five dollar's worth of grain and flour were wasted there each night. We might have refused the flour, but it was all there was to be had of that special brand, and we wanted it.

Farmers have strained every nerve to grow increased crops this year. Uncle Sam should see to it that there is none wasted in high places. To work as one must work for the garden and field crops and have them condemned because of damage in transportation is neither fair nor just. Unless the farm women extend their interest in matters outside of the house they will suffer from conditions for which the farmers themselves might find a ready remedy.

Saving Food

When food is scarce, there are two ways to meet the situation. The first is to reduce the amount of food we consume, substituting, as far as possible, the more plentiful and cheaper food for that which is scarce and high priced. The second is to increase production. Food is scarce now. Over half the world is at war. Some fifty million men have been taken out of productive occupations and set to work fighting one another. A large percentage of these men were food producers. Now they are food consumers. And engaged in the sort of work that makes it necessary for them to be exceptionally well fed.

The United States is the greatest surplus food producing country from which the people in Europe can get supplies, and, unfortunately, the food supply in the United States is below normal, and the prices are very high.

We have just joined with the other nations in the fight to save civilization. We are training about a million men to fight and are sending them over to the battle lines as fast as we can get them ready. We are making ammunition and war supplies just as rapidly and we are lending money to the people who are fighting with us. But our greatest and most important task is to feed ourselves and our allies.

The National Food Administration has recently arranged with the various state food administrations to make an appeal to the housewives of the entire country. They are to be enlisted in the army of food conservation. Pledge cards will shortly be distributed which read as follows:
"I pledge myself to use the practical means within my power to aid the Food Administration in its efforts to conserve the food supplies of the country."

We trust every family which reads *Wallaces' Farmer* will join in this food conservation campaign. Our own boys are going to the battle field by the thousands. When they get over there, they must depend upon the people at home to send them food and they must have plenty of it if they are to fight vigorously. It is well to remember that in saving food in our own homes, we may be by that very act providing food for our own particular boys on the other side.

Breaking in the Family

Eating is a question of habit: Those who have always had stale butter and eggs don't like the fresh. Rye bread tastes better than white to those who are used to it. We Americans need to approach the table with an open mind and not the critical air of one who is being a martyr to a cause in which he is not interested. This is our war which is being fought; we are lucky to get off with sending our boys and giving our time and money. The French and Belgians have seen their girls tortured and assaulted. Who dare refuse to substitute or go without because the family would rather have white bread with plenty of sugar? Approaching the subject tactfully is not so much for the sake of the family than for ourselves. To get the family on a war ration without their finding it out is much more of an achievement than to force a war ration down on them.

— *Stella Hart*

Camouflage Cookery

To be a successful camouflage cook the family must not be let into the secret. Neither must they be fed too abundantly on the dish. A bountiful helping these days makes the family suspicious. Give them small helpings — especially the hungry, growing boy — and when that is done artfully suggest that since he has been working hard, he may have a second helping.

An artist in camouflaging gets no laurels — she does her work so skillfully that her family never finds out. The sign that one has achieved the artist stage is the suggestion on the part of a member of the family that Hoover is asking for economy and conservation. Then the camouflage cook proudly hugs herself, puts another cup of corn meal in her fruitcake, substitutes coffee for milk and another tablespoonful of corn starch instead of an egg.

A good camouflage dish is **Meat Roll**. To make this take 2 cups of mashed potatoes, 2 tablespoons of milk, 1 tablespoon of chicken fat or drippings, salt and pepper to taste. Mix these ingredients well together, adding 1 raw egg. Bake in a hot oven for 10 minutes and serve with turkey sauce. We may explain that fine name. Turkey sauce comes from the fact that it is supposed to be served with roast turkey — this is readily seen as good camouflage. For turkey sauce take a pint of milk, a cup of bread crumbs (very fine), 1 sliced onion, pepper and salt to taste and 3 tablespoons of cream. Simmer the sliced onion in the milk until tender; strain and pour over the bread crumbs which should be put in a saucepan. Cover and let soak half an hour; beat smooth with an egg whip and the seasoning and cream, boil up once and serve.

May 25, 1923

Poor cooking is responsible for much of the stomach trouble from which Americans suffer. We women have not made an art of cooking as have the French.

We are absent-minded cooks. We have and we haven't "good luck with our cooking." Our girls are being taught differently. Take a group of eight girls who belong to the girls' club and they can cook and can demonstrate and get the same results every time. Luck does not enter into it. Scientific principles and attention to the process in hand are the secret.

Instead of cutting her unappetizing bread in thin slices, the housekeeper would better have figured the cause and the cost of the poor bread and made it into charcoal for the chickens. Poor bread is expensive any way one thinks of it. To save it by eating it is an extravagant thrift. Drunkards are made by poor cooks.

The Food We Don't Eat Will Win the War

At a downtown luncheon the other day a woman who has no one on the fighting line looked with brimming eyes at a few of us whose boys are serving and sobbingly said, "I feel so sorry for mothers of soldiers." Then she called for white bread and put three lumps of sugar in her coffee, after having fairly smothered a grapefruit with sugar. Doubtless she was sorry for the mothers, but not sorry enough to do without the foods which by shortening the time to win the war will save their boy's lives.

If we do our share we will lose sight of the high cost of corn meal and rye and bear in mind the value to our men of wheat.

Brown Cake

Emma Orton Schultz, South Dakota

To Hearts and Homes
The following recipe for brown cake may be useful to your readers who are trying to economize.

   1 cup molasses
   1 cup hot water
   1/3 cup butter
   I teaspoon baking soda
   I teaspoon cinnamon
   2 1/2 cups flour

Preheat the oven to 350 degrees F. In a medium size bowl, put in the molasses and hot water. Add the butter and stir until melted. Add the baking soda, cinnamon and finally the flour. Mix well and pour batter into two 8- or 9-inch cake pans. Bake until the cake is firm in the center and just beginning to pull away from the sides. Cool on wire racks and fill with white frosting or the boiled icing below.

   Filling: *1 cup sugar and 1/2 cup milk boil until soft ball. Then add one teaspoon of flour and beat until it is right consistency to spread.*

Casserole Cookery

The casserole may be housed in a silver frame or an ordinary bean pot. The taste of the viand is the same. Long slow cooking is the secret of the deliciousness of a casserole dish. A benefit to the thrifty housekeeper is that the casserole takes odds and ends of dishes and with the addition of onion or celery blends them into a harmonious dish.

The food is served in the casserole in which it is cooked. For a **Casserole Roast,** take three or four pounds of heal of beef, a slice of salt pork, diced, 1/4 each of a carrot, a turnip, and an onion and a head of celery. Cook the pork like bacon. Remove the crisp bits. Brown the meat on both sides in the fat. Put in the casserole with the vegetables around it add 2 cups of hot water or stock. Cook 3 hours, basting occasionally.

Casserole Hash

Boil 1/4 pound macaroni, drain and put in a buttered casserole. Add a little butter and grated cheese. Push the macaroni to one side and fill the center of the dish with chopped meat, seasoned to taste. An hour before serving, add a can of tomatoes.

King Corn the Wonderful

Corn is not only king of the field and of the feed lot, but he is just about the king of Mrs. Iowa's kitchen in these days of conservation with every loyal housewife doing her best to save meat, wheat, sugar and fat.

Here is a day's menu worked out by the home economist experts at Iowa State College that is wholesome, nutritious, appetizing and every meal saves meat, wheat, sugar and fat. Any housewife who does not have any of the recipes on this menu may obtain them by writing Ames for them.

Breakfast — Cream of rice and raisins, milk, raised honey muffins, butter, corn syrup, coffee, cream

Dinner — Corn tamale, potatoes au gratin, tomato relish, apple and cabbage salad, corn and wheat bread, date pudding, lemon sauce, coffee or tea

Supper — Cornmeal mush fried in corn oil, corn syrup, corn and wheat bread, cherry sauce, oatmeal crisps, tea, lemon

United States Conservation Dishes

With bread and butter, a square meal for five persons.

Fish Chowder

1/4 pound salt pork
9 potatoes, peeled and cut in small pieces
1 sliced onion
2 cups sliced carrots
3 cups milk, divided
3 tablespoons flour
Pepper, to taste
1 1/2 pounds fresh fish, salted or canned

Put pork, onions, carrots and potatoes in a kettle. Cover with boiling water and simmer until vegetables are barely tender. Remove the vegetables from the kettle and set aside. Mix flour with 1/2 cup cold milk and add to the cooking liquid. Simmer until thickened, stirring constantly. Return the vegetables to the kettle and add the rest of the milk and the fish. Cook until the fish is tender, about 10 minutes. Serve hot. You may substitute rabbit, fowl, or any meat may be used instead of the fish or tomatoes instead of milk.

Dried Peas with Rice and Tomatoes

2 cups dried peas
1 1/2 cups rice
6 onions
1 teaspoon salt, or less
2 cups tomatoes, fresh or canned

Soak the peas overnight in two quarts of water. Cook until tender in the soaking water. Add rice, onions, tomatoes and seasoning. Cook for 20 minutes.

The War is Won

In the fullness of His own time, the God of Hosts has brought to an end the greatest period of crime and death and suffering in the history of the world. The arch fiends are panic-stricken fugitives in foreign lands. The nation which blindly but willingly followed their leadership is in the throws of internal revolution.
— Wallaces' Farmer Editorial

Foods that are Plentiful

A statement from the Food Administration says: The world balance of food products shows a shortage of three billion pounds of fats and three million tons of high protein foods. Among the fats are included pork products, dairy products and vegetable oils. Commodities of which there are sufficient quantities if used with economy are wheat, rye, beans, peas, rice and foods other than those high in protein. Sufficient beef is in sight to load all refrigerator ships to their capacity. There is enough sugar for our normal consumption if other nations retain their present short rations. With the possible exception of high protein foods, the United States has sufficient foods and feed for its own people. But to fulfill its pledge of 20,000,000 tons to Europe by July 1, 1919 there must be continued conservation and avoidance of waste. Mr. Hoover says that conservation is needed now more than at any time since we became aligned with the enemies of Germany.

"The situation is such that Americans are put on their honor to avoid waste, to eat the foods which are plentiful and to eat only the food required. The fourth meal, the extra indulgence, are all at the expense of the starving." — *Mr. Herbert Hoover*

Great Majestic
The Range with a Reputation

Spanish Influenza

Spanish influenza is spreading terror thru the homes of the land. Anything relating to its prevention and cure is eagerly sought.

At Camp Dix, New Jersey, men who have Spanish influenza are put on a diet which calls for an abundance of fresh fruit. School children need the same diet. Let us keep out this disease by the above simple precautions.

CHAPTER 9

Home Economics

Thrift on the Farm
August 15, 1919

*Thrift is not altogether a matter of saving; thrift is
making everything do its best.*

*Thrift on the farm lies in putting a value on the best
and making that best thrive.*

*What is the best on the farm?
The heart of the family is the mother. Unless she is in health,
no part of the farm can thrive as it could if she were
in vigorous health. If there were modern conveniences which
will help her, she should have them. Running water in the house
should be the right of every farm woman. One prematurely
aged woman on her sick bed said: "I am so tired. The water
bucket was always empty and the slop bucket was always full
and there was no one but me to tend to them."*

*There is the arrangement of the rooms and the furniture
in them. Sometimes a kitchen is so planned that the
mileage of woman power is twice what is needed. And woman
power has a limited amount of "juice" in the health reservoir as
well as has the automobile.*

*To live more cheaply is not the ideal — to live better and easier,
but to live without waste, that is thrift.*

Economical Recipes

Fruit Pudding

Preheat the oven to 300 degrees F. Place in an earthen or granite baking dish a layer of juicy black raspberries. Add water or juice to more than cover the berries, 1 cup of sugar and a bit of butter (2 tablespoons). On this, place slices of stale bread to more than cover the fruit and over this more berries, adding sugar, butter and juices as in the first layer. Cover and bake slowly for an hour and a half. If carefully baked, the bread and fruit are united so that it would puzzle the uninitiated to know the combination of the pudding. Any kind of fruit may be used in place of the raspberries or two kinds of fruit, one sweet and one tart, such as peaches and apricots. Serve with whipped cream or jelly sauce.

RKE *This recipe is more dependent upon the size of your baking dish than actual measurements. You will need a sturdy home-made style bread for this to work. Modern loaf breads are too soft to make an appetizing dessert.*

Cracker Pudding

2 cups rich milk
2 eggs, separated
1/2 cup fine cracker crumbs
2 tablespoons coconut flavoring, or to taste
2 tablespoons sugar

Preheat the oven to 350 degrees F. Combine the egg yolks and milk, reserving the egg whites. Stir into the cracker crumbs and add the coconut flavoring. Pour the mixture into a small casserole dish. Place this dish into a pan of hot water and bake 1/2 hour or until the pudding is firm in the center. Just before the pudding is done, make a meringue by beating the reserved egg whites with the 2 tablespoons sugar until firm peaks form. Reduce the heat in the oven to 325 degrees F. Spread the meringue over the pudding and return to the oven to brown, about 10 minutes.

February 15, 1921

In every community will be found foreign women
who have secrets of cookery or needlework which
would bless both the giver and the receiver if she were
invited to share them. It may be we are too anxious
to show our foreign neighbors how we do things and
too slack in our interest in how they do.

Sponge Cake

1 1/4 cups flour
1 teaspoon baking powder
2 eggs, separated
1 cup sugar, divided
1/2 cup warm water

R\E *My mother-in-law had a recipe similar to this one. As she used to say, "Don't putter around when making this!" You need to get it in the oven as quickly as you can.*

Preheat the oven to 350 degrees F. Sift together the flour and baking powder. Begin beating the egg whites in a clean bowl with grease-free beaters. Gradually add 1/2 cup sugar and continue beating until the egg whites are stiff. Set aside. In a separate bowl, beat the egg yolks together with the remaining 1/2 cup sugar. Beat until thick and lemon colored. Gently fold the flour mixture into the egg yolks in the flour mixture, then fold in the beaten egg whites. Finally, fold in the warm water. Pour the batter into a greased and floured 9-inch square baking pan. Bake until firm in the center, about 25 minutes.

One Dish Meals

The family can be well fed on a meal of one dish only if they can be brought to think so. Provided that one dish is really a meal in itself. All of these are nourishing and if we do not let our eyes influence our attitude toward our food, these dishes will be sufficiently satisfying with bread and butter.

Corn and beans served as a succotash with butter or cream dressing is a combination which may occasionally take the place of meat and potatoes

Rolled steak with bread crumb dressing and gravy

Baked beans with bacon

Hot vegetable soup with cold meat shoulder of mutton or a neck piece, thickened with rice

Macaroni with cheese

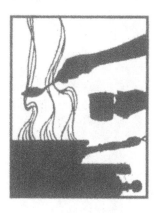

When Fresh Fruit is Scarce

To Hearts and Homes

At these times of the year when fresh fruit is scarce or so high in price that I feel that we can not afford to buy it, I turn to the various dried fruits with much satisfaction. Take the wholesome and nourishing date; its flavor combines especially well with rye and graham flour, molasses, apples and oranges and the ingenious housewife may combine many dishes having the zest of the unexpected. The child who rejects his morning cereal can usually be tempted by adding a handful of chopped dates five minutes before the porridge is removed from the fire. Raisins and chopped figs are both excellent to use in this way.

Fig Tarts: 1 cup chopped figs, 1 cup water. Stew in a double boiler for three hours then add 1/2 cup sugar and the juice of 1 lemon. Fill small pastry shells previously baked and have whipped cream on each before serving. (RKE: Stewing the figs in the microwave will make these tarts much more quickly.)

Prune Toast: Toast as many slices of bread as desired, butter and place on a hot serving dish. Have ready some large prunes which have been stewed and the stones removed. Place 4 or 5 prunes on each slice, moisten with the hot syrup in which they were cooked and serve at once. This is a very nutritious and wholesome dish for a school girl or boy.

Sponge Cake with Figs: Take stale sponge cakes and cut into squares. Heaped with stewed figs, prunes or dates, or a mixture of all three and ornamented with whipped cream, this makes an attractive dessert especially when an unexpected friend drops into luncheon and you have to prepare a dessert in a hurry.

Raisin Pie: Boil the peel of 1 orange or lemon. When tender, chop fine and add 1 small cup of light brown sugar, 1/2 cup of raisins, seeded, 1 beaten egg and the pulp of 2 oranges. Thicken with 1 teaspoon of arrowroot or corn starch. Bake between 2 crusts. (RKE: Instead, grate the rind and add to the brown sugar. This makes a small pie, 6 inches in diameter. Bake at 350 degrees F. for 35 minutes.)

Apple and Date Salad: 1 cup dates, stoned and shredded, 3 cups tart apples chopped, 1/2 cup chopped walnuts. Season with sugar and lemon juice or a cup of sweet cider.

In the home cooking as well as in that for company I think one should always plan to not upset anyone's digestion by serving rich, indigestible dishes simply because they look pretty and appeal to the taste when others just as pretty and tasty, and not harmful, may be substituted.

— *Mrs. Browning*

Thrift Luncheon

Macaroni Loaf

> 3/4 cup uncooked macaroni
> 1 cup cream or milk
> 1 cup soft bread crumbs
> 1/4 cup butter
> 1 teaspoon green pepper
> 1/2 cup grated cheese
> 1 tablespoon onion juice
> 3 eggs, well beaten

Partially cook the macaroni in water and drain. Add to the milk and finish cooking until tender. Add the remaining ingredients and mix well. Pour into a baking dish, and bake until firm, about 30 minutes. Serve with Tomato Sauce.

Tomato Sauce

> 1 cup tomato pulp and juice
> 1 slice onion, minced
> 2 teaspoons flour
> Salt and pepper to taste

Mix all ingredients together and cook over medium heat until thickened, stirring frequently.

Convenient Kitchen

By properly arranging her kitchen stove, table and sink in close proximity to the dining room and pantry, the housekeeper may save many steps in her tasks of the kitchen. In planning a new house or in remodeling an old one these three items are the most important of the kitchen equipment and should be installed first of all.

Equipment such as the ice box, dish cupboard and set tubs should be also located so that they will be convenient. These suggestions are taken from Farmer's Bulletin No. 607, "The Farm Kitchen as a Workshop."

In locating the stove or range, room must be allowed for the hot water boiler. It is not necessarily placed at the side of the range but may be suspended from the ceiling. Never place it below the level of the range as the water will not circulate and heat satisfactorily under this condition.

The floor under the stove or range should be made of, or covered with, some fireproof material.

When Meat is High

"What are we going to do for meat when the price is beyond us?" a young housekeeper asked. Our families can be weaned from the large helpings of meat they have had in former years, and their health be really bettered if they can but be coaxed to do without meat cheerfully. The deprivation to most of us in doing without is not so much in not having as in being willing to go without.

If the cook can make a body of a dish of macaroni, beans or potatoes merely flavor it with meat and call it meat macaroni, meat loaf or meat soufflé. She will satisfy the meat cravers better than by apologizing for the small amount of meat she is able to afford for the family table. The following dishes are aimed to supply a nourishing dish without a great amount of meat.

Beefsteak Roll Take a thin slice of round steak and fill with bread and onion stuffing. Roll and secure with toothpick. Bake in a medium oven until browned.

Shepherd's Pie Cut a pound of any kind of meat in small pieces and put it on to stew until almost tender. Cold meat will do almost as well as fresh. Make a gravy over it with cream and milk, and put in a baking pan. Cover the top with a thick crust of mashed potato without an egg and bake till brown. Grated cheese adds to the flavor.

Fall Sweets A delicious jelly is made of sour apples and mint. To 4 pounds of apples take 1 cup of finely chopped mint. Wash the mint and cook with the apples until they are well done, adding enough water to keep from burning until the juice starts. Strain and take 3/4 cup of sugar to each cup juice. When about ready to jell, enough color paste may be added to color the desired shade. This jelly looks well for a St. Patrick's Day lunch or for a green and white color scheme.

Chicken a la King One of the favorite dishes in a Des Moines lunch room is "Chicken a la King." This is brought out in small plates covered with glass covers to keep it piping hot when it reaches the customer. The following is the recipe used.

> *1 1/2 tablespoons chicken fat*
> *1 tablespoon corn starch*
> *3/4 cup of chicken stock*
> *1/2 cup milk*
> *1/4 cup cream*
> *1 egg yolk*
> *1 cup cold boiled chicken, cut in strips*
> *1/2 cup mushrooms, sliced*
> *1/2 cup canned pimentos cut in strips*

Melt the fat, add the corn starch and stir until well blended. Then pour in the stock, milk and cream. Bring to the boiling point then reduce heat and cook, stirring constantly, until thickened. Beat the egg yolk in a heat-proof cup, add a bit of the hot mixture and stir until the egg yolk is warmed. Add to the sauce and cook 3 minutes. Stir in the chicken, mushrooms and pimento and heat through. Serve over slices of buttered toast.

March 16, 1917
Corn Meal

The poets have sung in their beautiful song
Of food things to eat for ever so long;
They've sung of potatoes,
Of peas and tomatoes;
Of mutton, or pork and of veal
Of milk and of honey –
But isn't if funny
That they have neglected corn meal?

Corn meal was the food of our fathers, you know
And back to that food we should all gladly go,
For the high cost of living
Is causing misgiving
So, comrades to you I appeal –
Get back to corn dodgers
Ye modernized codgers
And eat your own home made corn meal.

Just think of corn meal and the things it will make!
How close to us all and how easy to bake!
Just think of the muffins,
The chitlins and stuffing
And doesn't the thinking reveal
That these and pot liquor
Will hit the spot quicker
With water-ground, home-made corn meal!

Then join us in singing to corn meal a song —
The product that made our grandfathers so strong;
Yes, join us in singing,
In chanting and ringing
Will all of our national zeal;
The praise of the dishes
That fill our food wishes,
And's made of our matchless corn meal

— *V. O. Ramnkin, quoted in* Wallaces' Farmer
from the Louisville Courier Journal

Five-Cent Meals

Miss Margaret Foster of Cincinnati spent three weeks in a tenement studying living conditions. Miss Foster has compiled menus which can be served to a family of seven for 35 cents. One day's menu was:

Breakfast – *Apples, 3 cents; bread and peanut butter, 8 cents; milk, 2 cents.*

Dinner – *Creamed lima beans, 13 cents; day-old bread and oleo, 7 cents; grape pudding, 13 cents; milk, 8 cents. This is slightly higher than 35 cents but is balanced by the cheaper breakfast menu.*

Supper – *Round steak, onions and gravy, 24 cents; baked potatoes, 10 cents; bread and oleo, 7 cents; rice, sugar and milk, 12 cents.*

A five-cent menu which a college girl prepared giving seventy-five calories was: Creamed eggs on toast, gingerbread and milk.

Enough for Five

People are rich or poor by comparison. The following list of necessary articles of diet for five people for one week would seem insufficient to the farm family, yet we have the assurance of Miss Aubyn Chinn, food expert of the Department of Agriculture, that it is sufficient. Miss Chinn says the cost of living has increased 58 percent since 1913. The following prices are based on Washington prices. Washington is said to be one of the dearest places in the county.

Bread, 14 1/2 pounds	*$1.16*
Butter, 2 pounds	*1.20*
Milk, 21 quarts	*3.78*
Eggs, 1 1/2 dozen	*.45*
Cereal, 5 pounds	*.18*
Sugar, 4 3/4 pounds	*.48*
Tea and coffee, 1 1/2 pounds	*.42*
Meat, 4 pounds	*1.76*
Potatoes, 16 pounds	*.15*
Vegetables, 15 pounds	*.45*
Fruits, 11 pounds	*.69*

Farmers can not estimate the cost of their food on what it would cost them to buy it in Washington, but on what they could sell it for at the local market. One reason the farm family sometimes thinks their meals lack variety is because they do not sufficiently emphasize the value of fruit in the diet. Fruit — fresh, dried or canned — is a necessary in a well-balanced diet, especially for children.

Menus for Families Doing Moderately Hard Work

Sunday Breakfast – *Eggs, hot muffins with butter and marmalade and coffee*

Sunday Dinner – *Chicken and gravy, potatoes, onion or squash or cabbage, prune pie and whipped cream*

Sunday Supper – *Welsh Rarebit, toast, fruit, cookies*

Monday Breakfast – *Cereal and cream, eggs, toast and coffee*

Monday Dinner – *Roast pork, sweet potatoes, fresh or stewed tomatoes, fruit*

Monday Supper – *Bread and milk, fruit salad or sauce, tea*
(For a heartier meal, add potatoes or bread and butter and jam for energy.)

Tuesday Breakfast – *Fruit, boiled ham, biscuit, coffee*

Tuesday Dinner – *Cottage cheese, creamed potatoes, lettuce or fruit salad, hot bread and preserves*

Tuesday Supper – *Tomato soup, baked potato, bread, butter, soft custard, angel or sponge cake*

Wednesday Breakfast – *Fruit, cereal and cream, toast, bacon and coffee*

Wednesday Dinner – *Tamale pie, spinach, bread and butter*

Wednesday Dinner – *Creamed or scalloped eggs, fried potatoes, bread, butter, baked apple, peanut cookies, milk*

You will note that some kind of green vegetable, fruit and eggs appear in each day's menus also that about one pint of milk is used per person each day. One pint for each child should be added each day.

November 12, 1926

The growing of soybeans as a substitute for par of the oats crop has been advocated. The great drawback has been the extreme difficulty in cutting, curing and threshing. A "combine" harvester-thresher changes all this. With a small machine, three or four men can harvest, thresh and put in the bin the bean crop from twenty or more acres in an eight or nine hour day.

Dear Hearts and Homes Editor

Will you please help me plan a budget? This is the first time I ever tried it. My husband is moving from a place where he was farming for himself to a place where he will work for $75 a month. He is doing this because the doctors say I must have a rest. The house we move into will be modern. Our house rent, meat, eggs, and wood for fuel will be furnished. We shall keep a cow for milk and cream but will have to buy our butter.

We must save $5 a month. I shall have a small garden, do plain sewing but nothing hard. Sewing tires me dreadfully, but I am a good buyer, I think, and I take good care of clothes when washing.

The problem is to pay for groceries. Oh! First let me tell you there are six children, the oldest ten years. All right – groceries, coal for furnace in severe weather, electricity (I wash and iron with it), water (we use city water), clothes for all of us; school supplies ($5 will do I believe); house furnishings (I must have about $50 for that); telephone, books and magazines, doctor and dentist bills and recreation, which will be Chautauqua, $6.

I know it is a hard problem but it has to be done and I shall be thankful for any help you may give me.

The Spending Plan

Note: Since the house rent, meat, eggs and wood are furnished we list these under income.*

Income

Salary for the year	*$900*
House, rent for one year at $15	*$180*
Fuel, wood	*$20*
Meat at butchering time	*$50*
Eggs hard to estimate, but about	*$50*
Total income	*$1,200*

Expenditures

Groceries	*$450*
Clothing	*$320*
Savings	*$60*
Doctor and Dentist	*$100*
Electricity	*$60*
Coal	*$50*
Miscellaneous	*$50*
Education and Recreation	*$50*
Household Equipment	*$50*
Total expenditures	*$1,190*
Balance	*$10*

In explanation of this budget we might say that the grocery bill may be kept down to a minimum thru the good use of the home garden and canning. Clothing is a great big puzzle. Mother's and father's clothes should have first consideration The smaller ones will, of course, wear the "hand-downs."

An authority on budgets says that money and illness are saved by going to doctors and dentists for examinations occasionally. School supplies are lumped off into the miscellaneous column along with the telephone which will probably cost around $10 a year and water for $5 a year. Any number of other little items will come out of this fund including birthday and Christmas presents and the like.

A balance was purposely left to be fitted in as the users of this budget see fit.

*Looking at these figures today, it is difficult to see how the $900 of actual cash income could cover the $1200 cash expenditures.

The Zero Hour in Meal Planning

There is a time in early spring which every housewife knows all too well. Fresh fruits and vegetables are expensive and difficult to procure if one is situated far from the larger markets; household supplies are somewhat exhausted and jaded appetites are rebelling against "canned" foods. Try some of these methods of serving food already on hand and see if they will not offer a welcome change.

French Style Green Beans

> *1 can green beans*
> *2 tablespoons butter*
> *Juice of half a lemon (about 1 tablespoon)*

Cook the green beans in the water they were packed in. Drain them and return them to the pan and heat until the beans are dry. Add the butter and lemon juice and shake over heat until the butter is melted.

Tomato Custard

> *1 32-ounce can stewed or chopped tomatoes*
> *1/4 cup minced onion, optional*
> *2 tablespoons sugar*
> *1/3 cup cracker crumbs*
> *2 lightly beaten eggs*

> **For the cheese sauce:**
> *1 1/2 cups white sauce, see recipe on page 15 of Vegetables chapter*
> *1/2 cup grated cheese*
> *1/8 teaspoon dry mustard*

Combine the tomatoes, onion and sugar in a medium sauce pan. Cook over low heat for fifteen minutes. Press the tomatoes through a sieve, or puree in processor or blender. Cool slightly. Stir in the cracker crumbs and then the eggs. Divide the mixture among 4 well buttered ramekins. Bake until custard is set. Top with the cheese sauce.

Quick Pea Soup

> *2 regular sized can peas (about 15 ounces each)*
> *1 quart liquid which may be light cream, beef or*
> *   chicken stock or half of each*
> *1/4 cup minced onion*
> *1 package frozen spinach*
> *1 tablespoon flour*

Drain the peas but reserve 1/4 cup of the canning liquid. Combine all ingredients and cook over low heat for ten or fifteen minutes. Press the mixture through a sieve, or puree in a processor or blender. Whisk together the flour with the reserved pea liquid. Stir this into the soup. Return it to the stove and cook, stirring constantly, until thickened.

■ **March 4, 1921** Harding inaugurated as President.

■ **February 22, 1921** First issue of Reader's Digest published.

■ **March 18, 1921** Ghandi imprisoned for civil disobedience.

■ **October 30, 1921** Mussolini governs Italy.

■ **December 2, 1921** *Wallaces' Farmer* article "Support for Acreage Reduction." *"With farmers selling their corn at less than half the cost of production and with the greatest piling up of corn reserves in history it was expected that a campaign for reducing the corn acreage would meet with high approval. Of course some men must have a cash crop. On good corn land soybeans yield about 20 bushels to the acre and each pound of seed has a feeding value equivalent to oil meal. On many farms it will pay to grow an acre or two of potatoes."*

■ **December 9, 1921** *Wallaces' Farmer* article "The Magic of the Wireless." *"The United States Bureau of Markets has established a number of stations to broadcast stock, grain and market reports and other items of interest to farmers at certain times each day. The messages can be received at any wireless station. There is no charge connected with the service."*

■ **November 26, 1922** Tomb of King Tutankhaman discovered.

■ **March 1923** Teapot Dome government scandal breaks.

■ **August 2, 1923** President Harding dies in office, Calvin Coolidge takes oath of office.

■ **November 1924** Calvin Coolidge with 382 electoral votes elected president over John W. Davis with 163 and William La Follette with 13. Election slogan: "Keep Cool with Coolidge."

CHAPTER 10

Canning

Canning Joy

Josephine Wylie August 31, 1928

There is something very fascinating about storing and locking fruits and vegetables away in cans that one almost forgets to be tired. And then one feels so virtuous afterwards, too. And so well compensated for weariness. Just to think of all that food put away! We ought to live pretty well thru still another winter.

I found myself easily identifying with the Wallaces' Farmer *writers as they described the toil and satisfaction resulting from "putting up" the garden produce in glass jars. Freezing food may be more convenient, and certainly cooler in the middle of the summer when all the vegetables and fruits are ripe for processing. To my mind and heart the end product shut away in the freezer can't compare with the joy of lining the kitchen counter with shiny glass jars filled with richly colored jams, jellies, pickles and other preserves.*

The directions for the recipes in this chapter are for those who are already experienced in home canning. I've elected not to include the specifics of the canning methods. If you have never tried this process there a few rules to remember. Everything must be scrupulously clean. Unless you are making a small amount for immediate use and storing it in the refrigerator, you should use jars specifically manufactured for home canning. Jars and lids should be sterilized. In most cases the filled jars should be processed in a boiling water bath to assure stability and a good seal. For methods and times consult the material in canning books, the inserts that come with new jars or on the Internet at sites such as the one maintained by the Kerr jar company at www.homecanning.com.

Chow Chow

1 peck green tomatoes
1/2 peck string beans
1/4 peck small onions
1/2 cup diced green and red peppers
2 large cabbages
4 tablespoons white mustard seed
2 teaspoons whole cloves
2 tablespoons celery seed
2 tablespoons whole allspice
1 2.5–ounce box dry mustard (approximately)
1 pound brown sugar
1 ounce turmeric
6 cups vinegar or more

Chop the vegetables into very small pieces using a food processor, grinder or knife. Combine in a very large kettle with the spices and sugar. Pour the vinegar over to just barely cover the vegetables. You may need to add more than the 6 cups. Bring to a boil over medium heat, then lower the heat and simmer until the vegetables are just tender. Pack in sterilized jars and process pint jars in a boiling water bath for 20 minutes.

September 16, 1898

Sweet Pickles of Ripe Cucumbers

2 pounds peeled, quartered cucumbers
1 tablespoon salt
1 quart vinegar
1 1/2 pounds sugar
1 tablespoon whole cloves
5 2-inch cinnamon sticks

Put the cucumber spears in water to cover, add salt. Bring to a boil and cook for two minutes. Drain. Combine the remaining ingredients and bring to a boil. Carefully add the cucumbers, remove from the heat and allow to cool. Keep the cucumbers in the syrup in the refrigerator for one week. Drain the liquid. Bring it to a boil. Add the cucumbers, remove from heat and allow to cool. Pack in hot sterilized jars, and keep refrigerated.

October 6, 1899
Golden Grains

A man is like a horseradish — the more it is grated the more it bites.

We never are as happy, or so unhappy, as we imagine.

The safety of the state depends upon the virtue of its women.

A man prays when he is in danger, a woman all the time.

Second thoughts are best. Man was God's first thought, woman his second.

Cold Catsup

1 peck ripe tomatoes
2 cups salt
2 cups finely chopped onions
2 cups finely chopped celery
1 cup sugar
1 quart vinegar

Peel tomatoes without scalding and cut in small cubes, add the salt and let stand over night. In the morning combine the sugar and vinegar and bring to a boil, stirring until the sugar is fully dissolved. Drain well and rinse off excess salt. Pour the syrup over the vegetables. Mix well and refrigerate.

May 10, 1918

View of the Farmer's Wife

I take great pride in my garden and in the fresh and canned fruits, berries and vegetables with which I supply my table both winter and summer.

Our nine-room house contains toilet, bath, hot and cold water, furnace, etc. with complete laundry equipment and churn operated by a gasoline engine in the basement with a larger engine in the engine house for sawing wood and grinding feed. Electric light lines are being put up here also, so we will soon have electric lights. We have an automobile and go where we please. Our farm consists of 395 acres, and we never have any trouble keeping a hired man as long as we want him. We also keep a horse for him (sometimes two), do his washing, and he has as good a room and bed as anyone in the house. He is treated like one of the family, gets the highest wages going and as good food and as well cooked as at any restaurant in town and plenty of it.

We are not living in a famine stricken land, not in the dark ages, but in the enlightened twentieth century and in the prosperous United States.

—A Contented Iowa Farmer's Wife

A Shelf Full of Relishes

Home-made sauces from home-grown fruits and vegetables are first aids in serving cold meats or stretching out the roasts. Every well-stored pantry should have its shelf of relishes; chutney to serve with chicken, corn relish with fish, cucumber catsup with steak and spiced grapes or currants with cold meats.

Apple Catsup

1 quart apple sauce,
1 teaspoon each ginger, cinnamon, cloves, black pepper, mustard and onion extract
1 teaspoon salt
2 cups vinegar
3/4 cup molasses

Combine all ingredients in a heavy kettle. Cook over medium heat until the catsup is thickened. Lower heat and stir frequently as the catsup nears completion.

Indian Chutney

24 medium sized ripe tomatoes, peeled, seeded and drained
6 onions
3 red peppers
3 green peppers
3 stalks celery
12 tart apples, peeled and cored
1 pound seedless raisins
2 quarts vinegar
1 1/2 cups sugar
1 1/2 cups corn syrup

Chop all the fruits and vegetables into 1/8-inch pieces using a food processor, knife or grinder. Combine all ingredients in a large heavy kettle. Cook over medium to low heat until the chutney is thickened, about 45 minutes. Stir frequently. Pour into sterilized jars and process in a boiling water bath.

Corn Relish

10 cups sweet corn, cut from cob
3 green peppers, chopped
2 red peppers, chopped
8 cups finely chopped cabbage
2 cups sugar
4 ounces dry mustard
2 tablespoons salt
1 cup light corn syrup
8 cups vinegar

Combine all ingredients in a large heavy kettle. Cook over medium heat until the corn and cabbage are tender, about 20 minutes. Put in sterilized jars and process in a boiling water bath, or keep in the refrigerator.

How to Can Beef

There is nothing that quite so fortifies the housekeeper as having a supply of meat on hand. Unexpected company for dinner or extra farm hands to cook for are not matters for concern to the woman who has her cellar shelves filled with a variety of canned meats.

In this article on canning beef, I intend getting a bit personal by telling you about some of the ways in which I have canned nearly 300 quarts of meat in the past two years.

The wash boiler makes a very good container for canning by the hot water bath method as a great many cans may be put in at a time. The water should come to a bubbling boil — this must not be mistaken by steam arising from the boiler — before a can should be put in. As more cans are put in, water may be dipped out so that the cans are under water of at least an inch. I keep a pencil handy and mark on the top of each jar the time it is to be taken out. This is quite important when you have a boiler full of jars that have been put in at different times.

I much prefer to use the pressure cooker in meat canning since is it possible to get temperatures from 10 to 36 degrees higher than when the jars are cooked by submerging them in boiling water. This not only insures death to any bacteria that might live through the ordinary boiling temperature, but shortens the time of cooking just about one-third. I have never had any spoilage from steaks cooked 50 minutes in the pressure cooker under 15 pounds pressure or 2 1/2 hours in the boiling water bath.

Carrot Pickles

4 cups baby carrots
2 cups vinegar
1 cup sugar
2 tablespoons mixed pickling spices

RKE *The original recipe in* Wallaces' Farmer *says, "This is a dainty and very delicious pickle and is also especially nice and colorful for garnishing dishes of cold meat and salads."*

Cook the carrots in salted water until tender, about 20 minutes. Make the pickling syrup by combining the vinegar, sugar and pickling spices. Simmer, stirring frequently, until the sugar is dissolved. Pack carrots in sterilized jars and pour the syrup over them. Seal and store in the refrigerator indefinitely.

July 31, 1925

Eat vegetables rather than so much meat during the hot days of July and August and you will feel much better. Drinking plenty of water, too, will add to the general comfort of this season.

Grape Pear Butter

1 cup water
2 pounds grapes
2 pounds Bartlett pears
Sugar

Combine the grapes and water. Simmer until the grapes are tender. Run the grapes through a good food mill or press through a colander. Peel, core and chop the pears and add to the grape pulp. Measure this and add 4 parts sugar to each 5 parts of pulp. Cook over very low heat, stirring almost constantly, until the butter is thickened. Pour into sterilized jars and store in the refrigerator.

April 5, 1929

Rhubarb Conserve

It won't be long now until we can count on fresh spring rhubarb to aid us in our campaign against empty jam jars.

2 cups rhubarb, cut in 1/4-inch dice
Juice from 2 oranges
2 teaspoons grated orange rind
2 tablespoons lemon juice
2 cups sugar
2 cups chopped almonds

Combine the rhubarb, orange juice, rind, lemon juice and sugar. Stir and let stand until the sugar is dissolved. Bring to a boil over medium heat and cook, stirring frequently, until the mixture is thickened and the rhubarb is transparent. Stir in the nuts and cook for 5 more minutes. Pour into sterilized jars and process in a boiling water bath.

Rhubarb Pineapple Conserve

This makes an excellent sandwich filling according to the original *Wallaces'* recipe.

2 cups crushed pineapple
2 quarts diced rhubarb, cut in 1/4-inch dice
1 orange, juice and rind
7 cups sugar
1/2 cup nuts

Combine all the ingredients except the nuts. Stir until the sugar is dissolved. Bring to a boil, reduce the heat and cook over medium heat until the mixture is thickened, stirring frequently. Add the nuts and cook for 5 more minutes. Pour into sterilized jars and process in a boiling water bath.

August 17, 1928

Mrs. Lane's Red Pimento Pickle

Cut the ends out of pimentos and remove seeds. Wash and let stand in cold water for 15 minutes. Then put into boiling water and boil 3 minutes. Dip immediately into cold water and let stand a few minutes. Then put back into hot water, but not the same hot water, for a few minutes. Put into cold water again and at last into hot. They are now ready to put into the jars.

Prepare a pickling syrup by bringing to the boiling point 2 cups vinegar, 2 cups water and 1 cups sugar. Pour boiling hot syrup over the pimentos in the jars.

RKE In the middle of the 1920s references to pimentos began appearing in recipes. Pimentos are red sweet peppers. Being only familiar with the commercially packed version, frequently popped into olives, I was somewhat bewildered at their appeal. Preparing this version, helped me realize the difference.

This process may seem a little tedious with all the moving about from hot water into cold water and back again, but you will be rewarded with lovely pimentos that remain whole and a beautiful red color. They are delicious for winter salads. They may be stuffed with cottage cheese and nuts and sliced or stuffed whole with cabbage.

July 5, 1929

Do You Plan as You Can?

For each member of my family I can the following fruits and vegetables. This budget allows for one serving each of canned fruit and vegetable per person per day. A stored vegetable, or an occasional one bought fresh, will provide a second vegetable thus meeting the ideal of two servings a day.

Vegetables: 40 quarts
— Greens served 2 times a week for 5 months equals 10 quarts
— Tomatoes served 2 times a week for 8 months equals 12 quarts
— Other Vegetables served 3 times a week for 7 months equals 18 quarts

Fruits: 43 quarts
— Rhubarb served once a week for 5 months equals 10 quarts
— Other fruits served 6 times a week for 7 months equals 33 quarts

	Yields
1 bushel peaches	*35 quarts*
1 bushel pears	*30 quarts*
1 bushel plums	*28 quarts*
1 bushel cherries	*20 quarts*
1 bushel whole tomatoes	*20 quarts*
1 bushel tomatoes for soup	*28 pints*
1 1/2 pounds spinach	*1 pint*
1 pound chard	*1 pint*
12-15 baby beets	*1 pint*
3/4 pound string beans	*1 pint*
2 1/2 quarts peas	*1 pint*
18 small carrots	*1 pint*

I shall never get along without a canning budget again. It has furnished healthful, nourishing meals all winter with variety and interest in the meal planning. It has eliminated worries and embarrassment when guests arrive unexpectedly. It has made possible, on thrice reduced wages, a very welcome tho very small bank account. It has interested the children in saving and budgeting and best of all, I believe, it is directly responsible for the present good health of the family. Before we had much sickness but this winter and early spring we have been fine. Altho we have been out of work two weeks this winter and have had our wages cut again, the budget went right on working and we have paid over half of what we owe.

Vegetables and fruit

1 half pint jelly, preserves or fruit butter each day.

Each week – 2 quarts corn
4 quarts tomatoes
1 quart green beans
1 quart strawberries
1 quart gooseberries
1 quart peaches
2 quarts apples
2 quarts mixed fruits

Once every two weeks
1 pint carrots
1 quart beets

Every four weeks
1 quart sauerkraut
1 quart squash
1 quart pickles
1 quart relish

Every day we like we could have potatoes and onions, and dried beans once in two weeks.

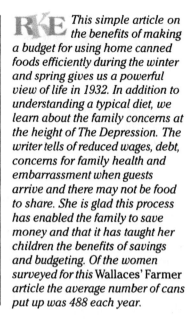

This simple article on the benefits of making a budget for using home canned foods efficiently during the winter and spring gives us a powerful view of life in 1932. In addition to understanding a typical diet, we learn about the family concerns at the height of The Depression. The writer tells of reduced wages, debt, concerns for family health and embarrassment when guests arrive and there may not be food to share. She is glad this process has enabled the family to save money and that it has taught her children the benefits of savings and budgeting. Of the women surveyed for this Wallaces' Farmer *article the average number of cans put up was 488 each year.*

Carrot Marmalade

Mrs. E.M. Carter, Iroquois County, Illinois

> *2 pounds carrots, ground*
> *1 teaspoon salt*
> *3 lemons*
> *3 oranges*
> *7 cups water, twice*
> *4 cups sugar*

Grind or process the carrots into very small pieces, about 1/16 of an inch in diameter. Grate the rind form the oranges and lemons and combine it with the carrots. Squeeze the fruit and and set aside the juice in the refrigerator until the next day. Sprinkle the salt over the carrot mixture, pour over 7 cups of water and set aside, in a cool place, overnight. The next day, drain the water from the carrot mixture and rinse it to remove the salt. Put carrots into a large, heavy stock pot. Add 7 cups of water again and the juice of the oranges and lemons. Bring to a boil and cook for an hour and a half or until the mixture is reduced about two-thirds. Add the sugar, mixing well and cook over medium heat until the marmalade is thickened, about another half hour. You will need to stir frequently to keep the mixture from sticking to the bottom of the pot and burning. Stir the marmalade as it cools to keep the carrots suspended in the syrup. Pour into clean jars and store in the refrigerator. Makes about 3 pints.

Bread and Butter Pickles

> *1 gallon small cucumbers*
> *8 small white onions*
> *2 green peppers*
> *1 1/2 cups salt*
> *4 cups cracked ice*
> *5 cups sugar*
> *1 1/2 teaspoons turmeric*
> *1 1/2 teaspoons ground cloves*
> *2 tablespoons mustard seed*
> *1 teaspoon celery seed*
> *5 cups vinegar*

Wash the cucumbers and slice very thin. Slice the onions and the green peppers into thin strips. Mix with the salt and cracked ice. Let stand in a cool place for three hours. Drain off the accumulated juices and rinse to remove excess salt. Combine the sugar, spices and vinegar in a large heavy kettle. Bring it to the boil over medium heat. Carefully add the vegetables, reduce the heat and simmer until the cucumbers become transparent. Pour into sterilized jars and seal.

Pickled Cantaloupe

6 slightly under ripe, medium sized cantaloupes
1/2 cup salt
1 1/2 gallons cold water
6 cups white sugar
6 cups vinegar
1 1/2 cups brown sugar
4 2-inch sticks cinnamon
1 tablespoon whole cloves
1 tablespoon whole allspice
1/4 teaspoon mace
1 small bay leaf

Peel and slice the melons into strips 1/2 inch by 3 inches. Combine the salt with the water and soak the melon strips in a cool place for 2 hours. Combine the sugars and vinegar. Tie the spices up in a cheesecloth bag and add to the syrup. Bring the mixture to a boil and continue boiling over medium heat for 10 minutes. Drain the melon strips and carefully add them to the boiling syrup. This will cool the syrup down, allow it to return to the boil, then remove it from the heat. Keep the melon strips in the cooling syrup. After about 6 hours, remove the melon strips and the bag of spices from the syrup. Bring it to a boil again and add the melon and spices. When it comes to a boil, remove from the heat as before. Repeat this process twice a day for 5 days. Keep the melon and syrup in a very cool place between boilings. On the 5th day, pack the melon strips carefully and firmly into hot, sterilized jars. Bring the syrup to a boil and pour over the melon in the jars. Seal the jars and keep refrigerated.

Por-Do

(Simple Chili Sauce)
Mrs. Lois J. Hurley

12 large ripe tomatoes, peeled and seeded
2 large green peppers
2 large hot peppers
3 large onions
2 cups vinegar
1 cup sugar
1 tablespoon ground cinnamon

Grind or process the vegetables in a food processor until they are like pulp. Combine with vinegar, sugar and cinnamon in a large heavy kettle. Simmer over medium heat until the mixture is thickened, stirring almost constantly so that it doesn't stick to the bottom of the pan and scorch. Pour into sterilized jars and process in a boiling water bath.

Canned Stuff New Ways

Grace M. Ellis

We may have the same old fruits and vegetables in the cellar, but if we vary the methods of serving we may keep appetites whetted until another season finds empty jars stored away and fresh stuffs appearing in orchard and garden. Hence a doggerel parodying the old sewing lines might pertinently state that:

> *Sally canned a lot of stuff.*
> *(She cooked with inspiration.)*
> *The family licked the dishes clean*
> *And chortled with elation.*

Corn Chowder

4 cups diced potatoes
2 tablespoons diced bacon
1 medium onion, diced
2 cups water
2 cups canned corn, drained
2 cups hot milk
Salt and pepper to taste

Combine the potatoes, bacon, and onion in a large sauce pan. Cook over medium heat, stirring frequently, until the potatoes are browned, the onion is transparent and the bacon is crisp. Add the water and stir to dissolve the browned bits from the bottom of the pan. Add the remaining ingredients and simmer over medium heat until the chowder is heated through.

Green Beans with Bacon

A recipe from an Amana Colony reader

6 medium potatoes, peeled and quartered
4 slices bacon, diced
1 onion, diced
2 tablespoons flour
2 cans green beans
1 1/2 cups water or drained bean liquid
1 tablespoon vinegar
1 teaspoon sugar
Salt and pepper to taste

Combine the potatoes, bacon and onion in a large pan. Cook over low heat until the potatoes are browned, the onion transparent and the bacon is crisp. Remove the vegetables and keep warm. Springle the flour into the bacon fat and cook, stirring constantly, until the flour is lightly browned. Gradually add the drained bean liquid or water and stir until the mixture is smooth. Return the cooked vegetables to the sauce. Stir in the green beans, vinegar, sugar and salt and pepper. Cook until heated through.

Grandmother's Carrot Relish

8 medium carrots, peeled
2 medium sized cabbages
9 green peppers, seeded
9 red peppers, seeded
9 onions, peeled
1/2 cup salt
7 cups vinegar
4 cups sugar
2 teaspoons mustard seed

Chop, grind or process in a food processor all the vegetables into very fine pieces. Mix with the salt and let stand in a cool place overnight. Drain off the accumulated juices and rise off the excess salt. Combine the vinegar, sugar and mustard seed in a medium saucepan. Bring to a boil and pour over the drained vegetables. Stir well and chill. It will be ready to eat in about 4 hours and will keep for several days.

August 17, 1935

Lazy Wife Pickles

1 gallon vinegar
1 cup salt
1 cup dry mustard
1 peck medium sized cucumbers, washed and dried thoroughly

Mix the vinegar, salt and mustard in a large container. The original *Wallaces'* recipe called for a big stone crock. Add the cucumbers and seal overnight. The recipe says you can add cucumbers all through the summer.

June 6, 1937

Does it Pay to Can?

Perhaps the satisfaction any woman takes in her own well done handiwork is sufficient answer to the question, "Does it pay to can?" However, such satisfaction bought at the price of health, family companionship or neglect of other important tasks is dearly bought.

As with home baking of bread, home sewing, the use of horses vs. tractors and a dozen and one other questions of home and farm management, the answer is an individual one to be decided by the circumstances of the homemaker herself. If those circumstances indicate that she has time, energy, equipment, and home grown vegetables and fruits to can, there is not need to consult extensive cost charts. She already knows it does pay.

■ **January 27, 1926** Television demonstrated in London.

■ **1926** *Wallaces' Farmer* begins campaign to stop farm thieves. Offers $50 rewards for thefts on farms where farmers have posted a Wallaces' Service Bureau sign at farm gate. *"'Your campaign to put the farm thieves in jail is the best thing you have started.' A farmer wrote us last week. 'Send me a new sign. Last night my neighbor had 175 chickens stolen and I do not want to take any chances.'"*

■ **April 13, 1926** *Wallaces' Farmer* article, "Odds and Ends." — *"I pointed out the effect of the tractor on creating a surplus of corn and oats speaking of the millions of acres which are not producing food which was formerly eaten by horses, but which now is eaten either by farm animals or humans. In reply Mr. Benjamin told me a proposition for making a mixture of alcohol and ether out of corn. It seems what with corn at 70 cents a bushel, a mixture of alcohol and ether can be made for 15 cents a gallon. This mixture has been substituted gallon for gallon with perfect satisfaction in automobiles."*

■ **August 20, 1926** *Wallaces' Farmer* article, "Odds and Ends" — *"I have watched and dreamed about this new method of corn breeding for so many years that I am becoming quite excited now that I see the time of practical application drawing near."* — H.A. Wallace

■ **September 3, 1926** *Wallaces' Farmer* article, "Tractor Demonstration Success" — *"That there is no slackening of the interest in power farming was demonstrated by the attendance of over one thousand farmers at the 'Cut the Cost' demonstration put on by the Hart-Parr tractor company. A count of parked cars showed farmers from over thirty counties and from eight neighboring states."*

■ **May 21, 1927** Lindburg flies the Atlantic.

■ **January 27, 1927** Nine million cars registered in the United States, one for every six people.

■ **April 30, 1927** Mississippi River floods 30 million acres. 200,000 left homeless.

■ **May 26, 1927** 15 millionth Model T rolls off the assembly line.

■ **September 30, 1927** Babe Ruth hits record 60th home run.

■ **October 6, 1927** First talking movie premieres, *The Jazz Singer*.

■ **December 1, 1927** Ford Motor introduces the Model A, top speed 71 miles per hour.

■ **March 28, 1928** Frantic trading on Wall Street. GM falls 8 points closing at 198.

■ **July 3, 1928** United States manufactured television set, sells for $75.

■ **September 15 1928** Penicillin isolated by Alexander Fleming.

CHAPTER 11

Modernization

A Gift of Time
February 2, 1917

*Too often women get along with an inconvenient kitchen
without a pantry, without even good cooking utensils, on the
grounds that what they can get along with is good enough. This
is not the right attitude. Conserving one's strength by refusing
to spend it in unnecessary drudgery is a potential saving, the
wisdom of which will be realized in later years
in increased strength and comfort. When mother considers the
calamity to her family of being deprived of her services
by poor health or death, she must acknowledge that personal
savings of her self are more than justified by her returns.
A good kitchen cabinet where all the tools for work and
the materials for baking are with in reach and the
compact, easily cleaned kitchen cabinet itself almost with
in reaching distance of the range makes the ordinary
baking and cooking operations a pleasure.*

*There is the vacuum cleaner, both hand and electric;
the fireless cooker, the gasoline and electric iron and many
other household conveniences none of which are too good
for the farmer's family. We need more comfort on the farm.
This is a busy age. We all are pressed for time. If there is
any household convenience which will give us more time,
let us by all means provide ourselves with it before
the rush of spring work begins.*

The Bread Mixer

To Hearts and Homes:

What a jolt it gives us sometimes to read an article that shows us that, after all, our trials and problems are the same as those studied by women everywhere, even in far away cities and states.

This came to me anew as I read the article in Hearts and Homes issue of January 11th, concerning bread mixers. Our experience is that at first it takes faith, and plenty of it, to use this new machine. For generations we have been taught by precept and example to "knead bread until it is smooth." Well, after that I say, it takes faith to use the mixer until accustomed to it. For the rough, sticky mess that meets the sight of the housewife when she lifts the cover at the end of three minutes is distressing. I know from experience. However, very careful measuring of both flour and liquid, strict adherence to rules, and good yeast and baking, and you will not be disappointed.

Make yeast sponge. In the morning warm to luke-warm, measure carefully a pint to a loaf, add the required amount of flour and it is ready to be turned by father or one of the boys while mother puts the breakfast on the table. Then it is ready to set in a warm corner until light enough to mold into loaves. One will soon learn their own particular brand of flour and the dough when mixed down to put into the pans will be the right consistency to mold the dough with well greased hands, thus saving the use of the board.

—*An Ohio Reader*

Basic Bread Dough

1 quart milk
1 cup sugar
1 cup mashed potatoes (do not use instant)
1 cup soft butter
2 packages instant yeast
1/2 cup warm water
2 tablespoons sugar
1 teaspoon baking soda
2 teaspoons baking powder
12 to 14 cups bread flour

R\E *The 1907 bread mixer would be perfect to make up the dough for this bread recipe. It makes a huge amount of bread dough — enough for 8 dozen rolls of various types. It may seem excessive, but this is one of the best bread doughs I've ever worked with. The rolls will freeze nicely, so go ahead, get up to your elbows and knead away.*

Scald the milk and add the sugar, butter and mashed potatoes. Set aside to cool. Proof the yeast by mixing it with the warm water and sugar. Put the mashed potato mixture into a very large mixing bowl, add the yeast mixture and begin stirring in the flour. Add the first 4 cups of flour, the baking soda and baking powder. Continue adding the flour until you have a stiff dough. Knead in the last 2 or 3 cups flour. Continue kneading until you have a smooth dough. You may want to divide it in half so you can knead more easily. Put the dough into a clean, well-greased bowl. Lightly grease the top of the dough, cover with a clean, damp towel and set aside in a warm place until the dough has doubled in bulk. Punch the dough down and form using one of the following recipes.

Hot Cross Buns

Knead into 1/4 of the dough:
1 teaspoon cinnamon
2 tablespoons sugar
1/2 cup currants
1/2 cup raisins

Form into balls about 2 inches in diameter. Place in well-greased pans and allow to rise until doubled. Cut a cross in the top of each roll with a very, very sharp knife just before baking. Bake at 350 degrees F. until the rolls are lightly browned and sound hollow when tapped, about 25 minutes. Cool on a wire rack.

Cheese Rolls

For 1/4 of the dough:
Finely grate cheese to yield 2 cups. Roll the dough out into a rectangle about 20 by 5 inches and fill with grated cheese. Roll into a cylinder and slice. Place in a greased pan cut side up and allow to rise until doubled. Bake in a preheated, 350 degree F. oven until the rolls are lightly browned and sound hollow when tapped, about 25 minutes.

Peanut Rolls

For 1/4 of the dough:
Knead in 1 cup finely chopped peanuts. Form into round rolls about 1 inch in diameter. Place in a well-greased pan, allowing space for them to rise until double. Bake in a preheated, 350 degree F. oven until the rolls are lightly browned and sound hollow when tapped, about 25 minutes.

The Fireless Cooker

From time to time we have urged our lady readers to give the man of the house no peace until he provides them with a fireless cooker. Some of our readers have done so, and there is a great contentment in the home when the old fashioned mush or porridge is brought upon the table with such cream as can only be found on the farm. Occasionally we receive letters asking how to make this cooker and we fear that we have not described its construction with sufficient accuracy. Therefore we quote from *The Industrialist,* published weekly by the Kansas Agricultural College at Manhattan. Its instruction as to the making:

The following articles will be required in its construction: (1) A tight box, barrel, or old trunk with a tight fitting lid. (2) Padding that will prevent loss of heat: hay, straw, wool, feathers, ground cork, asbestos or mineral wool. (3) Asbestos board to line the box and asbestos paper to be used as an inside cylinder. (4) Cheese cloth or flour sacking to cover the padding. (5) A granite bucket with a tight fitting lid in which the food is cooked.

The cooker is made in the following manner: The box is lined with asbestos board on bottom and sides. The bottom is covered with three inches of padding material on which is placed a cylinder piece of asbestos paper just large enough to allow the cooking bucket to slip into it. Between the sides of the box and the asbestos cylinder the padding is placed. The box should be large enough so that there will be at least three inches of this padding on all sides of the cylinder. A cloth bag with a round bottom should be made that will fit into this cylinder and extend over the over the top of the padding to the sides of the box where it should be tacked to prevent the padding from becoming scattered. A three-inch pillow of the padding material should be supplied to place over the cooking bucket before the lid of the box is closed down.

Food, boiling hot, placed in this box and left undisturbed will continue to cook and remain hot for ten or twelve hours. The box will be found useful for other cooking than that of cereals.

Now get after the man of the house. If there is no tight box or old trunk there are plenty of barrels and he can be trusted to put on a tight fitting lid. If there is nothing better on hand for packing material there is hay; and if the cows need that, there is straw. Asbestos board and paper can be had at the nearest hardware store. And is not expensive. Now if a man cannot follow these directions and make a fireless cooker, he is made out of poor stuff.

Usually men folk are more hungry on the Sabbath than during the week. The meal is a little later and there is no urgent need of haste to eat and get back to work They also want a hot meal and as a rule, gravy. To us, gravy has always been the "last straw" of the meal. Everything is dished up, the tea or coffee is made, the members of the family are eager to be seated at the table, but the gravy must be made! We like the fireless cooker because the gravy can be made when the meat goes in and forgotten. It is like making a discovery to get a hot meal, deliciously cooked, out of the fireless cooker when one comes from church in her best clothes and sits down like other people.

Cooking on the Sabbath

Chili Con Carne
1 pound chopped meat, stew beef or hamburger
2 tablespoons vegetable oil
1 cup diced onion
1 can kidney beans, 2 cups approximately
2 cups tomatoes
1 cup chopped celery
Chili powder to taste

Brown the meat in the oil. Add the onions and sauté until transparent. Add the beans, tomatoes, celery and seasoning. Cover and simmer until the Chili is thickened, stirring from time to time. If you make this in your crock pot — today's version of the fireless cooker — follow the directions on your machine.

Serve with 4 cups cooked white rice, dusted with paprika, Cinnamon Rolls, Hot slaw.

Spiced Pork Tenderloin

R E *This recipe calls for canned tomato soup. I prefer to use one of the healthy, non-condensed varieties with less salt.*

1 pound pork tenderloin
3 tablespoons butter
2 onions, sliced
1 cup water
1 tablespoon vinegar
3/4 teaspoon cinnamon
3/4 teaspoon cloves
1/2 bay leaf
1 16-ounce (approximately) can tomato soup

In a frying pan, brown the pork in the butter and remove to a crock pot. Sauté the onions until they are transparent and put them into the crock pot along with the butter remaining in the pan. Pour the water into the frying pan. Simmer to remove any browned bits and pour into the crock pot. Add the remaining ingredients. Cover and simmer until the meat is tender, 2 to 4 hours depending on the diameter of the meat and the temperature range of your crock pot.

Casseroled Chicken

"The chicken may be kept warm by wrapping several thicknesses of newspapers around it before you head to church."

4 or 5 pounds chicken
4 tablespoons butter or oil
3 carrots
1 bunch celery
1 medium onion
1 green pepper
1 1/2 tablespoons flour
1 cup milk

R E *If the homemaker wanted to have her Sunday dinner completely prepared, meat cooked, gravy thickened before leaving home, she could follow this advice. Note the cooking time of 3-plus hours. She would certainly have to get up before the chickens to follow this method.*

Preheat the oven to 325 degrees F. Brown the chicken in butter. Place the meat in a large casserole. Cut the carrots and celery into 1-inch slices, dice the onion and pepper. Brown the vegetables and add them to the chicken. Add 1 cup water to the casserole, cover and bake 3 hours, or until the chicken and vegetables are tender. Remove them to a serving dish. Combine the milk and flour into a smooth mixture. Pour into the pan juices and cook over medium heat, stirring frequently, until the sauce is thickened. Pour the sauce over the chicken and vegetables.

An Effective Iceless Refrigerator

The accompanying illustration shows a home-made iceless refrigerator or milk cooler. This consists of a wooden frame covered with canton flannel or similar material. It is desirable that the frame be screened, altho this is not absolutely necessary. Wicks made of the same material as the covering rest in a pan of water on top of the refrigerator, allowing the water to seep down the sides. When evaporation takes place, the heat is taken from the inside with a consequent lowering of the temperature. On hot, dry days a temperature of 50 degrees can be contained in this refrigerator.

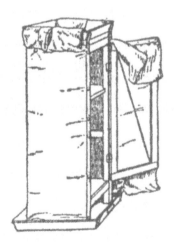

Eavesdropping over the Telephone

The rural telephone has been a great blessing to the farmers all over the western country. It has done very much to break up the isolation of the farm as well as to save long trips to town. It is a wonderful help in time of sickness and at threshing time; in short, it is an improvement which farmers would not get along without at any reasonable cost.

There are, however, some very grave abuses in the use of these rural telephones. They are so constructed that when a call is made for one member it is heard by all and any person who wishes to go to the 'phone whenever the bell rings can be in touch with the gossip of the whole community. In other words, the telephones are used for eavesdropping. How can a child be impressed with the essential meanness of eavesdropping if parents rush to the telephone and listen purposely to the conversations that their neighbors may be carrying on? The remedy is easy. Never take down the receiver except in response to your own call, and never allow a child to do so.

Some farmers are taking out their party telephones simply because they do not wish to have their conversations with intimate friends, or with their physician, or with the buyer of livestock listened to by their neighbors; and in this they are doing exactly right.

There are other abuses connected with the rural telephone system. But all could easily be corrected if the managers would limit conversations, as they have done in town, to three minutes and charge for longer use of it. Any farmer or farmer's wife can say all that needs to be said in three minutes, whether it be about buying a new horse, the baby's teething, John's cold or the new dress pattern, or the prospects for weddings in the neighborhood. The rural telephone is a wonderful help to farmers, but like all other good things it may be, and in some cases is, very greatly abused to the moral detriment of those who abuse it.

Ginger Ale Salad

1 3-ounce package lemon Jell-O
1/2 cup hot water
1 cup ginger ale
1/3 cup grapefruit sections, cut in smaller chunks
1/2 cup minced celery
1/3 cup diced apple
1 small can crushed pineapple
2 tablespoons minced candied ginger

Combine the Jell-O and hot water, stirring until the powder is completely dissolved. Slowly add the ginger ale. Stir in the remaining ingredients and chill. Once the Jell-O begins to set, give the salad a good stir to distribute the fruit evenly and put in molds, if you prefer.

The Pressure Cooker

We were especially interested at the Iowa State Fair in watching the demonstrations with pressure cookers. Many of our readers who appreciate the savings in time in cooking by steam are reluctant to use one lest it explode or in some way harm the user. The college reports showed that this is not possible unless the cook is careless.

The advantage in dish washing in cooking the entire meal in one pot was also touched upon. Also that the high temperatures used in cooking to 20 pounds of steam pressure destroys organisms that might cause food poisoning.

The following recipe for the pressure cooker was distributed at the 1919 Iowa State Fair

Vegetable Beef Stew with Dumplings

2 pounds stewing beef, chuck preferred
3 cups boiling water
1/2 small onion, chopped
1 cup carrots, peeled and diced
2 tablespoons vinegar
1/4 teaspoon ground cloves

Biscuit dough

RKE *All pressure cookers are different. Before using this recipe see what the capacity and amount of liquid your cooker requires and make adjustments as needed.*

Cut the meat into 1-inch serving pieces. Brown the meat in a little oil in the pressure cooker. Add the remaining ingredients. Cook for 40 minutes at 10 pound pressure. Cool and release the pressure. Bring the stew back up to boiling. Drop the biscuit dough on top of the stew and cook, covered until the dumplings are done, about 10 minutes.

August 16, 1907

Have a kitchen stool of the right height in your kitchen
to use when preparing vegetables, washing
dishes, etc. and save your feet much needless
weariness and pain.

Esperanto Sauce

R̶E *Esperanto was an attempt to have a world-wide common language.*

2 tablespoons butter
2 tablespoons flour
1 cup hot water
1 tablespoon minced red pepper
1 tablepoon Worcestershire sauce
Juice and grated rind of one lemon

In a small saucepan melt the butter and stir in the flour until smooth and bubbly. Add the hot water, stirring constantly until smooth. Add the minced pepper, Worcestershire sauce and lemon juice and rind. Simmer until the sauce is thickened, stirring to keep it from forming lumps. Serve over Hamburger Steak.

Why Have a Radio Set?

Entertainment, Education and Profit from the Air

It seems to me that farmers need and can use a radio set better than any other class of people. In the first place the information disseminated by radio is intended especially for the farmer or relates closely to his work. Take the weather forecasts. No worker is more dependent in his operations on weather changes than the farmer and prompt and reliable forecasts often mean the difference between profit and loss on some farm work.

One of the radio services most valuable to the farmer is the broadcasting of market reports. Think what a wonderful advantage this is over the old way when all the advantage was with the grain dealer or stock buyer, who could buy with later market information than the farmer had available.

In addition to the above, many agricultural colleges and other institutions are radio-casting lectures and extension talks on various phases of farm and home work.

The Old Time was when "down on the farm" was synonymous with isolation and loneliness, when for weeks at a time the farmer's family were completely isolated and scarcely saw their nearest neighbors. Much of this has, of course, changed with closer settlements of communities, with better roads and automobiles, telephones, rural mail delivery and daily papers, phonographs and so on. But even yet, at certain seasons and under bad weather conditions, there is still much isolation and loneliness.

But how different it is with the farm home equipped with a good radio receiving set! In cold, wintry weather when radio-casting and receiving conditions are the very best, the family can all sit comfortably by their fireside and tune in on a lecture or speech by some distinguished individual, a solo by some beautiful song or player artist, an after-dinner or ball-room concert, or, in fact, any of the widely varied programs put out by radio-casting stations within their receiving range.

October 24, 1924

Tomali Pie

1/2 cup corn meal
1 1/2 cups water
2 cups tomato sauce
1/4 cup diced green pepper
1/4 cup diced onion
2 cups cooked, diced meat, beef, chicken or pork
1/4 cup grated cheese, cheddar or pepper jack

RKE *Not only is the name spelled differently, the original recipe did not call for any of the spices we use in Mexican recipes today. You may wish to add a teaspoon of chili powder, a dash of Tabasco sauce or use a can of seasoned stewed tomatoes instead of the tomato sauce, onion and green pepper.*

In a medium saucepan, stir the corn meal into simmering water and cook, stirring frequently, until thickened. Set aside to cool slightly. Preheat the oven to 425 degrees F. Combine the tomato sauce, green pepper and onion and simmer until the vegetables are just tender. Stir half of the mixture into the corn meal with the diced meat. Press into a well-greased tin pie plate, about 9 inches. Put into the oven, reduce heat to 350. Bake for 15 minutes, sprinkle cheese on top and cook for 5 minutes more, or until the pie is heated through and the cheese is melted. Serve with reserved tomato sauce.

July 31, 1925

Locating the Bathroom

Usually one of the most desired improvements to be put in when an old home is to be remodeled is a bathroom. The bathroom should by all means have the best protected and most easily heated place in the home. Nothing is much more disagreeable than a chilly bathroom.

A small compact bathroom is usually to be preferred to a big roomy one since it is much more easily kept clean and warm. The 5 by 6 foot bathroom is probably too small where more room can be secured, but even that would be preferable to one 10 by 15 feet.

Just a few words as to the fixtures. Bathroom equipment should be looked upon as a permanent home investment, since high-grade equipment when installed will keep in good shape for years and years.

If possible all pipes should be kept out of the outside walls and put in inside partitions to decrease the danger from freezing.

Few Farms Have Adequate Plumbing

The 1920 census reports showed that only one farm home in ten has water piped into the house, which means that 9 out of 10 homes, or even a greater proportion, do not have adequate plumbing and toilet and bathing facilities.

Just why our farm homes have lagged behind city people in adapting good plumbing facilities is a little bit hard to understand.

Probably one of the greatest factors has been the labor problem of getting them installed. The farmer is used to hiring good willing labor at from 30 to 40 cents an hour and that is about all he expects for his own labor and he rather dislikes to pay a town workman $1.00 to $1.50 an hour, especially when the latter doesn't seem to be in any hurry about his work and expects to be paid for the time spent in coming and going.

This matter of plumbing work has been somewhat of a mystery to the average farmer because the plumbers are naturally interested in keeping it so; but there is no question that the farmer needs more plumbing and that the main thing is to get him to realize better what he can do himself along plumbing lines.

The United States Department of Agriculture, along with most of the state agricultural colleges, have wonderfully good bulletins on farm water supply, plumbing, sewage disposal, and so on, which will be sent free to any interested farmer.

Electricity on the Farm

Probably no other type of farm power has been so rapidly and so widely adapted in this country as has electric power. So far, however, the gas engine farm lighting plant is perhaps the easiest secured type of electric power for the farm. When of good size and properly installed and cared for, it goes a long ways towards solving the housewife's power problems. With this the farm lighting can be changed from drudgery to a joy and delight with plenty of light and nice fixtures in each room, no groping or stumbling thru pitch dark rooms but plenty of light at the turn of a switch. Plenty of light in the barn and other buildings so the chores can be done easily and efficiently and with no danger of fire; the washing and ironing can be done out on the shady porch if desired; the electric vacuum sweeper does away with the broom and hand sweeper; there is power for the sewing machine, electric fans, hair dryers, curling irons, soldering irons, and other conveniences which to the city household have become almost matters of habit. In addition to these, the small power uses around the home can be started and stopped with the movement of a switch.

Electricity on the farm can be developed from any of the several possible sources, is adding efficiency of the farm worker and the homemaker, increasing leisure time and making both work and play more enjoyable.

Harvest Your Ice

The ice crop is ripe and harvest time is here. This is the one crop which matures in the winter and the one crop which does not drain a farm of its fertility. Perhaps it is because of its abundance and cheapness that more farmers do not harvest it at the time when they have little else to do. In the city, they think they can not get along without ice, but in the country it is just as much needed.

The average family in the city uses about three 20-cent pieces of ice a week during the summer. Even families with moderate incomes think it is a necessity during June, July and August and their ice bill probably amounts to about $7.80 for the season. Ice is not a luxury; it enables them to preserve perishable food products and is really economical.

One of our subscribers who keeps ten cows and who had always sent his cream to the local creamery said his ice supply had been worth at least $200 to him in one season. When we asked him how that comes, he said the local creamery would have paid him only about $750 for the butter during the year and that by having the ice he was enabled to sell his cream to an ice cream manufacturer for nearly $1000. Without the ice he could not have kept the cream sweet during the hot weather and the ice cream man would not contract for any of it unless it could be supplied in the hot weather months as well as during the cooler months.

It is a good plan to put up 50 percent more than you think you will need, because some of it will melt regardless of the precautions you take. The hardest part is getting at it in the first place and a few extra loads will not be noticed. A large body of ice keeps much better than a small body, other conditions being equal. So the loss will be proportionately less. By a little figuring, one can tell approximately the amount he will need for cooling his dairy products and for household uses. The average family should have at least 12 or 15 tons and this would give him approximately 150 pounds daily for four months, June, July August and September. While a ton of ice contains 36 cubic feet. One should figure on about 42 cubic feet to the ton as it is packed in the ice house. With ice a foot thick on the pond he would need an area about 27 feet long and 20 feet wide to supply fifteen tons.

Chocolate Ice Cream

1/2 cup of grated unsweetened chocolate, 2 squares
2 cups milk
1 1/2 cups sugar
2 eggs
2 cups cream

Grate the chocolate either with a four-sided grater or with the grating feature of a food processor. Put the milk into a 2 quart sauce pan over medium heat. As the milk begins to warm, gradually add the sugar, whisking until it is dissolved. Beat the eggs. Add a bit of the hot milk mixture to them to raise their temperature then add to the remaining milk. Stir in the chocolate. Lower the heat and cook until the mixture is thickened. Add 1 cup of the cream and put the mixture into the freezing compartment of the refrigerator until is it very cold, but not frozen. Whip the remaining cream, fold into the chilled mixture. Finish freezing the ice cream in an ice cream freezer according to the directions.

Grape Juice Sherbet

2 cups unsweetened grape juice
1 cup sugar
1 quart milk

RKE *This is an unexpect-
edly refreshing
combination. Purple grape juice
will make a lavender sherbet, the
white juice is a light cream color.*

Combine the grape juice and sugar in a saucepan and simmer until the sugar is dissolved. Chill and add the milk. Freeze according to the directions on your ice cream freezer.

Ice Creams and Ices

Now is the time when cold deserts in the form of ice creams and ices are thoroughly appreciated and enjoyed. With the arrival of peaches our attention is called to the delicious and delicate colored cream containing this fruit. The turning at first is done slowly and regularly about 40 revolutions a minute for from 5 to 8 minutes. One may then turn faster, but regularity should be maintained.

Peach Ice Cream

4 eggs
3 cups sugar
3 cups peach pulp and juice
6 cups half and half
6 cups milk

For a gallon of ice cream: Beat eggs and sugar together until light and foamy. Add fruit juice, cream and milk and stir all together. Cook in the top of a double boiler until thick. Chill in the freezer compartment of the refrigerator until ice is just beginning to form around the edges. Then finish processing in an ice cream freezer.

Peach Sherbet

5 cups milk
3 cups sugar
4 cups peach pulp and juice
Juice of 1 lemon

For a gallon of sherbet: Combine the milk and sugar, stirring until the sugar is dissolved. Add the peach pulp, juice and lemon juice. Stir well and chill in the freezer compartment of the refrigerator. Finish processing in an ice cream freezer.

Lemon Ice

6 cups water
3 cups sugar
1 1/2 cups strained lemon juice

Combine the water and sugar in a large sauce pan. Bring to a boil, reduce heat and simmer for fifteen minutes. Cool slightly and add the lemon juice. Pre-chill in the freezer compartment of the refrigerator and finish in an ice cream freezer.

Why Do You Bake Your Own Bread?

R*KE* Even with all the benefits of modern homemaking and farming equipment, folks on the land expressed concerns for the changes they brought. In 1931 Wallaces Farmer asked their readers to write on the topic "Why Do You Bake Your Own Bread?"

Mrs. O. T. Nolte's winning letter expressed the importance of continuing the effort to make bread in the home. In the midst of the Depression, it is not just money savings that keep her kneading her own loaves. The value homemade bread carries is central to the role of the farm wife as the center of the family.

First Prize Winner

Mrs. O.T. Nolte, Mower County, Minnesota

I am inclined to think that bakery bread is like Henry Ford's synthetic milk — it has body but no soul. Speaking of bread's having a soul makes me think of the little boy in one of Zona Gale's stories who said, "If you want things to grow, you have to love them before you plant 'em down." Perhaps it holds true that one must love their dough before they can work it down.

At any rate, I like to make bread. When the loaves come from the oven, golden brown and smelling so sweet they really are a source of pride to me. I can't write poems, or paint pictures, but I can make a loaf of bread.

We buy flour here at $2.35 for 98 pounds. Such a sack will last us 30 days. Out of this comes all the baking — pies, cakes, cookies, pancakes, puddings and bread. The sugar, lard, salt and fuel used in making bread must be added to its cost so figuring as closely as I can, each loaf costs 4 cents which makes a savings of 6 cents a loaf (from the cost of bakery bread).

I use what we call "starter" I save some each time for the next baking so my bread is always uniform. When I used to buy yeast, I sometimes had trouble due to its being stale. The starter, of course, costs me nothing, so there's another little saving and "many a mickle makes a muckle, you know."

Some farm women think they haven't time for baking bread, but we can always find time for what we really want to do.

January 9, 1932

Blue Ribbon Breads

Margaret Sereg, Mahaska County, Iowa
Blue Ribbon for White Bread, 1931 Iowa State Fair

1 1/2 cups milk
2 tablespoons shortening
1 tablespoon sugar
1 package instant dry yeast (original recipe used homemade starter)
3 1/2 to 4 cups bread flour
1 1/2 teaspoons salt

Scald the milk, stir in the shortening and let cool to lukewarm. Mix in the yeast and sugar and allow it to get foamy. Pour the milk mixture into a large bowl. Add the flour and knead until smooth and elastic. Form the dough into a ball and put it in a lightly greased bowl. Set it in a warm place to rise until double. Punch the dough down and allow to rise until double one more time. Form the dough into a loaf and place in a lightly greased 1 1/4 pound loaf pan to rise until double a third time. Preheat the oven to 400 degrees F. Bake the bread for 15 minutes then lower the heat to 350 and finish baking until the top is golden and the bread sounds hollow when tapped, about 20 more minutes.

March 9, 1929
Why Farmers are Leaving the Farm

Our experience indicates that as a result of low farm income, too many of out first-class farmers are going to town. If the drift to the city is taking our efficient farmers along with inefficient farmers, then both the country and the nation are losing.

Doctor Galpin of the Department of Agriculture has been in charge of a survey designed to dig into the results of this situation. He suggests that to stop this city-ward drift of the farm's best people, we need not only more income for the farmer but better ways of converting that income into comfortable homes and fine rural communities.

CHAPTER 12

Meats

The Meat Problem
January 22, 1909
Mrs. Ada Parsons

Perhaps the most important task of the whole winter is butchering and caring for the meat. Everyone dreads it, yet we are learning every year how to lessen the work until it is not nearly the bug-bear of former times.

We are learning how to get so much more satisfaction from our meat supply than formerly. By co-operation among neighbors, farmers may now have the choicest corn-fed beef throughout the winter, and everyone enjoys it better than pork in cold weather.

May 6, 1898

Salmon Salad

1 can salmon, drained
3/4 cup mustard salad dressing
    Use a commercial honey mustard or
    the Old Fashioned Boiled Dressing from
    the Vegetable chapter

R̶K̶E̶ Wallaces' Farmer
*printed several recipes
featuring canned salmon at the
turn of the 19th century. Today we
could use canned, pre-cooked or
our own leftover fresh salmon.*

Combine the salmon with the dressing, chill and serve over shredded lettuce.

September 8, 1898

Baked Salmon Dish

For those who like salmon, this is a real treat.

1 1/2 cups fine dry or stale bread crumbs
1 cup milk
2 eggs, lightly beaten
1 can salmon, drained

Preheat oven to 350 degrees F. Combine the bread crumbs and milk. Let stand 10 to 15 minutes until the milk is absorbed. Stir in the eggs and lastly the salmon. Pour mixture into a well greased baking pan. Bake until firm and slightly puffed.

August 4, 1899

Meat Fritter

2 cups stale bread crumbs
Salt and pepper, to taste
1 teaspoon butter, melted
2 eggs
1 to 2 pounds cooked meat, chopped
1/2 cup corn meal
Butter for frying

Combine the bread crumbs, salt and pepper, melted butter and eggs. Mix with the chopped meat. Form into patties, and coat with corn meal. Melt about 3 tablespoons butter in a heavy frying pan. Fry the patties until lightly browned on both sides.

Irish Beef Stew

Maureen

2 pounds beef chuck roast cut in 2-inch cubes
3 tablespoons flour
3 tablespoons butter
3 medium onions, sliced
1 quart boiling water
5 carrots, sliced
1 turnip, diced
2 medium potatoes, diced
Salt and pepper to taste
2 tablespoons additional flour
1/2 cup cold water

Combine the beef with the flour in a plastic bag and shake until the meat is well coated with flour. Melt the butter in a large stew pan. Add the onions and sauté until they are transparent. Add the beef cubes and cook over medium heat until they are browned, stirring frequently to keep from sticking and burning. Add the boiling water and cover. Cook until the meat is almost done, 1 to 1 1/2 hours. Add the vegetables and simmer for another half hour until they are tender. Add salt and pepper. If you like a thicker stew you may combine the remaining flour with cold water in a jar and shake until smooth. Remove the meat and vegetables from the juices in the pot and stir in the flour mixture. Bring to a boil and cook until thickened, stirring constantly.

November 10, 1922

Hamburger Steak

RKE *Or you can make patties and cook on a grill or in a frying pan.*

A few years ago we used to call this "Liberty Steak."

2 pounds ground beef
1 tablespoon minced parsley
1 egg, lightly beaten
1/2 teaspoon onion juice
2 tablespoons melted butter
1/4 teaspoon ground pepper

Combine all ingredients and mix with your hands until just blended. As with most ground meat mixtures, you don't want to handle it too much. The more you mix it, the tougher it may be. Form into a loaf and bake in a 350 degree F. preheated oven for 45 minutes.

Cottage Pie

6 potatoes
2 carrots, cut in 1/2-inch chunks
2 turnips, cut in 1/2-inch chunks
2 tablespoons butter
2 tablespoons flour
1 cup milk
2 eggs, separated
1 onion, cut up fine
3 cups cooked, chopped pork

Cook the potatoes and mash them. Set aside to cool to lukewarm. Cook the carrots and turnips and drain well.

Make a white sauce by melting the butter in a 2- to 3-quart saucepan. Stir in the flour and cook until bubbly. Add the milk and lightly beaten egg yolks. Cook, stirring constantly, until the sauce is thick. Add the onion, vegetables and chopped pork.

In a large grease-free bowl, whip the egg whites until stiff. Fold in the mashed potatoes.

Preheat the oven to 350 degrees F. Lightly grease a 9-inch square pan. Put half the potato mixture in the bottom, pour in the pork mixture and top with the remaining mashed potatoes. Bake until the top is a rich golden brown, about a half hour.

Yankee Doodle

Mrs. H.L. Wahlgren, Washington County, Nebraska

Here is a tasty satisfying dish for frosty days.

1 large onion, sliced thinly
1/2 pound cooked beef
1 cup tomato sauce
1/2 pound macaroni, cooked and drained
Butter

Preheat the oven to 350 degrees F. In a 2- or 3-quart baking dish with a cover layer the onion, beef and cooked and drained macaroni. Pour the tomato sauce over and dot with butter. Cover the dish tightly and bake for 1 and 1/2 hours.

April 2, 1932

Baked Chicken with Milk

Mrs. A.R.C., Jones County, Iowa

> Chicken pieces
> Flour
> Milk

R/**E** *The key to this recipe is in the original directions to "pack" the chicken into the pan. You need to select a deep pan that will hold the chicken compactly, otherwise there will be too much milk.*

Preheat the oven to 350 degrees F. Remove the skin from the chicken. Dredge the chicken with flour and pack into a deep roasting pan with a cover. Bring the milk just to a boil and pour over until the chicken is just covered. Cover and bake until the chicken is tender, about an hour. Remove the cover and continue baking until the sauce is thickened and the chicken is golden. Remove the chicken to the serving platter. Strain the sauce through a fine sieve either over the chicken or into a gravy boat.

June 25, 1932

Swiss Steak with Vegetables

Mrs. Charles Knox , Hardin County, Iowa

> 1/4 cup flour
> 1 teaspoon pepper
> Salt to taste
> 1 pound round steak
> 2 potatoes
> 4 carrots
> 2 onions
> 1 cup cabbage
> 1 cup tomato sauce or stewed tomatoes

R/**E** *The readers and editors of* Wallaces' Farmer *didn't complain much about economic conditions during The Depression and the years of low farm prices before it. They just went on about their business as well as they could. However, sometimes hints of the struggles can be found even in the home-making columns. I didn't think much about it until I tested this recipe. This is easily enough to feed 4 to 6 people as the original recipe said, however each person gets a lot of vegetables and just a bit of the round steak.*

Preheat the oven to 325 degrees F. Mix the flour, pepper and salt. Dredge the meat well with this mixture and brown it on top of the stove in a well-greased frying pan. Place the meat in a casserole dish. Peel and chop all the vegetables. Put the vegetables around and over the meat. Pour the tomato sauce over the top and cover. Bake until the vegetables are tender and the meat is done, about 2 hours.

January 21, 1933

Spiced Pork Chops

Mrs. Steward S. Foster, Frement County, Iowa

Pork chops
Apple butter (1 tablespoon per chop)
Cracker crumbs (1 teaspoon per chop)
Butter (1/4 teaspoon per chop)

R E *The original recipe suggested coating both sides of the chops with cracker crumbs, however those on the bottom layer simply got soggy from the butter and apple butter and stuck to the bottom of the pan. I eliminate the crumbs on the bottom of the chops. The apple butter is terrific, however.*

Preheat the oven to 350 degrees F. Take as many pork chops as you need and brown them in a frying pan. Spread the tops and bottoms with apple butter and place in a lightly buttered baking dish, in a single layer. Dust the tops with cracker crumbs, dot with butter and bake until done, about 30 minutes.

March 4, 1933

Spanish Rice

Mrs. Anton Arp, Dickenson County, Iowa

2 cups cooked long grain rice
4 slices bacon
1/2 onion, chopped
1/4 teaspoon paprika
2 cups stewed tomatoes

Preheat the oven to 350 degrees F. Cook the bacon, remove the crisp slices and sauté the onion in the bacon fat until it is transparent. Crumble the bacon and add it with the onion to the rice. Stir in the paprika and stewed tomatoes. Pour the mixture into a greased casserole and bake until heated through, about 20 minutes.

April 1, 1933

Southern BBQ Ham

Mrs. Clive Butler, Audubon County, Missouri

1 1/2-inch thick ham slice
3 tablespoons vinegar
1 tablespoon dry mustard
3 tablespoons brown sugar, firmly packed
1 teaspoon paprika

Preheat the oven to 350 degrees F. Combine the vinegar, mustard, brown sugar and paprika. Rub into both sides of the ham steak and place in a baking dish. Bake until the meat is heated through and browned, about 30 minutes.

March 17, 1934

Creamed Spaghetti with Carrots

3 tablespoons butter
3 tablespoons flour
2 cups milk
1/2 teaspoon black pepper
1 1/2 cups cooked spaghetti
1 1/2 cups sliced carrots, cooked

Make a white sauce by melting the butter in a 2-quart sauce pan. Add the flour and cook over medium heat, stirring constantly until the mixture bubbles. Stir in the milk and continue cooking and stirring until the sauce is thick. Add the pepper. While the sauce is cooking, boil the spaghetti and carrots. Add the carrots to the drained spaghetti and blend in the white sauce.

January 19, 1935

Ham in Casserole

Mrs. G. DeWitt, Polk County, Iowa

1 slice ham, about two pounds
1/4 cup brown sugar, firmly packed
6 new potatoes, cut in half
2 tablespoons butter
1 regular-sized can apricots in light syrup or juice, about 15 ounces

Preheat the oven to 350 degrees F. Place the ham in the bottom of a casserole. If it is too large to fit, you may cut it and layer it. Sprinkle the top of the ham with brown sugar. Place the potatoes on top of the ham, cut side down and dot with butter. Pour the juice from the apricots over the ham and potatoes, reserving the apricot halves. Cover the casserole and place in the oven. Cook for a half hour. Arrange the apricot halves around the ham and return to the oven for another half hour.

February 16, 1935

Casserole of Chicken and Corn

1 regular-sized can of whole kernel corn, about 15 ounces
1 cup cooked chicken, diced
1/2 cup cracker crumbs
1 egg
3/4 cup milk
1/2 teaspoon sugar
1 tablespoon green pepper, diced

Preheat oven to 350 degrees F. Drain the corn and combine with rest of the ingredients. Spread mixture in a small, well buttered casserole. Bake until lightly browned on top, about 30 minutes.

Barbecue Sauce

1 onion, diced
1 green pepper, diced
1 cup diced celery
2 tablespoons brown sugar, firmly packed
1 regular bottle catsup, about 15 ounces
Juice of half a lemon
1 teaspoon dry mustard
2 tablespoons vinegar
3 tablespoons Worcestershire sauce, optional
3 1/2 cups brown, beef stock

RKE Brush this sauce over beef, pork or chicken during the last 10 to 15 minutes of cooking. Keep unused portion in the refrigerator.

Combine all the ingredients in a large sauce pan. Bring to a boil. Lower the heat and simmer until thickened, about 1 1/2 hours. Stir frequently as the mixture thickens.

Delicious One-Dish Meal

Mrs. Lewis P. Peterson, Fillmore County, Minnesota

4 3/4-inch thick or thicker pork chops, with bones removed
1 cup cooked rice
1 medium onion, thinly sliced
1 teaspoon black pepper, or to taste
1 regular sized can chopped tomatoes, about 15 ounces

Preheat oven to 350 degrees F. Brown the pork chops on both sides in a frying pan in a little oil or butter. Put the chops in the bottom of an oven-proof dish large enough to hold them in one layer. Place 1/4 cup rice over each chop. Cover with sliced onion and pour the tomatoes over the top. Cover and bake until the chops are done and tender, about an hour.

March 12, 1938

One of our friends whose guesses on the hog market very often turn out to be correct assures us that there is a fair chance that heavy hogs may sell as high as light hogs sometime this spring. The increase in lard exports, coupled with the low supply of lard held in storage, makes him feel that packers will be willing to bid up a bit on lard hogs before long.

Baked Barbecued Spare Ribs

R|E *This recipe works equally well with pork or beef. Boneless short or country-style ribs are particularly good. You could even use this technique and recipe with chicken wings or turkey tenderloins.*

3 to 4 pounds meaty spare ribs
Salt and pepper to taste
2 medium onions, thinly sliced
3/4 cup catsup
3/4 cup water
1/8 teaspoon red pepper
1 teaspoon paprika
1/2 teaspoon black pepper
1 teaspoon chili powder

Preheat the oven to 325 degrees F. Cut the meat into serving pieces and place them in the bottom of your roasting pan. Dust with salt and pepper to taste. Cover with onions. In a small bowl or large measuring cup, blend the catsup and water and stir in the spices. Pour over the meat, stirring to coat. Cover roaster and bake for 2 hours, basting occasionally. Take off the cover during the last 20 minutes to brown the ribs.

Lillian's Swiss Steak

R|E *This is an interesting variation of usual Swiss steak, as the meat and vegetables cook in the gravy.*

About 2 pounds round steak, cut 3/4 of an inch thick
Flour, about 2 - 3 tablespoons
Salt and pepper to taste
3 cups milk
6 tablespoons flour
3/4 cup water
1/2 teaspoon pepper
2 small onions, sliced
6 stalks celery, cut into 1-inch pieces
8 carrots, cut into 1-inch pieces
4 medium potatoes, peeled and cut in quarters

Preheat oven to 350 degrees F. Have the butcher tenderize the round steak, or pound it well to tenderize it yourself. (The original recipe says to "pound until the surface is pulpy".) Rub the surface well with flour and salt and pepper. Heat shortening, butter or oil in a skillet and brown the meat on both sides.

Remove the meat to your roasting pan and make the gravy in the skillet using the following method. Lower the heat to medium. Pour in the milk. Combine the 6 tablespoons flour with water to form a lump-free paste. Stir the paste into the milk and cook over medium heat, stirring frequently, until the gravy is thickened.

Put the vegetables around the meat in the roasting pan, pour the gravy over, cover and bake until tender, about 1 hour.

March 12, 1938
The Song of the Lazy Farmer

Mirandy thinks that I should try some hybrid corn;
the reason why is that she says that corn will yield more bushels
from off ev'ry field. It's bred some scientific way to help us make
corn growin' pay with stiffer stalks and thicker root and bigger
ears thrown in to boot. In fact she says that hybrid seed is just
the kind of stuff we need to fill our cribs and fat our swine
and get the milk from out the kine. It sure is scientific stuff
and if I'd only buy enough to plant our acres she believes them
fields will be a sea of leaves with ears a-pepin' out between,
the finest sight you'd ever seen.

I guess Mirandy's right at that, I know the corn that is begat
from that there scientific seed will just produce the corn we
need. At least it did on neighbor's land and tho I can not under-
stand inbreeding and detasseling, I guess that it's all right, by
jing, for after they cross-pollinate it makes the corn stalks strong
and straight; they stand against the wind and hail, and
grasshoppers can not assail that corn, for it's so very tough that
tho they chew away and puff and eat until their jaws are sore
that corn keeps growin' more and more. So I'll git me some
hybrid seed and raise a bumper crop indeed.

Sauerbraten

This is a favorite old German dish which may be made of very tough beef. Take a 4 to 6 pound piece of rather tough beef and almost cover it with a mixture of 3 parts water to 1 part vinegar. Add 1 bay leaf, 2 cloves, 1 clove of garlic, 1 1/2 half teaspoons salt, and a dash of pepper to the kettle. Let the meat stand in a cold place in the seasoned vinegar for at least 48 hours turning it occasionally so that all parts will have a chance to absorb the vinegar. Then drain the meat, reserving the marinade. Brown on all sides in hot fat. Add 1 cup of the juice in which the meat was soaked and simmer or bake very slowly. covered for abut 3 1/2 hours. Add more of the marinating liquid if necessary. Make gravy in the pot after the meat has been removed. Serve with potato dumplings.

Butcher's Meat Balls

For the Meat Balls:
1 pound ground beef
1/2 pound ground pork
1/2 cup bread crumbs
1 teaspoon scraped onion
1 teaspoon salt, optional
1/2 teaspoon pepper
1 tablespoon flour
1 egg

For the sauce:
3 tablespoons butter, divided
1 tablespoon cooking oil
1 tablespoon flour
1 cup tomato sauce or puree

Preheat the oven to 300 degrees F. Combine all ingredients. Form into balls about 1 inch in diameter. Brown in a frying pan in 2 tablespoons butter and oil, mixed. Remove the meat balls from the pan when they are browned on all sides Add 1 tablespoon butter and 1 tablespoon flour to the pan and cook over low heat until blended. Stir in the tomato sauce and mix until thickened. Pour the sauce over the meat balls and bake for about an hour.

■ **March 4, 1929** Hoover takes office.

■ **May 16, 1929** First Academy Awards presented.

■ **June 25, 1929** Color television broadcast demonstrated by Bell Labs. Three commercial television stations broadcasting in New York city showing animated silhouette movies.

■ **October 27, 1929** Black Tuesday. 16.4 million shares sold on New York Stock Exchange. Losses in 1929, $40 billion in paper losses.

■ **1929** Severe drought in Arkansas leads to starvation in winter 1929-1930. Farmer laborers working for 25 cents for a ten hour day. Contributions to the Red Cross are urged in *Wallaces' Farmer*.

■ **March 8, 1930** William Howard Taft dies.

■ **June 17, 1930** Smoote-Hawley tariff bill enacted.

■ Grant Wood paints American Gothic.

■ **1930** Unemployment reaches 6 million. Wheat selling for 37 cents per bushel.

■ **1930** Americans own 30 million automobiles.

■ **1930** Severe drought hits Mississippi Valley.

■ **May 1, 1931** Empire State building opens.

■ **May 23, 1931** Report on Status of the Drought in *Wallaces' Farmer*. From July 1, 1930 to May 31, 1931

	Normal inches	Actual this year	Difference
Iowa	24.3	17.2	- 7.1
Illinois	29.8	20.4	-9.4
Indiana	32.8	21.5	- 11.3

■ **September 4, 1931** James Doolittle flies across country in 11 hours and 16 minutes with 3 fuel stops.

■ **January 22, 1932** Reconstruction Finance Authority enacted by President Hoover. Budget at $2 billion.

■ **July 2, 1932** FDR elected in landslide victory over incumbent President Hoover. 472 to 59 electoral votes. Slogans "Happy Days are Here Again" and "Keep Rosy with Roosevelt."

■ **August 22, 1932** 11 million Americans out of work. By the end of 1932, 12 to 14 million are jobless.

■ **August 29, 1932** *Wallaces'* reports new corn crop price is to be 11 cents. One farmer sold his half interest in forty acres of corn for $140.

■ **October 7, 1932** One writer in *Wallaces'* reports, *"A two-row picker came to Jim's field today. He is hiring 25 acres picked for $12 and supplying the food and caring for the corn."*

CHAPTER 13

The Depression

Country Air
March 14, 1931
By a Farm Woman

Quite recently I've seemed to be a bit off balance in my reading, radio listening and conversation. That is, I've taken in a lot of discussion in the name of Economics. I've been reading "Your Money's Worth," by Chase and Schlink, from the WOI Book Club and "The Road to Plenty" by Foster and Catchings (Houghton, Mifflin) and I even pushed back the kettles during lard rendering last Friday (1 p.m.) to listen to Dr. Jules Klein over the WGN Executives' Club hour. Everyone seems to have valuable and witty comment upon the "why" of the present situation, but few have many sweeping remedies to suggest. In spite of all our mental progress we don't seem to get very far. Each generation of thinkers has it all to do over again. Things go up and down and up again. But it's something to talk about and anybody who comes along with a book or a lecture of explanation is hailed as a great person.

Making Do

There is very little complaining about The Depression economic conditions in the pages of *Wallaces' Farmer*. Instead, readers and editors alike focused on ways to cope with low farm prices and little ready cash. This article is an imagined dialogue between the Master Home-maker and one who is trying to make do on "Nothing Plus."

Economy Substitutes

You may manage without:
1. Fresh meat and cod liver oil, butter, whole milk and sunshine

2. Fresh spinach, canned peaches or liver

3. Fresh oranges and fresh lettuce

If you have:
1. Canned meat, plenty of eggs, greens, liver

2. Canned greens, strawberries, eggs

3. Canned tomatoes, strawberries or raspberries, raw green cabbage, carrots, sauerkraut, and plenty of whole wheat apricots, bread and whole cereals.

Keeping Fit on Nothing Plus!

Grace M. Ellis

One look at the list of food staples which are being given the starving Arkansas families should emit a prayer of thanksgiving from those of us who still have canned strawberries and tomatoes in our cellar shelves. But in between those unfortunates who were literally "wiped clean" by the drought and those few favored folk among us whose heaped storage bins and basement shelves may be supplemented at any time by generous purchases of fresh lettuce and oranges and meal from the grocery stores, there are those of us who are feeling the decided hamperings of cream checks cut in half and 15-cents-a dozen eggs. Frankly there isn't much money at hand to spend upon needed groceries. Does this mean that we, too, must stick to a restrictive diet?

"You wouldn't need to, really, that is if you have any supply of canned or stored foods left in your cellar," came the quietly comforting reply from a woman who had as evidence of her own handling of such confusing problems as unrestricted diets and restricted cream checks, a tiny medal bearing the words "Master Homemaker."

Living on Nothing Plus: What about cod liver oil? If we should have it, we should have it, I suppose. But at $1 a bottle and eight of us on a schedule of from one to three tablespoonful a day. I've just figured that we might easily spend $20 a month for that alone were I to follow the advice.

Master Homemaker: If one of the children seems bothered with a continual cold or has a tendency toward poor teeth or rickets, I'd believe that I'd spend the money if I could and feed the cod liver oil. That's the chief source of the sunshine and anti-rickets vitamin D. But this is a sunshiny winter and your children get a good deal of it.

NP: Tomatoes cabbage, strawberries, eggs, butter and greens! How many times you've mentioned them and how many more expensive things they may be made to substitute for.

MH: Indeed they may. And that they the are not any one of them as important, probably, for the standpoint of winter health as a good quart of milk per person per day. I've just been wondering, do you use that much?"

NP: I doubt it. In fact I'm quite certain we don't. We've been selling it a bit close, but it brings in cash and —

MH: But at 8 or 10 cents a quart it can't possibly bring in enough cash to buy its own food value in a single other product. It's an economy substitute for a dozen or more other things that would take far greater toil in cream checks and grocery bills.

April 4, 1931
Children need gardens

More than anyone else, the garden enthusiast is at heart a child and the child who has garden lovers for parents has an advantage over his playmates. Let the three, four, and five year old share in the delight of pouring over the brightly colored seed catalogs with his father and go through the fascinating and instructive process of garden planning and planting.

Sunny hours in the open, contact with the earth and with green things growing, wholesome exercise with development of responsibility and initiative are only a few of the benefits the small child may get from his own garden. Picking and arranging the flowers affords much pleasure and is one means of developing appreciation of color, feeling for beauty, and grace and control of his muscles.

Potato Water Wisdom

In these hard times American housewives may well tear a leaf from the cook book of their French cousins across the sea. To the thrifty Frenchwoman, what seems like economy in this country appears the wildest extravagance.

True domestic economy may well begin with potato soup. Almost every day in many homes the water in which the evening potatoes were cooked is thrown down the sink. The housewife may know that potato water is good for soup, but when she is serving boiled or mashed potatoes she is not interested in the rich deliciousness of potato soup. Liquids from carrots, from cabbage, from onions all rich in flavor and in mineral salts go the way of the potato water.

Potato Water Soup

Why not use these valuable and well-flavored juices? Instead of pouring the potato water down the sink, put it in the refrigerator until tomorrow. Then add more potatoes to it — one to a pint of water — and as many onions and cook them until they are soft. Strain the potatoes and onions through a sieve back into the water, add butter, milk and thickeners and heat again. Serve steaming to a delighted family.

Irish Potato Soup

    6 large Idaho potatoes, peeled and diced
    2 medium onions, peeled and diced
    1 cup diced celery
    3 cups water
    1 1/2 cups cream
    Salt and pepper to taste (I didn't use any salt and a
    tablespoon of pepper)

RKE *This later recipe improves on the potato water version, but only slightly. I was delighted to discover how good these simple soups are, comprised of the pureed vegetables and a little milk.*

Combine all ingredients in a large pot. Bring to a boil, reduce heat, cover and simmer until all the vegetables are tender, about 25 minutes. Puree the soup until smooth by pressing through a sieve or potato ricer, in a blender or food processor. If you use the blender or food processor be sure not to over-process. You will want to leave a few lumps. Over processed soup has a consistency close to glue, and is unappealing.

Baked Bean Soup

1 cup baked beans
5 cups milk
2 tablespoons minced onion
1/4 teaspoon pepper
2 teaspoons minced parsley
3 tablespoons tomato catsup
2 tablespoons soft butter
1 tablespoon flour

RKE *One excellent way to stretch that last cup of Baked Beans is to convert it to this satisfying soup.*

Mash the beans and combine with the milk in the top of a double boiler. Add the onion, celery, pepper and parsley. Simmer for 20 minutes. Combine the catsup with the butter and flour. Stir into the soup, blending well to prevent lumps. Simmer for 10 more minutes.

Augsut 29, 1931
Country Air

And now, not to neglect the well-known topic
of The Depression — a friend says, "This is nothing compared
to the depression of a hundred years ago. Even the insurance
companies failed then." Fancy that. It didn't even pay to die.

Country Air

A letter from a Chicago man who signs himself "an Ex-Iowa Country Banker" disagrees with my wager that no one who reads this column will go hungry this winter. He says that *Wallaces' Farmer* and *Iowa Homestead* is constantly out of the racks in the Chicago Public Library and the Country Air seems frequently to be read by men whose appearance might indicate that they were among the hungry and jobless. Yes, Mr. Ex-I.C.B., I directed that remark at my rural readers and while I doubt that enough "food and milk in Iowa goes to waste to feed the entire starving and bankrupt city of Chicago," I do know that we'd gladly turn the surplus of our gardens and orchards over to the hungry if they would only come and get it. Every Iowa farm wife knows that overproduction is as absurd as under consumption so long as there are hungry people in the world. It's the system of distribution that is the broken link between gardens "going to waste" and undernourished human beings. Many farm women have dropped wearily, down in the evening to share the daily paper with their husbands who are almost too tired to keep awake even at the World Series or the comic strips — to ponder as they read of bread lines, doles and hundreds of people without work and to calculate how many of these same unemployed could have been used to advantage on the farm that day. Too much to do for some — no work at all for others. Funny world! Still I guess it's wagged on this way for quite a spell — centuries, in fact. Even Cain was pretty busy tilling the soil while Able got about more or less over the countryside in the course of his business.

December 16, 1927
The Voiceless Soil
"I am speaking for the voiceless land"
– Uncle Henry

Oh, who will speak out for the voiceless soil,
Her face upturned to God,
With her hills and plains and homeward lanes,
And the urge of new-turned sod?

Her soul is the deeps of our human need,
Her heart the smile of Spring,
And her pulse the beat of myriad feet
That o'er her daily swing.

But some still live for their day alone
And in gold they count their gains;
While the birds fly by with a plaintive cry
To the land where life remains.

Oh, who will give voice to the voiceless soil,
And guard her tenderly?
For the humble clod is a trust from God
For the ages yet to be,

— H.R. Gross,
Iowa Congressman, 1949-1975

Pocketing Pin-Money

RKE Wallaces' Farmer *requested letters telling what farm wives did to earn important "pin money." Here are the winning letters.*

What we need, what we want, and whether we get either or not – all three of these problems are solved by that one little hyphenated word "pin-money."

We need or want so many things, but it takes more than merely needing or wanting. If we've had a lean year, we don't get them. Then is when the ingenious housewife turns to pin-money. And such varied methods there are for pocketing the pin money yet so simple and practical that you ask yourself, "Now why didn't I think of that?"

There's Mrs. Theodora P. Rayner of Johnson County, Iowa. "I don't for the life of me see why we can't buy a can of corn without its being three fourths cob!" her husband said to her after he's had several encounters with the cob in a 25-cent can of corn. Straight away Mrs. Rayner's alert mind set to work. Corn at 25-cents a can! A tin-can canner that she'd long coveted, yet considered the initial cost of $22 as too large an investment! And that acre of sweet corn that they'd always planted — and then fed the left-over surplus to the hogs!

"I'd never made it a practice to can my corn, for I never could get a large enough percentage of the glass cans sealed tight enough to keep," she said. Yet, fired with the idea of making her tin-can canner pay for itself, she took the plunge.

She sold the first dozen cans to her brother who lived in a town of about 5,000 and soon, unsolicited, six orders came from the brother's friends. Those six orders at 20 cents a can paid for the canner, "and that was last year. This year," she said, "I already have orders for more corn and vegetables that I can fill. People wish beans, peas and other vegetables too, but with the possible exception of beans, I consider the margin of profit over the work required too small.

"Of course, I have my husband's cooperation. Working together we can easily fill 100 cans in an afternoon. At 20 cents a can, the 100 filed cans bring us a total of $10. Deducting the $3.50 for the case of new cans, that leaves us a profit of $6.50 for our afternoon's work. This year I hope to manage 500 cans without overworking or interrupting my regular routine.

There were the cooks famous for cookies, cakes, cheese, or good home-made bread who succeeded in finding a market for their wares. There were clever seamstresses who marketed everything from gingham aprons to mittens. And there were the animal lovers who raised everything from guinea pigs to canaries. Each contestant, however, solved the two questions: what shall I do? And where shall I sell?

Five different women wrote local news for their paper and earned from 5 to 10 cents an inch that way. One woman tutored failing high school students. Developing Kodak pictures filled another's pocketbook. Another woman found a market for bittersweet. Ever so many women planned and canned for fair premiums. Oh! The pocket-money methods were unlimited in originality and variety.

Mrs. Raynor, who capitalized on the lowly sweet corn, was awarded first place and a $5 prize. Mrs. Cartier, who potted parsley, basing her pin money on the unusualness of her product — unusual because it was out of season — took second place and received $3. The canary project of Florence Peters was given third place and $2.

Depression Holiday Dinner

Mrs. Frank Miller, La Salle County, Illinois

For a family of six I prepare the following: Dressing — 1 loaf of bread cut into small pieces. Add 1 level teaspoon of salt, 1 teaspoon sage, 1 scant teaspoon pepper, 1 rounding tablespoon of butter and pour over this 1 cup of boiling water.

Let steam then mix and add 1 quart of canned beef or pork and distribute through the dressing. If a few oysters are available they will add greatly to the flavor. Place in a roaster and keep the oven temperature at about 250 degrees F., then increase the heat to 350 for browning and finishing the roast. Serve with tart applesauce.

Swelling Family Incomes

You can't keep farm women down. When income from hogs and corn goes down, they start piecing quilts and selling them. When live poultry prices slump, they eliminate the middleman by dressing and selling their own chickens. When they want some improvements in the house and cash is lacking they trade eggs and butter to the carpenter and the hardwareman. Several women reported trading vegetables, canned meats, hams and eggs to the doctor and the hospital. In return the hospital and doctor delivered a baby.

Our contest on swelling family incomes has brought in 300 entries. Dozens wound up with the sentence "I hope this will help others to get along."

One woman said very frankly, "I don't want to do this sort of work always. When prices of hogs and corn go up, I hope I can have more time to be with my family and enjoy life. However right now it has been a godsend that I have been able to do some work that we get cash and goods for"

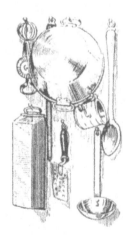

*We have sold or swapped corn, cucumbers, chickens and other farm
produce. Here are some examples of the swaps: Canned corn and honey
for a permanent wave and another swapped for in advance. Corn and kraut
for alfalfa, hay and oats; honey for chickens; chickens for vanilla and louse
powder; canned corn and kraut for radio repair service and corn for an express
wagon for the boys. Honey and potatoes have partially paid a doctor bill
and I've made arrangements to pay the hospital with produce.
Canned corn brought me a Dicky-bird who cheered me thru many weary
weeks of recuperation. I used to think swapping was primeval a method
for old-time horsetraders. But –*

*I've swapped for this and I've swapped for that;
I've swapped for everything but the cat!
When hubby looks for his green cravat,
It may be swapped for a gander, fat!*

*Now when my days below are o'er
And I must meet St. Peter at his door,
I fear, from my robes I may unfold
Something to swap for a harp of gold!*

*— Mrs. Grace Comer
Black Hawk County, Iowa
May 17, 1933*

CHAPTER 14

Cornmeal, Pineapple and Prunes

Soaking Corn Meal
March 29, 1918

To Hearts and Homes

In all that I have read regarding the cooking of corn meal, I have not seen anything about putting the meal to soak — an idea I received from Ames years ago. Perhaps you have practiced it yourself. Anyway, if the meal can soak for only half an hour it helps, but all night or all day makes a big difference. When I am going to have griddle cakes or muffins I measure out the milk and stir in the meal and let it stand. Entire wheat flour is much improved that way, too. We are all hoping to put in good "licks" on the farm the coming season and help to whip the Kaiser.

— Lucy V. White

As I read through the recipes in Wallaces' Farmer *I was struck by the appearance of certain ingredients over and over again. Corn meal was expected. It was the primary ingredient in pioneer bread and came into prominence again during World War I when most of our wheat flour was sent to Europe. Prunes and pineapple were big surprises. Certainly dried fruits filled a need in the Midwestern kitchen, but why were prunes mentioned in recipes more than any other?*

A little research provided an answer. In the early 20th Century, America was the world's leading grower of specialized prune plums and producer of dried prunes. Beginning in 1914, the World War in Europe and continuing depressed economic conditions greatly diminished the export market for American prunes. Prunes were now plentiful. Military cooks served them to servicemen, and in the decade after the War, prunes were lauded in food columns as a way to continue to promote the use of this tasty, economical fruit.

Pineapples from Hawaii and the Caribbean were once exotic fruits, however once Hawaii became a United States territory and major fruit packers invested in pineapple plantations, canned pineapple became a readily available ingredient for salads, desserts, even meat dishes.

Corn Cakes

Mary B. Wade

We are all familiar with fried mush, but possibly there are some who have not tried baking it. It is an old fashioned method of preparing corn meal. My grandmother used to bake it often in the winter and serve it for breakfast or supper under the name of corn cakes. Into a skillet put boiling water, about a dessert spoon of salt, a tablespoon of lard and 3 tablespoons of molasses. Stir in slowly corn meal till thick enough to drop from a spoon in cakes. Add water and meal till the quantity desired is made. Let it cook a few minutes stirring all the time. Grease the baking pans and drop in the mush to form cakes. Set on the bottom of the oven to bake. When the cakes are brown on the bottom, turn over to brown on the other side. Baking the mush imparts a rich nutty flavor that is wholly lacking in fried mush. Split the cakes and eat while hot with butter or they may be treated the same as fried mush and served with syrup.

Here is a recipe for Corn Bread reduced to about the quantity needed for 2 persons. Our favorite pan for this is a frame of 11 iron gem pans such as may be bought at any hardware store for 25 cents, but any kind of pan will do. One of the beauties of this recipe is that it will stand almost any kind of abuse and still be good so long as it is well stirred just before being put into the hot pan.

— Abigail Jane

Corn Bread

3 tablespoons flour
3 tablespoons sugar
6 tablespoons corn meal
1 teaspoon baking powder
1 teaspoon baking soda
1 egg, lightly beaten
1 cup milk

Preheat the oven to 425 degrees F. Combine the dry ingredients. Combine the egg and milk and quickly stir into the dry mixture. Pour batter into 12 well greased gem muffin cups or other preferred pan. Bake until lightly browned.

Army Strawberries

War is over! But in its day it brought not only soldiers and ammunition to the front, but prunes as well. What the strawberry is to the food world so was the prune to the army, hence the name "army strawberries."

Since the army had trained its soldiers to eat prunes and like them, the art of cookery has cooperated with the army to present prunes to the eating public in an appetizing and quite unexpected way. The first contribution is prune pie. We might also call it peace pie since the war brought peace as well as prunes.

To make prune pie the following materials are used:

> *1 cup mashed prunes*
> *1/2 cup lemon juice*
> *1/4 cup flour*
> *1/2 cup sugar*
> *2 egg yolks*
> *1 cup milk*
> *1 teaspoon vanilla*
> *1 teaspoon lemon juice*
> *2 8-inch pie shells, baked*

Mix sugar and flour, add beaten egg yolks and enough of the milk to make a thin paste. Scald the rest of the milk, gradually stir in the milk paste. Cook until thick and creamy. Add the prunes and lemon juice to this custard. Fill previously baked shells with the custard mixture and top with meringue.

At the institutional tea room at Iowa State College one of the guests complained about the service of such food to civilians. "Prunes may be all right in the army," he said, "but they have no place on the ex-soldiers table." Thru courtesy to the manager he condescended to taste the pie. Altho it is not generally known among his friends who heard his criticism, he requested a second piece of pie.

Good Things from Prunes

RYE *The moist packed prunes available now eliminate the need to plump the prunes before using them in many of these recipes.*

Prune Cake

1/2 pound moist prunes, chopped
2 1/2 cups flour
1 1/2 teaspoons baking powder
1/4 teaspoon baking soda
1/2 teaspoon nutmeg
1/2 teaspoon cinnamon
1 1/2 cups sugar
1 cup thick sour cream
2 eggs
2 tablespoons soft butter
1/4 cup sugar

Preheat the oven to 350 degree F. Stir the flour, baking powder, baking soda and spices together. Stir in the sugar and prunes. Next add the sour cream and lightly beaten eggs. Lastly stir in the very soft butter. Pour into a 9-inch square pan that has been greased and floured or sprayed with a non-stick spray. Bake until the cake is firm in the center and has just begun to pull away from the sides, 50 to 60 minutes. Sprinkle with the remaining 1/8 cup sugar and place under the broiler to glaze. You will want to have this about 5 inches away from the broiler and watch carefully so that it doesn't burn.

Prune Skillet Cake

6 tablespoons butter
1 cup brown sugar, firmly packed
1/2 pound moist prunes
1/2 cup butter
1 1/4 cups sugar
3 eggs, separated
2 cups flour
3 teaspoons baking powder
1 teaspoon vanilla
3/4 cup milk

Preheat the oven to 325 degrees F. Melt the butter in a 10- or 11-inch cast iron frying pan, or larger. Sprinkle the brown sugar evenly over the melted butter. Arrange the plumped prunes over this topping. Prepare the cake batter: Cream the butter and sugar. Add the egg yolks, milk and vanilla and beat well. Stir in the flour and baking powder. Fold the stiffly beaten egg whites into the batter and carefully spread it over the prunes. Bake about 45 minutes. Run a knife around the edge of the cake and allow it to stand five to ten minutes. To serve, place a serving platter over the frying pan and turn it upside down.

New Chicken Salad

Miss Ethel Schmitt, Marshall County, Illinois

>1 1/2 cups diced, cooked chicken
>1 cup diced celery
>1/3 cup crushed pineapple, well drained
>1 to 2 cups mayonnaise
>Olives for garnish

Combine all ingredients and chill before serving.

Pineapple Betty

>1 1/2 cups crushed pineapple
>   (1 20-ounce can pineapple packed in juice)
>1 cup soft bread crumbs
>1 tablespoon brown sugar, firmly packed
>1/4 teaspoon cinnamon
>1/4 cup pineapple juice, drained from the can

>**For the topping:**
>1/2 cup graham cracker crumbs
>2 tablespoons butter

Preheat oven to 375 degrees F. Drain the canned pineapple, reserving the juice. Combine the pineapple, bread crumbs, sugar, cinnamon and the 1/4 cup pineapple juice by tossing with 2 forks. Put mixture into a well greased small casserole dish, 6 to 7 inches in diameter. Combine the graham cracker crumbs and butter and sprinkle over the top. Bake until browned on top and heated through, about 30 minutes.

Pineapple Pie

>1 cup sugar
>1/2 cup melted butter
>3 eggs
>1 cup cream
>1 20-ounce can crushed pineapple, well drained to yield
>   about 1 1/2 cups of packed pineapple
>1 9-inch unbaked pie shell

Preheat oven to 350 degree F. Combine the ingredients in the order given and pour into the pie shell. This will fill the shell fairly high so make sure the shell has a raised, fluted edge. Bake until the filling is set, about 55 to 65 minutes. Cool the pie thoroughly and then chill in the refrigerator. Serve with whipped cream.

Date Cornmeal Muffins

1/2 cup chopped, dried dates
1 cup hot water
1 cup corn meal
2 tablespoons brown sugar, firmly packed
1 1/4 cups milk
2 tablespoons butter
1 cup flour
4 teaspoons baking powder
1 egg

Preheat the oven to 375 degrees F. Combine the dates with hot water and microwave for one minute, or simmer on top of the stove for 5 to soften the dates. In a 2-quart saucepan, bring the milk just to a boil. Quickly stir in the corn meal, brown sugar and butter. Set aside to cool to lukewarm. Drain the water from the dates and add, with the remaining ingredients, to the corn meal mixture. Stir until just blended. Put batter into well greased muffin cups. This mixture makes 12 regularsized muffins and 12 gem sized muffins. Bake until browned, about 20 to 25 minutes.

September 2, 1933

Prune Drop Cookies

Mrs. T.J. Green, Cherokee County, Iowa

1 cup butter
2 cups brown sugar, firmly packed
2 eggs
1 teaspoon vanilla
1 cup chopped moist prunes
1 teaspoon baking soda
2 teaspoons baking powder
1 teaspoon cinnamon
3 cups flour
1/2 cup milk
1/3 cup chopped nuts

Preheat the oven to 350 degrees F. Cream the butter and sugar and stir in the eggs. Beat until fluffy. Add the vanilla and the chopped prunes. Stir in the baking powder, cinnamon and half the flour. Add the milk, then the remaining flour. Stir in the nuts. Drop by teaspoons on lightly greased cookie sheets. Bake until firm in the center, about 10 minutes.

Custard Cornbread

Mrs. R.E.L., Holt, Nebraska

> 2 eggs
> 1/2 cup sugar
> 1 cup sour milk
> > may be made by combining 7/8 cup milk with 2 tablespoons
> > of vinegar and letting it stand for 10 minutes
> 2 cups fresh milk, divided
> 1 teaspoon baking soda
> 1 cup yellow corn meal
> 1 cup flour
> 2 tablespoons butter, melted

Preheat the oven to 400 degrees F. Beat the eggs and sugar with a wire whisk. Add 1 cup of the fresh milk, the sour milk and baking soda. Stir in the corn meal and flour. Melt the butter in a large shallow pan (9 x 12 inches works well. The original recipe called for a dripping pan.) Pour in the batter and then pour the remaining cup of milk evenly over the top of the batter. Do NOT stir. Bake until firm in the center, about 25 to 35 minutes. Serve warm from the pan.

Pineapple Oatmeal Cookies

Mrs. L.V. Couch, Antelope County, Nebraska

> 1/2 cup shortening
> 1 cup sugar
> 2 eggs, slightly beaten
> 1 1/2 cups flour
> 1/4 teaspoon soda
> 1 teaspoon baking powder
> 1/2 teaspoon salt
> 1/2 teaspoon cinnamon
> 2/3 cup sour milk
> 1/2 cup raisins
> 1/2 cup nutmeats
> 1 cup oatmeal
> 1 2/3 cups crushed or grated pineapple

Preheat the oven to 350 degrees F. Cream the butter and sugar. Stir in the eggs. Add the dry ingredients alternately with the sour milk. Stir in the raisins, nuts, oatmeal and pineapple. Drop by teaspoons on lightly greased cookie sheets and bake until the cookies are firm and the edges are just beginning to brown, about 15 minutes.

Cornbread

Mrs. Clive Butler, Audrain County, Missouri

My family thinks this cornbread is unusual. Just to experiment one day I tried beating the egg whites with the sugar as you would for a meringue, and then folded the mixture into the batter. As a result the corn bread was much lighter in texture.

4 eggs, separated
6 tablespoons sugar
1 1/2 cups flour
1 1/2 cups corn meal
1 1/2 tablespoons baking powder
1 teaspoon salt
1 1/2 cups milk
1/2 cup melted butter or other fat

Preheat the oven to 425 degrees F. In a perfectly clean and grease-free bowl, beat the egg whites until they begin to get stiff. Continue beating while adding the sugar, 1 tablespoon at a time. Beat until stiff peaks form. Set aside. Sift flour, then measure. Resift with the other dry ingredients and place in a large mixing bowl. Combine the egg yolks and milk. Stir in the cooled melted butter. Stir these liquid ingredients quickly into dry ingredients. Fold the beaten egg whites into batter. Pour into greased pans and bake at 425 degress F. for 25 minutes.

Upside Down Ham Loaf

Mrs. Elsie Lucas, Holt County, Nebraska

6 or 8 canned pineapple slices
1/2 cup brown sugar, firmly packed
1/2 teaspoon ground cloves
3 tablespoons fruit juice from the canned pineapple
1 pound ground ham
1 pound lean ground pork
1 cup bread crumbs
1/2 teaspoon dry mustard
2 eggs
1 cup milk

Preheat the oven to 350 degrees F. Put the pineapple slices in the bottom of an 8- or 9-inch baking pan. Sprinkle with brown sugar and cloves. Drizzle with pineapple juice. Combine the meats, bread crumbs, mustard, eggs and milk. Pat over the top of the pineapple. Bake until done, approximately 1 1/2 hours. Turn loaf upside down on a serving platter.

■ **January 21, 1933** *Wallaces' Farmer* article "Farms That Vanish Checking Soil Erosion on the Rolling Land of Southern Iowa. *"If the present rate of erosion of the rough lands in southern Iowa continues another fifty years, considerably more than one-half the land in many counties will have become worthless for cropping purposes."* Urges adoption of terracing, and the application of barnyard manure.

■ **January 30, 1933** Hitler named German Chancellor.

■ **February 1933,** Farm prices hit lows.

■ **April 28, 1933** Farm Relief Bill passes. Senate provisions include withdrawal of land from production, government guarantee for the cost of production, refinance farm mortgages at 4.5 percent. Stabilize farm prices at 1909-1914 levels.

■ **June 16, 1933** National Recovery Agency provides 1.6 million new jobs.

■ **December 5, 1933** Prohibition ends at 5:32 as Utah becomes the 36th state to ratify the 21st Amendment.

■ **May 12, 1934** *Wallaces' Editorial* "We're on the Uphill Road." Since February 1933, farm prices have risen 51 percent.

■ **May 31, 1934** President Roosevelt signs treaty annulling the Platt agreement giving up US rights in Cuba passed in 1902. US retains rights to Guantanamo Bay.

■ **August 19, 1934** Hitler named president after the death of Hindenberg.

■ **April 11, 1935** Increasingly severe dust storms in west Kansas, eastern Colorado, Wyoming, western Oklahoma and all of Texas.

■ **April 13, 1935** *Wallaces' Farmer* article "Let's Stop Destroying Our Wealth" urges soil conservation. *"We destroy national wealth and injure farm income when we take crops for which there is no market from land that should be grass. Getting more land back to grass helps: 1. To build farm income by reducing the volume of crops to the amount needed by the market. 2. To end destruction of soil resources form erosion on overcropped land."*

■ **August 14, 1935** Social Security enacted.

■ **January 28, 1936** England's King George V dies, Edward VIII crowned.

■ **March 3, 1936** Nazis enter Rheinland.

■ **July 31, 1936** Spanish Civil War begins.

■ **September 5, 1936** Beryl Markham is the first woman to solo the Atlantic.

■ **November 3, 1936** Roosevelt reelected.

■ **December 3, 1936** Edward the VIII abdicates.

■ Falling Water built.

CHAPTER 15

Eggs, Nuts and Cheese

October 6, 1930

When vegetables are featured as the main dish at a meal
they are usually combined with other ingredients which
give flavor and food value and make the dish both tasty
and hearty enough to substitute for meat. Combinations
of vegetables with cheese, eggs, nuts, ham or bacon
are specially well adapted to luncheon or supper and
occasionally appear as the main dish at dinner.

December 1898

Nut Salad

Take equal amounts of:
Diced apples
Diced celery
Nuts, you may use walnuts, almonds or peanuts.

Bind with a boiled dressing.

RKE *This recipe uses a mustard boiled dressing as a binder. You can find a recipe at the beginning of the vegetable section, or you could get a similar flavor by using a commercial cream-style honey mustard dressing.*

January 4. 1907

Baked Eggs

If one is tired of the continual round of fried pork, fried eggs, fried potatoes, a nice change will be found in baked eggs. Grease a small pan and break the eggs into it, taking care not to break the yolks. Pour in a little milk, half a cupful to 3 or 4 eggs is about right. Dash of pepper and salt over the top, but do not stir the mixture. Bake 5 or 10 minutes in a moderate oven.

January 2, 1925

Baked Eggs

Mrs. G.J. Struthers, Palo Alto County, Iowa

1 cup leftover chicken gravy
1/2 cup chopped mushrooms
6 eggs
1/4 cup buttered bread crumbs

Preheat oven to 325 degrees F. Combine the gravy and mushrooms and pour into a small baking dish. Heat until warm. Break in the eggs. Sprinkle over the buttered crumbs and bake until set, about 15 minutes.

February 14, 1931

Swiss Eggs

Combine 1/2 cup cream with 1 teaspoon prepared mustard. 1/4 teaspoon salt, and 1/8 teaspoon paprika. Butter a shallow baking dish cover the bottom with 1 cup grated cheese doted with 1 tablespoon butter and cover with half the mustard cream mixture. Break 6 eggs into the baking dish, pour the remaining mixture over the eggs and bake in a slow oven, 10 or 15 minutes until the eggs are set.

May 24, 1907

Nut Sandwiches

1/2 cup each hickory, walnut and pecan nutmeats
3/4 cup diced hard boiled eggs
2 tablespoons or more of good quality mayonnaise

R E *Nut fillings were popular in the early part of the 20th century. Nuts were seen as a good protein source and part of a healthful diet.*

Mix all the ingredients thoroughly. Spread between slices of sturdy bread.

March 22, 1907

Bread Omelet

2 cups stale bread crumbs, fairly dry
2 cups milk
1 cup grated sharp cheese
3 eggs, well beaten
1/2 teaspoon pepper

Soak the bread crumbs in the milk. Add the cheese, pepper and well beaten eggs. Pour the mixture into a well greased frying or omelet pan. Cook over low heat until the middle is set. Fill with desired filling — mushrooms, tomato sauce, steamed vegetables. Fold the omelet over the filling and carefully slide out of the pan.

May 31, 1907

Cheese Soufflé

Appetizing and easily prepared.

3 ounces bread without the crust, crumbed
3/4 cup milk
3 ounces butter
6 ounces cheese, grated
2 egg yolks
1/2 teaspoon salt
1/2 teaspoon mustard
2 stiffly beaten egg whites

Preheat the oven to 375 degrees F. Boil the milk and bread crumbs until the crumbs are soft. Blend in the butter, cheese and egg yolks. Fold in the egg whites. Pour into a lightly greased dish and bake 5 to 10 minutes.

Bread and Cheese Casserole

Mrs. J. P., Sarpy County, Nebraska

Preheat oven to 375 degrees F. Cut stale bread into 1-inch cubes and place a layer in the bottom of a buttered casserole. Dot with 1 tablespoon of butter and then sprinkle generously with grated cheese. Repeat until your baking dish is full. Beat 2 eggs (use 3 if your dish is large) add 1 teaspoon of salt and 1 cup of milk and pour over the bread and cheese mixture. Pour on enough more milk to cover the bread. Set the casserole in a larger dish of hot water and bake until the mixture is firm. The product is a smooth, flavorful custard. Serve hot.

Bird's Nest Eggs

6 slices of bacon
6 eggs

Preheat the oven to 350 degrees F. Half cook the slices of bacon in the microwave or frying pan. Line the sides of each muffin cup with one piece of bacon. Carefully break an egg into the center of the muffin cup. Bake until the egg is set, about 10 minutes.

Eggs and Tomato Tortilla

4 teaspoons butter
1 can stewed tomatoes, drained
3 eggs, well beaten

Melt the butter in a medium sized frying pan. Add the tomato and cook until warmed through. Add the eggs and stir until set. Serve over hot, buttered toast.

Cheese and Olive Canapé

1/2 cup grated cheese
1/4 cup softened butter
1 teaspoon Worcestershire sauce
2 teaspoons paprika
Sliced olives as garnish

Combine the cheese, butter, Worcestershire sauce and paprika. Spread on thin slices of bread or crackers. Garnish with a border of sliced olives.

Nut Scrapple

1 cup corn meal
3 cups water
2 cups chopped nutmeats

Combine the corn meal and water. Cook over low heat until the water is absorbed and the mixture is quite thick. Stir frequently to keep from sticking and burning. Add the nutmeats. Line a loaf pan with sturdy plastic wrap. Spray with cooking spray and pack the mixture in very firmly. Chill overnight. When ready to serve, slice off thin slices, about 1/4 of an inch, and brown in butter. Serve with hot maple syrup.

April 27, 1929

Egg and Ham Timbales

When eggs are plentiful, try this dish.

2 tablespoons butter
1/3 cup dry bread crumbs
1 cup milk
1 teaspoon chopped parsley
1 cup cooked ham, chopped
2 eggs, lightly beaten

Melt the butter in a small saucepan. Add the bread crumbs and milk, cook, stirring constantly, for 5 minutes. Add the remaining ingredients. Pour into buttered custard cups and bake for 30 minutes. Turn out onto a hot platter and sprinkle with sieved hard boiled egg yolk. Serve with tomato or cream sauce.

December 9, 1930

Peanut Butter Loaf

RHE *This Depression era recipe highlights creative solutions for affordable protein.*

1/2 cup peanut butter
1/2 cup heavy cream
2 cups cooked rice
1 egg, lightly beaten
1/2 cup raisins
Juice of one lemon

Preheat oven to 350 degrees F. Stir the peanut butter into the cream until smooth. Add the egg and blend well. Stir this mixture into the cooked rice and add the raisins and lemon juice. Form into a loaf and bake 30-40 minutes until firm.

October 1, 1897
Mowing

The swish of the scythe in the grass
Is yet in my ears,
As I think of mowing time
In my early years
Such a thing as that out there
Was never seen!
I wonder how I'd a-flet
Atop a mowing machine.

By the sweat of the brow it is said;
I like the old ways
Anne used to bring us jugs
O' porridge in them days,
An' buttermilk. Only to see her
Was restin' Yes, science is gre't,
An comes mighty nigh in these times
Abolishin' sweat.

I remember a summer forenoon
Just like today –
Tarnation I am sweet with the smell o' the hay
Anne came across the fields
With a luncheon for me;
An' we set together awhile
In the shade o' the gre't elm tree.

There was berries a-soak in the sun
By the old stone wall.
An' young birds hoppin' about –
I remember it all.
Her short gown was printed in stripes
With rosebuds between;
An' to think that's her gran'son out there
On that mowin' machine!

— Mary F. Butts

Cheese Loaf

3 eggs, separated
1 cup scalded milk
1/2 cup American cheese, shredded
1 tablespoon butter
1 cup dry bread crumbs

Preheat the oven to 350 degrees F. Whip the egg whites until they are stiff in a clean bowl with grease-free beaters and set aside. Add the cheese and butter to the slightly cooled milk. Stir until they are both melted. Add the dry bread crumbs and egg yolks. Fold in the egg whites and pour into a loaf pan. Place the pan in a larger pan and fill it half-way up the side with hot water. Bake until the loaf is firm, about 20 to 25 minutes.

September 28, 1935

Cheese Noodle Ring

A new and very popular dish at a certain far-famed Midwest tea-room is Cheese Noodle Ring.

6 ounce package egg noodles, broken into 1-inch pieces
1 1/2 cups grated cheese
Dash pepper
3 eggs, well beaten
1 cup scalded milk

Preheat the oven to 325 degrees F. Cook the noodles in boiling water until they are tender. Drain and rinse with cold water. Add the cheese, pepper and eggs to the noodles and mix well. Gradually stir in the scalded milk. Pour the mixture into a lightly greased ring mold. Set the mold in a pan of hot water and bake until set, about 45 minutes. Unmold and fill the center with buttered carrots or creamed peas.

Fried Apples with Cheese

Wash, core and slice into rings as many apples as desired. Sprinkle generously with brown sugar. Fry in a little butter until tender. Remove from the fire and sprinkle generously with grated cheese. Cover until the cheese melts and serve hot.

CHAPTER 17

Contributions and Contests

Hearts and Homes,
Mrs. H. O. Minnis Sharpsberg,
Illinois, October 1, 1897

I have been reading "Hearts and Homes" for some time, but had not thought of making you a call until I noticed one of the sisters asked for a recipe for Angel Food Cake, and having an excellent one, I thought I would send it in.

It is as follows:
Whites of 11 eggs, 1 1/2 tumblers pulverized sugar, 1 tumbler flour, 1 teaspoon cream of tartar.

Sift flour and sugar together 4 times then add cream of tartar and sift again. Bake 40 minutes. Heat oven as for any loaf cake, do not open for 20 minutes after putting in cake. Do not grease your cake pans. When taken out of the oven turn pan upside down on something thick and soft and let it fall out. Put something under the edge of the pan to hold it up so that it will not strain out.

This will make a lovely cake if baked nicely. You will think the batter very thin, but it is all right.

*From the beginning of the "Hearts and Homes" column,
the* Wallaces' Farmer *readers responded positively to Nannie
Wallace's request in the very first column. As she wrote in
September 1895, "We ask your earnest cooperation in
making this department a step forward in a good cause.
We cordially invite contributions on all topics of interest or
current events. The young people and children are included
in this invitation. 'Hearts and Homes' would not be complete
without their cheering presence."*

*Almost immediately a sisterhood of readers developed.
Some would send in favorite recipes. Others would write
asking for the best way to make certain dishes and within
one or two issues another sister would respond
with her suggestions.*

*Over the years contributions from readers continued.
Beginning in the late 1920s* Wallaces' Farmer *editors began
asking readers for specific recipes. Perhaps as a way
to encourage reader participation, perhaps as a way
to reward members of the* Wallaces' Farmer *family during
hard times on the farm, the paper ran contests. Winning
entries received prizes of five dollars. The creativity of these
entries is remarkable. Some are serious, for example
presenting ways to stretch the farm budget in hard economic
times, others covered lighter themes. I've included excerpts
from several of these contests. My personal favorite is one
of the less serious contests. In responding to "What I Cook
When My Wife is Away," Mr. Don L. Wheery wrote an essay
that makes me smile every time I read it.*

Pickles

Mrs. Susan White

RKE *One way church ladies raised money was to sell single recipes, flavorings with a recipe or cookbooks.*

As this hot summer has come and almost gone, I have enjoyed the woman's page in this paper very much. One young girl asks for recipes and as we are fast approaching Fall I will send a few recipes for pickles which I have used for some years and found to be "excellent," as Mrs. Wade says. The value of the this one may be increased when I tell you it was sold by a certain church in Council Bluffs for a dollar a recipe.

French Pickles
1 peck of green tomatoes, sliced
1 teacup salt
2 quarts vinegar
1 quart water
3 pints vinegar, additional
2 pounds brown sugar
2 tablespoons cinnamon
2 tablespoons whole cloves
2 tablespoons whole allspice
2 tablespoons ground mustard

Mix the tomatoes with the salt and let stand overnight. Drain off the accumulated juices. Cook the tomatoes in the vinegar and water mixture for 20 minutes. Drain. Combine the 3 pints of vinegar and the remaining ingredients. Bring to a boil. Add the tomato slices and simmer until tender. Seal in sterilized jars or keep in the refrigerator.

Recipe for Cake

Ethel Ashby, Warren County, Iowa

I noticed that Alice Harmon wanted some recipes. I send her my recipe for cake which I have tried with success.

The whites of 6 eggs
1 cup butter
1 1/2 cups sugar
1 cup milk
3 cups flour
2 teaspoons baking powder
1 teaspoon lemon or vanilla

Preheat the oven to 350 degrees F. In a perfectly clean bowl with grease-free beaters, whip the egg whites until stiff and set aside. Cream the butter and sugar. Add half the flour and all of the baking powder, then the milk and finally the remaining flour, mixing well after each addition. Stir in the flavoring you prefer. Gently fold in the beaten egg whites. Pour the batter into a well-greased and floured pan. Bake until the cake is firm in the center and just beginning to pull away from the sides.

Chopped Pickles

May I step in this afternoon and give Cora Coster and others my recipe for making chopped pickles.

> 1 gallon chopped and drained tomatoes
> 1 gallon chopped cabbage
> 12 onions
> 30 large green cucumbers
> 1 cup salt

First pickling mixture:
1/2 gallon good vinegar
1/4 cup ground cinnamon
1/2 cup black pepper
2 cups white mustard seed
1 pound sugar

Second pickling mixture:
1 cup ground mustard
2 ounces celery seed
1/2 ounce ground turmeric
2 cups salad oil

Layer the vegetables with the salt and weight them down. Let stand in a very cool place overnight.

In the morning drain and rinse them well. Add the first pickling mixture. Let the mixture come to a boil and simmer for 20 minutes, stirring nearly all the time. Remove from the stove and add the second pickling mixture. Bring to a boil, seal in sterilized jars.

The turmeric can be left out, if you desire, but it gives to it a nicer color, I think.
How I do enjoy the Hearts and Homes page.

Aunt Ruth, Harrison County, Iowa

Frosted Creams

Who would have dreamed there could be so many different ways to make the delicious confections known as frosted creams? Forty-two recipes and no two of them the same have been received by Hearts and Homes department in answer to a Sac County reader's request.

Method for making Frosted Creams: The method for mixing and baking these cookies is the same for all versions. Preheat the oven to 350 degrees F. Cream the lard (or butter) and sugar. Stir in the eggs and molasses and mix until light. Add the spices, leavening and half the flour. Mix well. Stir in the milk, coffee or boiling water and then the remaining flour. The original recipes called for rolling the dough out and placing in a large pan. I've found the dough works well when I pat it gently into my large jelly-roll pan (12 x 18 x 3/4 inch deep). You can, of course, drop this batter by tea spoons onto the cookie sheet. Lightly grease a large baking pan. Spread the batter in the pan and bake until firm in the center, about 20 minutes. Cool, frost with vanilla frosting, and cut into 1-inch squares.

RYE *My neighbor Alice exclaimed, "I Love frosted creams" when I brought her samples from these three recipes. She had her favorite. I had mine. The editors picked a handful from the 42 sent in. None of them were like the very old one I had in my files from a 1900 issue of* Wallaces' Farmer. *I wonder if that was the one the reader from Sac County was seeking.*

Frosted Creams
Wallaces' Farmer
May 11, 1900

1 cup sugar
3/4 cup butter and lard
   (I use all butter)
2 egg yolks
1/2 cup molasses
1 tablespoon ginger
1 teaspoon baking soda
1/2 cup boiling water
3 1/3 cups flour

Mrs. Polly Erwin,
R.F.D. No. 2, Vinton, Iowa
1 cup lard (I used butter)
1 cup sugar
4 eggs
1 cup molasses
1 teaspoon ginger
1 teaspoon cinnamon
1 teaspoon baking soda
4 cups flour
1 cup cold coffee
(See directions above.)

Betty E. Dunston, Manchester, Iowa
2/3 cup lard (I used butter)
1 cup brown sugar, firmly packed
1 egg
1 cup molasses
1/2 teaspoon ginger
1 teaspoon cinnamon
1 teaspoon nutmeg
1 teaspoon baking soda
2 teaspoons baking powder
1/2 cup milk
3 cups flour
(See directions above.)

Vanilla Frosting:
4 tablespoons butter, melted
1 teaspoon vanilla
1/4 cup milk or coffee
2 1/2 cups powdered sugar, or more to make desired consistency.

Combine all the ingredients and mix until smooth. Add more sugar or a very small amount more liquid if needed.

What I Cook When the Wife's Away

R E *In the 1920's and 30's* Wallaces' Farmer *frequently asked readers to send in answers to a topical question. One of the most amusing resulted in this column. Winning entries would receive $5.*

H.A. Wallace, one of the judges, says, "It takes a brave man to admit in print how good he really is in preparing meals for himself. I congratulate these men on their courage and hope their wives never read what they have so rashly written. Some of them have displayed their bravery by eating the products of their messing. After reading these efforts I am tempted to relate my own efforts which have convinced me that cooking should be limited to eggs and potatoes. The chief reliance should be placed on bread and milk, crackers and cheese. But then I am not doing much hard physical labor, and if I were, I might be able to eat even the cooking of Don L. Wherry, who seems to have won first prize."

Josephine Wylie says "After reading the letters in the contest I am convinced that wives should go away more often. Not only would the absence give greater opportunities for practice, which the man may or may not need, but it would keep wives blissfully ignorant as to what is going on behind their backs, averting any domestic tragedies that might arise as to who is the best cook in the family."

Ms. Wylie continued, "I recommend this with but one exception, and that is in the case of the impeccable Mr. Wherry, who wrote the first prize letter. And whom I shall always picture in the doorway of his home, taunting the returning wife with remarks about his most excellent cooking. His wife should seldom, if ever, go away."

Winning entry from Don L. Wherry of Jones County Iowa. He wrote: "There was always a good deal of argument when I kept house during a weekend if my mother or later my wife was away. Invariably they complained I met them with the remark: I had some of the blamedest best pancakes while you were away that I ever ate."

Mr. Wherry continued, "But it's true! If a man keeping house does not have a little sour milk or, for that matter, all sour milk, he's an unusual man. So given the ever present sour milk, flour, soda and baking powder, plenty of eggs and a pinch of salt (man sized) any man who has lonesome visions of his wife's hot cakes, when absent, doesn't deserve hot cakes at any time. And so the method: Sift 2 cups of flour, 1 teaspoon baking soda, 2 heaping teaspoons baking powder and a pinch of salt in one bowl. 4 egg whites (more if you like) in another and the egg yolks in another. (Be prodigal of the dishes, the wife might come home in time to wash them.) Beat the contents of the two latter bowls well (keeping them separate). Add the yolks, 1 cup of sour milk and beat. Then mix the dry ingredients with the yolks and milk, gradually adding more sour milk and beating well. Batter should be somewhat thick. Have your griddles hot, mix in 2 big tablespoons of melted butter (now lay aside your cigar, let not the children or the hired man interrupt you) quickly fold in the beaten egg whites. A thin coating of grease for the first griddle full is sufficient. Avoid smoking up the house (it smells like fury when you come in for supper) by letting the butter be added to the batter to prevent sticking."

Mr. Wherry described this dish, "Someone might call it an omelet — he's the chef. Some might balk at the eggs and butter — he's an army cook. But I'll wager that chef or army cook wouldn't let any minor difference stand between him and another stack.

"Then there's supper. It's pretty slick to find a small can of kippered snacks in the cupboard. Frizzle the fish in butter, pour over 1/2 dozen eggs and 1/2 cup of thin cream. Scramble and consume voraciously with bread and butter. Fresh kippered salmon is the chosen whale for this dish, but lacking this, kippered herring or snacks serve very well. Be sure to wash the dishes that night however. (Grandpa says they make the kitchen smell badly by morning.)"

Mr. Wherry concluded, "I can have a lot of fun when my wife's away. There's potatoes with the skins on, apple fritters, cheese pudding, fried onions. You can fry anything as long as there is grease and a clean skillet, but O' my gosh, the dishes!"

In another entry to the contest Earl C. Marsh of Hardin County says, "Many years ago I learned my first lesson in cooking. Mother was away so father sent me to the house one evening to cook some rice for supper. So I put on a stew pan full of rice and poured in enough water to cover it nicely and dad and I had rice three times a day for quite a spell with plenty to spare for Shep and the cats."

April 22, 1927

One Dish Company Supper

Mrs. Arthur G. Eddy, Route 2, Cherokee, Iowa

> 1 4-pound chicken, cooked and cut in pieces
> 1 small can mushrooms, drained
> 1 can peas, drained
> 2 cups corn flakes
> 4 cups chicken stock (or could be half milk)
> 2 tablespoons butter
> 2 tablespoons flour
> 2 eggs, separated
> Salt and pepper to taste

Preheat the oven to 350 degrees F. Combine the boned chicken, mushrooms and peas in a large mixing bowl. Crush the corn flakes and add. Make a sauce of the chicken broth by melting the butter in a medium sauce pan, stir in the flour and cook over medium heat until it bubbles. Stir in the broth, or broth and milk combination. Add the lightly beaten egg yolks and cook over medium heat, stirring frequently, until the sauce is thick. Stir it into the chicken mixture. In a clean, dry bowl, whip the egg whites until they form stiff peaks. Gently fold them into the chicken mixture. Pour the mixture into a lightly buttered casserole. Bake until casserole is firm in the center, about 30 minutes.

February 23, 1929

Wash-day Dinners

R&E *Here are the results of another* Wallaces' Farmer *contest.*

Wash-day Dinner menus at last! And you'll all be glad to read the pick of the 300 letters that have come in with their suggested menus. One and all the housewives seemed to agree that wash day was the day to conserve time in meal preparation and in dishwashing — always keeping the balanced menu in mind.

First Prize Winner
M.S.W., Iroquois County, Illinois

Looking over my wash-day dinner menus I find this one which seems to please my husband and the boys the best this time of year.

Fresh Pork, Potatoes and Peas en Casserole
Perfection Salad
Bread, Butter and Jelly
Canned pears, Cake

My wash day is usually on Monday so I can have some baking left over from Saturday. The cake is made on Saturday. Likewise the salad and dressing. The **Perfection Salad** is made of lemon Jell-O, shredded cabbage, diced celery, and raw carrots. Any other vegetables could be substituted.

Fresh Pork, Potatoes and Peas en Casserole

Use 1 1/2 to 2 pounds of meat. I place it and a whole onion with pepper and salt in a casserole dish or crock which has a heavy lid. The potatoes are peeled, cold pack peas are opened and the cream is whipped and sweetened while my clothes are soaking.

At 9 o'clock a little boiling water is poured over the meat in the casserole dish and it is placed in the oven. At 11:15 the potatoes and peas are added to the meat and at noon the casserole is taken out and a little flour and water is stirred in to thicken the gravy

Pepper Pot

Mrs. Jay Carter from McLean County, Illinois sent in her recipe

>   *3 pounds lean pork, cut in 2-inch pieces*
>   *2 large onions sliced*
>   *6 green peppers, sliced*
>   *3 large tomatoes, peeled and seeded*

Fill the pot with water, place it on the back of the stove to simmer for 4 or 5 hours. Half an hour before serving drop in enough potatoes, peeled and cut in halves lengthwise, for the family. The sauce will be rich and deliciously flavored and the meat tender and toothsome. Just try it!

Who Says We Don't Like Salads

By a mere but skeptical man

I'll admit that I said it once myself, but then my idea of a salad was based pretty much upon the old restaurant variety — the kind that varies in consistency between a poultice and a cold stew, and in flavor from zero to less. At home we had potato salad in summer and pink gelatin salad in winter (the kind with oranges showing thru here and there and sliced bananas roaming around on top). I liked them, but it is a darn shame to limit your salad appetite to just those two kinds where there are so many crackling good ones to dip into.

From the standpoint of plain common food sense it shouldn't be necessary to convince a good livestock feeder that, particularly from January 'till June, human beings need just the sort of stuff that a good salad is made of, that silage will pep up a sluggish appetite is no news to a dairyman.

I have noticed there are three things which good salads are: they're crisp, they're cold and they have real flavor!

They say there aren't any restrictions on the kinds of combinations of things that can be used to make a salad, but I do know that a man likes to have at least one thing in the combination that has real "kick" of flavor. The two worst salads which I have ever tasted were made one of sea-shell macaroni, whipped cream and cooked peas and the other of cabbage and bananas with a flat and mushy dressing. There isn't anything to do about food combinations like that except to eat them, say nothing and vow next time to bring along your own apple, orange, tomato or onion to "pop" the thing up.

Favorite Combinations
Cinnamon apples, cottage cheese and celery
Ground carrots, chopped celery, cabbage and coconut
Shredded cabbage, pineapple and nutmeats with sour cream dressing
Celery, string beans, pickles and French dressing
Shredded cabbage, diced beats and horseradish
Apples, celery, pineapple and nutmeats
Diced beets and olives
Prunes stuffed with cottage cheese
Peas, cheese and celery

Good Machinery
Gets more *profit*
from your Corn

ADVANCE RUMELY
Ball-Bearing Silo Filler

One-Dish Meals Galore

Who would have guessed there were 1500 one-dish meal combinations. It has been a real job deciding which ones to run. A good many recipes were original, some were brought from Germany, England, Switzerland and, in fact, from all over the world.

Baked Fish Dinner

Mrs. Asa Brown, Crawford County, Iowa

> *2 1/2 cups diced potatoes*
> *1/2 cup diced onion*
> *1/4 cup diced celery*
> *1 1/2 cups flaked canned fish, tuna or salmon*
> *3 cups canned peas*
> *1/2 pimento, cut in strips*
> *1/8 teaspoon pepper*
> *Juice of half a lemon*
> *1/2 cup milk*
> *3 tablespoons butter*
> *Biscuit dough or refrigerated biscuit dough*

Preheat the oven to 425 degrees F. Cook the potatoes, onions and celery in boiling water until tender. Drain but reserve the cooking liquid. Lightly grease a 1 1/2- to 2-quart baking dish. Combine the drained vegetables with the fish, peas, pimento and pepper. Put in the baking dish. Squeeze the lemon juice over and pour over the milk and 1/2 cup of the reserved cooking liquid. Dot with butter. Place biscuit dough on top of this mixture and bake until the biscuits are done, 10 to 15 minutes.

Syrian Casserole

Mable Roming, Antelope County, Nebraska

> *1 medium eggplant, cut in 1/8 inch thick slices*
> *Flour for dredging*
> *3 tablespoons oil*
> *2 medium onions, sliced*
> *1 pound ground beef*
> *1 cup tomato puree*
> *Salt and pepper to taste*

Preheat the oven to 350 degrees F. Dredge the eggplant in flour and fry in the oil until lightly browned. Drain on paper towels. Grease a 2- to 3-quart casserole dish. Layer the eggplant, onions and ground beef, sprinkling each layer with salt and pepper. Pour the tomato puree over the top. Bake for an hour with casserole covered for the first 1/2 hour, and bake for 1/2 hour. Serves six to eight.

Dutch Recipe

Leona Hamm, Van Burean County, Iowa

1 pound pork sausage
1 cup uncooked rice
1 egg
1 large can sauerkraut
Warm water to cover

Preheat the oven to 325 degrees F. Make small meatballs with the pork, rice and egg. Put a layer of sauerkraut in the bottom of a 2-quart baking dish. Arrange the meat balls on top and cover with more kraut. Cover with warm water and place a lid on the dish. Bake for two hours.

Old German Dish

Mrs. F.C. Reinhardt, Hamilton County, Iowa

RKE *This is a very large recipe. It is good reheated and would be terrific to take to a potluck.*

Bottom Layer:
2 cups boiled potatoes, cooled
2 cups diced raw potatoes
2 apples
1 onion
2 eggs, well beaten
1 cup cream
2 cups flour
1 tablespoon sugar
1 tablespoon baking powder

Second layer:
2 eggs, well beaten
1/2 cup sugar
1 cup stewed pumpkin
1/4 teaspoon ginger
1/4 teaspoon cloves
1/4 teaspoon allspice
1 1/2 cups milk
1/2 pound stewed prunes

Preheat the oven to 350 degrees F. Grind or process together the raw potatoes, apples and onion. Mix in the eggs, cream, flour, sugar and baking powder. Spread over the bottom of a lightly greased 9 x 12 x 2- or 3-inch baking dish. Combine the ingredients for the second layer and gently pour over the first layer. Dot with prunes. Cover with a lid or foil and bake three or four hours.

Lima Bean Casserole

Opal Couch, Antelope County, Nebraska

4 cups cooked lima beans
2 cups sliced cooked carrots
2 medium onions, diced
2 cups cooked tomatoes
4 tablespoons butter
2 teaspoons brown sugar, firmly packed

Preheat the oven to 350 degrees F. Combine all ingredients and bake for 45 minutes. "Serve with cole slaw and corn muffins."

CHAPTER 16

Cookies

Gingersnaps
October 23, 1925

There is something about crisp fall days that always
makes me want to put on a big kitchen apron, build a roaring
fire in the range and turn out a full batch — 144 — of those
utmost of delicacies of sugar and spice — gingersnaps.
I remember that the recipe copied from grandmother's cook
book said, "these cookies will last for six months if kept in a
tight jar." But aside from the times a can full was hidden
away on the top shelf and forgotten about, I never actually
knew any to last that long.

November 11, 1898

Thanksgiving Cookies

Mrs. C. B. Harding

> 2 cups sugar
> 1 cup butter
> 4 eggs, beaten
> 1 teaspoon lemon extract (you may also add some grated lemon peel)
> 2 teaspoons baking powder
> 4 cups flour

Preheat the oven to 350 degrees F. Cream the butter and sugar. Add the eggs and mix until fluffy. Stir in the lemon extract and peel, if desired. Add the baking powder and half the flour. Mix well. Add the remaining flour. Drop by very small teaspoons onto well greased cookie sheets. Bake until firm in the center and just beginning to brown around the edges, 5 to 8 minutes.

November 6, 1908

Mother's Sugar Cookies

RKE *The mother mentioned in the name of this recipe is probably Mrs. Henry Wallace. Her daughter Josephine wrote many of the recipes in the early days of the Hearts and Homes column.*

> 1 cup fat (I use butter)
> 1 2/3 cups sugar
> 2 eggs
> 1 cup milk
> 2 teaspoon baking powder
> 5 cups flour

Preheat oven to 400 degrees F. Cream the butter and sugar. Add the eggs and mix well. Add the baking powder, 2 1/2 cups of the flour and mix well. Stir in the milk and then the remaining flour. Divide the dough and roll out until very thin. Sprinkle with granulated sugar and cut into squares. Place cookies on a lightly greased cookie sheet and bake until just beginning to brown, about 10 minutes.

January 6, 1899

Holiday Cookies

1 cup butter
1 1/2 cups sugar
3 eggs
1 teaspoon lemon extract
1/2 teaspoon baking powder
1/2 cup walnuts, very finely chopped
3 1/4 cups flour
Sugar for top of cookies

RKE *These are simply wonderful cookies. They are good keepers. The combination of the lemon flavor with the ground walnuts is very delicate. Use a knife or food processor to chop the nuts. You want the pieces to be fairly fine, a little be bigger than coursely ground corn meal.*

Preheat the oven to 350 degrees F. Cream the butter and sugar. Add the eggs and beat well. Stir in the lemon extract Then add the baking powder, walnuts and half the flour. Mix well, then add the remaining flour. Roll the dough out on a lightly floured surface, about 1/8 inch thick. Sift sugar on top, press in with the rolling pin and cut into squares. Place on a lightly greased cookie sheet and bake until firm and just beginning to turn brown around the edges, 10 to 15 minutes depending on how thick you roll them out.

February 5, 1909

Marguerites

Mrs. H. C.

Very nice when unexpected company comes, or for school lunches.

Unsalted saltine crackers
Chocolate icing
Caramel icing
Walnut halves

RKE *I thought this recipe sounded really good, but could not figure out how to make it until I talked to a long time cracker delivery man one day in the aisle of the Fairway grocery store. Years ago soda crackers came in large squares — 16 of our standard crackers today in one square. I had read the directions thinking I would need to split a cracker and open it up. His theory, and it makes sense, is closer to the written directions to "cut a cracker in half." So to make it today, use unsalted saltines and sandwich. Ready made frostings make this even easier to prepare.*

For each Marguerite:
Take two crackers. Spread the top of one with chocolate icing. Put the second cracker on top and spread it with caramel icing and garnish with a walnut half.

Caramel Frosting:
Boil 1 cup granulated sugar with 6 tablespoons cream until waxy consistency. Flavor with vanilla and beat until cool.

Chocolate Cookies

Mrs. Walter Cerrent, Cuming County, Nebraska

1/2 cup butter
1 1/2 cups brown sugar, firmly packed
2 eggs
2 cups flour
1/2 teaspoon baking soda
1 teaspoon baking powder
1/2 cup milk
1 square unsweetened chocolate, melted

Preheat the oven to 325 degrees F. Cream the butter and sugar. Add the eggs and mix until fluffy. Add 1 cup of the flour, baking soda and baking powder and mix well. Stir in the milk and then the remaining flour. Mix well. Add the melted chocolate, and finally the nuts.

Drop small amounts of dough on well greased cookie sheets. The dough spreads to form very thin cookies. You want no more than an amount equal to a standard measuring teaspoon for each cookie. Bake until the cookies are brown around the edges and firm in the center, about 12 minutes. The cookies will puff up and then sink down as they bake. Allow them to cool on the sheet for one or two minutes to firm up before removing to a cake rack. Frost when cool.

Frosting:
2 cups sugar
2 tablespoons cocoa
1/2 cup milk
2 tablespoons corn syrup
2 tablespoons butter
1/8 teaspoon baking powder
1 teaspoon vanilla

Combine the sugar and cocoa in a 2 1/2-quart saucepan. Add the milk and corn syrup, mixing well. Cook over medium heat until the soft-ball stage is reached (236 degrees F. on a candy thermometer). Remove from the heat and stir in the remaining ingredients. Continue stirring until cool.

Oatmeal Cookies

1/2 cup butter
1/2 cup sugar
1 tablespoon milk
2 eggs
2 cups oatmeal
2 cups flour
1/2 teaspoon cinnamon
1/4 teaspoon baking soda
1/4 cup chopped raisins

Preheat the oven to 350 degrees F. Cream the butter and sugar. Add the milk and eggs and mix well. Stir in the oatmeal, flour, cinnamon and baking soda and mix well. Stir in the raisins. Roll the dough out on a well floured surface. Cut into shapes or simply use a flutted cutter and cut into squares. Place on lightly greased cookies sheets and bake until crisp, about 10 minutes.

September 26, 1921

Hermits

2 cups brown sugar, firmly packed
1 cup lard or butter
3 eggs
1/4 cup milk
1 teaspoon baking soda
1 teaspoon cloves
1 teaspoon cinnamon
1 teaspoon nutmeg
4 cups flour
2 cups chopped raisins

R E *By chopping the raisins for these Hermits, you release their flavor and texture into the body of the cookie. It really is worth the trouble. You can chop them with a knife or in the food processor, it just depends on what you want to wash up. They just need to be cut in quarters or a bit smaller.*

Preheat the oven to 350 degrees F. Cream the sugar and butter. Stir in the eggs and milk and beat until fluffy. Add the baking soda, spices and flour. Stir in the chopped raisins. Drop by teaspoons on well greased cookies sheets. Bake until firm and lightly browned, about 10 minutes.

November 7, 1936

If there are cookies in the oven, let the telephone ring.
A three-minute overdose of baking can do to a perfectly good cookie
what an overdose of strychnine did to the family cat.

Chocolate Cookies

2 eggs, separated
1 cup sugar
1/2 cup butter
1 teaspoon vanilla
2 squares melted semi-sweet chocolate
3/4 cup flour
1 cup nuts

Preheat the oven to 350 degrees F. Whip the egg whites until firm peaks form in a grease-free bowl and set aside. Cream the butter and sugar. Stir in the egg yolks, vanilla and melted chocolate. Add the flour and nuts. Drop by small teaspoons on well greased cookie sheets and smooth the dough out to make a thin cookie. Bake until firm in the center and just beginning to brown on the edges, 10 to 15 minutes. You need to watch these carefully, there is a fine line between not done and overdone.

December 19, 1924

Gingersnaps

1 cup sugar
1/2 cup butter
1/2 cup lard
1 cup molasses
3/4 teaspoon baking soda
2 teaspoons ginger
5 cups flour
1 1/2 teaspoons baking powder

Preheat the oven to 350 degrees F. In a medium to large sauce pan, combine the sugar, butter, lard and molasses. Heat over medium heat until the mixture just begins to boil. Carefully add the baking soda and stir it in. The mixture will bubble up. If there is room in the pan you can add the remaining ingredients. Or you can pour the molasses mixture over the remaining dry ingredients in a large mixing bowl. Mix and knead into a firm dough. Roll out as thin as possible on a well floured surface. Cut into shapes or squares. Place on well greased cookies sheets and bake until crisp. This could take as little as 3 minutes depending on how thin you were able to roll the dough.

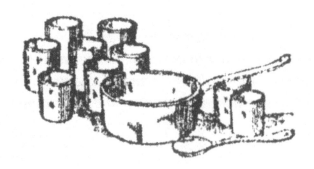

Swedish Nut Bars

1/2 cup shortening
1 1/2 cups sugar
2 eggs
1/4 cup milk
2 2/3 cups flour
2 teaspoons baking powder
1 teaspoon vanilla
1/2 teaspoon almond extract
2/3 cup chopped pecans

Preheat the oven to 350 degrees F. Cream the butter and sugar. Add the eggs and beat well. Stir in the vanilla and almond extract. Add the baking powder and half the flour, beating well. Add the milk and stir until well blended and then the remaining flour. Spread batter into a 9-inch square baking pan. Top with chopped pecans, pressing them into the dough. Bake until light brown around the edges and firm in the center, about 20 minutes. Cut into pieces about 1-inch square while still warm and in the pan. Cool and serve.

Holland Lace Cookies

1/2 cup softened butter
2 cups brown sugar, firmly packed
1/2 cup lukewarm water
1 cup flour
1 teaspoon cinnamon
1 teaspoon nutmeg
1 cup finely chopped almonds

R\E *You need a day when you have lots of time and patience to make these cookies successfully, at least I do. They need to bake until they are dark brown, but not burned and they need to cool on the sheet until they are firm, but not crisp and stuck to the pan. However, they are definitely worth the attention and care.*

Preheat the oven to 350 degrees F. Cream the butter and sugar. Add the lukewarm water, beating all the time. Quickly stir in the dry ingredients and mix well. Stir in the nuts. Drop very small amounts of this batter about 3 inches apart on well greased cookie sheets. The batter spreads and becomes lacy in texture and appearance. For the best luck, do not use more than a scant measuring teaspoon. Bake until the cookie is uniformly spread out and thin, dark brown in color — about 7 to 10 minutes. Remove cookie sheet from the oven and allow to cool 2 to 3 minutes, until the cookies are crisp, but not stuck to the pan. Carefully remove the cookies from the baking sheet with a thin-bladed spatula and allow to finish cooling on a wire rack. Store in an air-tight container. Makes about 8 dozen 2- to 3-inch cookies.

Dutch Christmas Cookies

2 cups butter
2 pounds brown sugar (5 1/2 cups), firmly packed
2 cups sour cream
2 cups molasses
2 cups corn syrup
2 teaspoons soda
1 teaspoon nutmeg
1 teaspoon allspice
1 teaspoon anise
1 teaspoon cinnamon
1 teaspoon cloves
1/4 pound raisins
1/2 pound currants
1 cup nuts
1 pound mixed dried fruits:
  dates, figs, pineapples, cherries, citron, lemon and orange peels
3 cups flour

R\E *This makes a large batch of cookies. However, the dough rolls freeze well. When you want a couple dozen remove a roll from the freezer, slice and bake.*

Cream the butter and sugar. Add molasses and corn syrup and mix well. Stir in the sour cream. Add the baking soda, spices and flour. Stir in the raisins, currants, nuts and mixed fruits. Form the dough into long rolls and set aside to chill overnight in the refrigerator. When you are ready to bake, preheat the oven to 350 degrees F. Slice cookies 1/4-inch thick or thinner and place on a lightly greased cookies sheet. Bake until the cookies are firm, but not browned, about 10 minutes.

Cream Cookies

Mrs. L. Z., Wells County, North Dakota

2 cups sugar
1 cup butter
2 eggs
1 cup sour cream
4 cups flour
1/4 teaspoon nutmeg
1 1/2 teaspoons baking soda

Preheat the oven to 350 degrees F. Cream the butter and sugar. Stir in the eggs and sour cream. Add the nutmeg, baking soda and flour. Mix well. Drop by teaspoons on well greased cookie sheets. Bake until firm in the center and just beginning to brown around the edges, 12 to 15 minutes.

Walnut Slices

Elsie R. Novak, Colfax County, Nebraska

This recipe has won first prize in two county fairs

For the crust:
1/2 cup butter
1 cup flour

For the filling:
1 1/4 cup brown sugar, firmly packed
2 tablespoons flour
1/4 teaspoon baking powder
2 eggs
1 tablespoon water
1 teaspoon vanilla
1/2 cup coconut
1 cup walnuts

For the topping:
1 1/2 cup powdered sugar
2 tablespoons melted butter
2 tablespoons orange juice
1 tablespoon lemon juice
1/2 cup walnuts

Preheat the oven to 350 degrees F. Grease a 7- x 10-inch baking dish. Make the crust layer by cutting the butter into the flour. Press the mixture into the bottom of the baking dish and bake until just beginning to brown, about 10 to 12 minutes. While the crust is baking prepare the filling. Combine the sugar, flour and baking powder in a small mixing bowl. Stir in the melted butter, eggs and vanilla. Mix well. Add the coconut and walnuts. Pour the filling over the hot crust layer and return to the oven until the filling is set and lightly puffed, 20 to 25 minutes. Allow the dessert to cool and frost with the mixture of powdered sugar, melted butter, orange and lemon juices. Sprinkle remaining walnuts on top.

Three Fudge Recipes

Cooking Method

Place the chocolate in a 2- or 3-quart saucepan. Melt over very low heat until smooth. Remove from the heat and stir in the sugar. Gradually add the water and milk, stirring until well blended and the sugar is dissolved. Return the pan to the heat and bring to a boil. Cook, stirring occasionally until the soft-ball stage is reached (236 degrees F. on a candy thermometer). Add the butter and vanilla and remove from heat. Place the pan in cold water for about 2 minutes, or until the fudge mixture begins to stick to the bottom of the pan. Remove the pan from the ice water and begin beating by hand until the fudge begins to thicken and lose its shine. Pour onto a buttered platter or tin and allow to finish setting up.

Black Fudge

2 squares chocolate
1 cup white sugar
1/4 cup molasses
1 cup brown sugar, firmly packed
1/2 cup cold water
2/3 cup milk
2 tablespoons butter
1 teaspoon vanilla

Plain Fudge

2 squares chocolate
2 cups sugar
1/2 cup cold water
2/3 cup milk
2 tablespoons butter
1 teaspoon vanilla

Additions to plain fudge include:
Nuts, marshmallows, candied cherries, raisins, or figs. Add just before pouring the cooled fudge into the pan.

Creamy Fudge

2 squares chocolate
2 cups sugar
2 tablespoons corn syrup
1/2 cup cold water
2/3 cup milk
2 tablespoons butter
1 teaspoon vanilla

Sugar Cookies

2 cups sugar
1 cup fat, I use butter
2 eggs
1 teaspoon lemon extract
5 cups flour
2 teaspoons baking powder
1/2 teaspoon baking soda
1/2 teaspoon nutmeg
1 cup cream or rich buttermilk

Preheat the oven to 350 degrees F. Cream the sugar and fat. Add the eggs and lemon extract and mix until fluffy. Stir in the baking powder, baking soda, nutmeg and half the flour. Stir in the cream or buttermilk and then the rest of the flour, mixing well after each addition. Roll the dough out to 3/8-inch thick. Cut into shapes or simply into squares. Place cookies on a lightly greased cookie sheet and bake until firm in the center and lightly browned, about 10 minutes.

Soft Ginger Cookies

Mrs. Alfred E. Ahrens, Delaware County, Iowa

1 cup sugar
1 cup butter
1 egg
1 cup molasses
1 teaspoon baking soda
4 teaspoons baking powder
1 teaspoon cinnamon
3 teaspoons ginger
5 cups flour
1 cup sour milk

Preheat the oven to 350 degrees F. Cream the butter and sugar, stir in the egg and molasses and beat well to combine. Add the baking soda, baking powder and spices along with half the flour. Stir in the milk and then the remaining flour. Drop by teaspoons onto a greased baking sheet. Bake until firm in the center, approximately 12 minutes.

Brown Cookies

Mrs. Ida Lutz, Crawford County, Iowa

1/2 cup sugar
1/2 cup butter
1/2 cup molasses
1 tablespoon vinegar
1 teaspoon ginger
1 egg
1 teaspoon baking soda
3 cups flour (you may need a bit more)

Preheat the oven to 375 degrees F. Mix this cookie dough by hand. Make certain you select a fairly large bowl, as the batter foams up. Put the first three ingredients in a microwavable bowl and heat until they melt together. Cool slightly and add the ginger and egg. Mix well. Stir in the baking soda and then the vinegar. At this point the batter will foam up and expand to about twice its volume. Stir in the flour and knead to form a non-sticky dough. Roll out very thin on a well floured surface. Sprinkle the dough with sugar and cut. Place cookies on a well greased cookie sheet and bake until firm. These bake quickly — 5 minutes — if they are very thin.

Butterscotch Cookies

Mrs. Howard M. Hansen, Cerro Gordo County, Iowa

RE *When I was growing up we used to call these icebox cookies and they were a family favorite.*

2 cups brown sugar, firmly packed
1 cup lard and butter mixed
2 beaten eggs
1 teaspoon vanilla
1 teaspoon baking soda
1 teaspoon cream of tartar
4 cups flour
1 cup almonds, or any other kind of nuts

Cream the sugar and butter. Stir in the eggs and vanilla. Mix in the baking soda and cream of tartar. Blend in the flour. Stir in the nuts. Form the dough into two rolls, wrap in plastic wrap or foil, and refrigerate overnight. When you are ready to bake, preheat the oven to 350 degrees F. Slice 1/4 inch thick cookies from the roll and place on lightly greased cookie sheets. Bake until firm and lightly browned, about 12 minutes.

April 14, 1916
The Child's Curiosity

There is, I think, no surer or better way to satisfy a child's curiosity than offer to explore with him, and instead of merely answering questions to help him find out. In this way you teach him by your very companionship and without one word that would lead him to think he is being taught the habit of satisfying his own curiosity.

For children old enough to use them, there should be a few good reference books. Care should be taken to teach them the use of these books. Not by precept, but by example. The child who sees his parents turning to some book of authority for the disputed answer to a question will take a certain pride in consulting the books himself.

His book shelf should have on it a few good books on the natural sciences. A good book on astronomy, on geology, on botany, on natural history, on chemistry, a good book of maps, one or two histories, these are worth their weight in gold to him. When, with your help, he has learned as a tiny fellow to take a pride in trying to satisfy his own curiosity, these books will answer many questions for him.

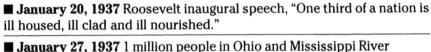

■ **January 20, 1937** Roosevelt inaugural speech, "One third of a nation is ill housed, ill clad and ill nourished."

■ **January 27, 1937** 1 million people in Ohio and Mississippi River basins homeless in flood.

■ **February 16, 1937** DuPont invents nylon.

■ **May 12, 1937** George VI coronated.

■ **May 6, 1937** Hindenberg airship blows up in Lakehurst, New Jersey.

■ **July 18, 1937** Amelia Earhart lost.

■ **November 1, 1937** Home televisions are demonstrated.

■ **January 1, 1938** 7.9 million American jobless. Total employment — 44 million.

■ **March 14, 1938** Nazis take over Austria.

■ **June 25, 1938** Congress sets minimum wage at 40 cents per hour.

■ **August 13, 1938** *Wallaces' Farmer* article describes *"The Story of Hybrid Corn" "Hybrid corn brings to agriculture for the first time the industrial technique of standardized parts and mass production. It is based on the fact that certain characters can be fixed in a corn plant by inbreeding and that after that the crossing of these inbreds in a certain way will always produce the same results."*

■ **October 30, 1938** Orson Wells broadcasts drama, "War of the Worlds."

■ **October 5, 1938** Hitler invades Sudatenland, Czechoslovakia.

■ **March 15, 1939** Nazis in Poland.

■ **April 30, 1939** New York World's Fair opens.

■ **September 30, 1939** Britain and France declare war on Germany.

CHAPTER 18

Cakes

March 19, 1935

It was an exciting business testing out the recipes
in the recent *Wallaces' Farmer* cakes and cookie contest.
And we've eaten so much extraordinarily good baked
stuff that we wouldn't mind a slice of "fallen" cake
for a change. It does have a nice, chewy quality, you
know — and isn't it filling!

Seriously, tho, the one fact which does creep to the
top of a recipe contest such as the one just closed is this:
The "sprinkle of this and a dash of that" sort of cook
may occasionally contribute a praiseworthy dish to
a neighborhood gathering. But rarely does he have a
praiseworthy — or shall we say followable — recipe.
"Pinches" and "handfuls" are personal matters.
Occasionally they may turn out delectable dishes for
the woman who "knows her own," but they are tricky
measurements for the neighbor who wants to beat
up your particular brand of Walnut Spice Cake
in her mixing bowl.

Layer Cake

Mrs. H. F. Benedict, Floyd County, Iowa

> *3 eggs*
> *1 1/2 cups sugar*
> *2 teaspoons baking powder*
> *2 cups flour*
> *1 cup cream*

Preheat the oven to 350 degrees F. Beat the eggs and sugar until they are thick and lemon colored. Stir in the baking soda and 1 cup flour. Add the cream and mix well. Blend in the remaining cup flour. Divide the batter between 2 greased and floured round baking pans. Bake until the cake is firm in the center, about 30 minutes. Cool on wire racks for about 5 minutes in the pans and then carefully turn the cake out of the pans and allow to finish cooling. Fill between layers with Lemon Filling.

> **Lemon Filling:**
> *1 cup sugar*
> *2 tablespoons flour*
> *1/2 cup water*
> *Juice and rind of 2 lemons*
> *1 teaspoon vinegar*
> *1 egg, well beaten*

In a small saucepan, combine the sugar and flour. Add the water, lemon juice and rind and vinegar and mix well. Stir in the well beaten egg. Simmer the mixture over low heat until it is thick. Set aside to cool, stirring from time to time so that it does not form a hard skin on top.

Great Filling for Chocolate Cake

> *6 prunes*
> *6 figs*
> *3 cups confectioner's sugar (approximately)*

Put the prunes and figs in a microwaveable bowl. Pour water over them. Cover the bowl with plastic wrap and microwave until the fruit is very soft. Drain the water, pat dry and process the fruit in a blender or processor until smooth. Stir in enough confectioner's sugar to make a thick paste.

May Cake

Mrs. L.L.B.

RE *These small cakes are wonderful. They almost melt in your mouth.*

2 egg whites
1 egg
1/2 cup sugar
1/2 cup flour
1 teaspoon baking powder
1/4 cup melted butter
1 teaspoon lemon extract

Preheat the oven to 350 degrees F. Beat the egg whites and egg, gradually adding the sugar about a tablespoon at a time. Sift the flour and baking powder together and fold into the batter. Fold in the melted butter and lemon extract. Pour the batter into a greased and floured 9-inch square cake pan. Bake until firm in the center, about 15 to 20 minutes. Cool in the pan for 10 minutes then carefully remove and finish cooling on a cake rack. When completely cool, cut into 1-inch squares and frost on all sides with a lemon glaze.

Lemon Glaze:
4 tablespoons melted butter
1 teaspoon lemon extract
3/4 cup confectioner's sugar

Combine ingredients and spoon a very thin layer over the squares of cake, coating all sides. Repeat after the first layer has set.

Chocolate Cake

1 ounce sweet German baking chocolate
1 tablespoon butter
6 egg whites
1/2 cup butter
1 cup sugar
1 1/2 cups flour
1 teaspoon baking powder
1 teaspoon vanilla
1/2 cup milk

Preheat the oven to 350 degrees F. Heat the chocolate and butter in the microwave at half power for 1 minute, or until the chocolate is melted. Whip the egg whites until stiff in a clean, dry bowl, and set aside. Cream the butter and sugar. Add the vanilla and melted chocolate, mixing well. Stir in half the flour and the baking powder and mix well. Add the milk and then the remaining flour, mixing well after each addition. Fold in the beaten egg whites. The batter is quite stiff, but it will work. Pour the batter into 2 well greased 8-inch cake pans. Bake until the cake is firm in the center, about 25 minutes.

Coconut Cake

1 cup sugar
1 cup flour
1 teaspoon baking powder
2 tablespoons melted butter
1/2 cup milk
1 egg

Topping:
2 tablespoons sugar
1/2 cup coconut

R E *This simple cake is perfect to take on a picnic. The coconut topping has the sweetness of frosting, but is much easier to carry. The cake is as good the second or third day as it is the first.*

Preheat the oven to 350 degrees F. Combine the sugar, flour and baking powder in a medium sized mixing bowl. In a small bowl or measuring cup, combine the melted butter, milk and egg and mix well. Using a large spoon, stir the milk mixture into the flour mixture until just blended. Spread this batter into a greased and floured 9-inch round cake pan. Sprinkle the 2 tablespoons sugar and 1/2 cup coconut over the top. Bake until the cake is firm in the center and the coconut is just browned, about 20 to 25 minutes.

Gingerbread

"Another Reader"

1/2 cup sugar
1/2 cup butter
1 cup molasses
1 cup boiling water
2 teaspoons baking soda
3 cups flour
1 teaspoon cloves
1 teaspoon cinnamon
1 teaspoon ginger
2 eggs

R E *Most recipes of this period, and earlier, instruct the cook to dissolve the baking soda in hot water before adding it to the batter. This step starts the soda action. I'm suggesting just beginning this preliminary mixing action on top of the batter.*

Preheat the oven to 350 degrees F. Cream the butter and sugar. Stir in the molasses. Sprinkle the baking soda on top of the batter and pour the boiling water over. Stir in quickly. Add the flour and spices, mixing well. Stir in the eggs. Pour the batter into a well greased and floured pan. Bake until the center is firm, 45 to 50 minutes.

Christmas Cake

2 cups sugar
3/4 cup butter
1 cup milk
2 1/2 cups flour
2 1/2 teaspoons baking powder
5 egg whites
1 teaspoon almond extract

Filling:
1 cup walnut meats
1/2 cup figs
1/2 cup raisins
1/4 cup candied cherries

RKE *The original frosting for this cake is a version of the boiled sugar, beaten egg white icing common during the era. A plain white confectioner's sugar icing works just fine.*

Process or chop fine the nuts and fruit into 1/16 of an inch pieces. Mix with a 1/4 cup white icing to bind.

Yellow Angel Food Cake

1 1/2 cups sifted flour
1 teaspoon baking powder
1/2 teaspoon cream of tartar
4 eggs, separated
1 1/3 cup sugar
1 tablespoon cold water
1/2 cup boiling water
1 teaspoon vanilla

RKE *This cake is a bit more substantial than the usual egg-white-only angel food. The flavor mellows a bit. I think it tastes better the second day.*

Preheat the oven to 325 degrees F. Combine the sifted flour, baking powder and cream of tartar and sift three more times. Set aside. Separate the eggs. Whip the egg whites until stiff in a grease-free, non-plastic bowl and set aside. Beat the egg yolks, sugar and cold water until the sugar is dissolved and the mixture looks very light, about 5 minutes. With the mixer running, gradually add the boiling water. Stir in the sifted dry ingredients a little at a time. Add the vanilla and mix well. Fold in the stiffly beaten egg whites. Pour the batter into an ungreased angel food cake pan and bake until firm, about 50 to 60 minutes. Turn the pan upside down to cool completely before carefully cutting around the side to release the cake from the pan.

February 14, 1931

Applesauce Cake

Mrs. Leo F. Bedard, Black Hawk County, Iowa

1 cup sugar
1/2 cup butter
1 1/2 cup applesauce, sweetened chunky home-style is good
1 tablespoon hot water
2 teaspoons baking soda
2 cups flour
1 teaspoon cinnamon
1 teaspoon cloves
1 cup raisins
1/2 cup nutmeats

For the topping, combine:
1 teaspoon cinnamon
3 tablespoons sugar

Preheat the oven to 350 degrees F. Cream the butter and sugar and add the applesauce. Put the baking soda into the batter and pour the hot water directly over it. Blend well. Add the flour and other spices, then the raisins and nuts. Spray an 8 x 15-inch baking pan with non-stick spray. Pour in the batter and sprinkle with the cinnamon and sugar mixture. Bake for 25 minutes or until the cake is beginning to pull away from the sides and is firm in the middle.

May 23, 1932

Ginger Coconut Cake

1/2 cup butter
1/2 cup brown sugar, firmly packed
1/2 cup molasses
2 eggs
1 teaspoon cinnamon
1 teaspoon ginger
1 1/2 cups flour
1/4 cup cold water
2 cups coconut

Preheat oven to 325 degrees F. Cream the butter and sugar. Stir in the molasses and eggs and beat well. Combine the dry ingredients and add half to the creamed mixture. Blend in the water and then the remaining dry ingredients and coconut. Pour batter into a well greased 9-inch square pan. Bake until the cake is firm in the center and slightly pulled away from the side.

Marble Cake

Ruth Quinn, Washington County, Nebraska

Instead of simply adding chocolate to a portion of the cake batter to make the marble part, this recipe calls for making two different batters. It is well worth the extra dirty mixing bowl.

Dark Part:
1/2 cup butter
1 cup sugar
1/2 cup molasses
2 cups flour
1/2 teaspoon salt
1 teaspoon baking soda
1/2 teaspoon each ground nutmeg, cinnamon and cloves
1/2 cup sour milk
4 egg yolks

Cream the butter and sugar, add the molasses and mix well. Sift the dry ingredients and add alternately with the sour milk. Last add the well beaten egg yolks.

White Part:
1/2 cup butter
1 cup sugar
2 cups flour
2 teaspoons baking powder
1/2 cup milk
4 egg whites
1 teaspoon vanilla

Preheat the oven to 350 degrees F. Cream the butter and sugar. Sift the dry ingredients together and add to the creamed mixture alternately with the milk, beating thoroughly after each addition. Fold in the stiffly beaten egg whites and vanilla.

Grease and flour two 9-inch round cake pans. Drop in the white cake batter in lumps around the pan. Fill in between with large spoonfuls of the dark batter. Run a knife thorough the batters to blend them slightly to create the marble look. Bake until the cake is firm in the center and slightly pulled away from the sides, about 30 minutes. Frost with a caramel or vanilla frosting.

Lightning Chocolate Cake

Mrs. C.W. Zuinn, Polk County, Iowa

> *1 1/2 cups flour*
> *1 cup sugar*
> *1/2 cup cocoa*
> *3 teaspoons baking powder*
> *1 cup milk*
> *1 egg*
> *1/2 cup melted butter*

Preheat the oven to 350 degrees F. Sift together the flour, sugar, cocoa and baking powder into a large mixing bowl. In a small bowl combine the milk, egg and melted butter into a smooth mixture. Pour the liquid ingredients into the dry ones and, using a spoon, mix them well. Pour into two greased and floured 8- or 9-inch round cake pans. Bake until the center is firm and the layers are just beginning to pull away from the sides, about 20 minutes. Frost with maple icing

Spiced Coffee Cake

Mrs. Frank Giles, Logan County, Illinois

> *2 cups hot coffee*
> *1 cup raisins*
> *1 cup currants*
> *1/2 cup shorting or butter*
> *1 1/2 cups sugar*
> *3 eggs*
> *2 teaspoons cinnamon*
> *1 teaspoon ginger*
> *3 1/2 teaspoons baking powder*
> *3 1/2 cups flour*

Preheat the oven to 350 degrees F. Combine the hot coffee with the raisins and currants and set aside for the fruit to plump. Cream the shortening and sugar. Add the eggs and mix well. Stir in the cinnamon, ginger, baking powder and half the flour. Add the coffee and fruit and mix well. Stir in the remaining flour. Pour the batter into well greased cake pans and bake until the center is firm and the edges are just beginning to pull away from the sides, 25 to 35 minutes.

This recipe makes: 2 loaves
4 small loaves
2 8- or 9-inch squares or
2 9-inch round layers or
1 10 x 13-inch cake

Lemon Sponge Cake

LuLu M. Stevens, Cottonwood County, Minnesota

3 eggs, separated
1 lemon, juice and rind
6 tablespoons cake flour
1 cup sugar
1 1/2 cups milk

As this cake bakes the batter separates into a light cake layer floating on top of a custard. This is a very light version of this dessert. It is best baked in a straight-sided casserole or soufflé dish.

Preheat the oven to 350 degrees F. Beat the egg whites until stiff in a grease-free bowl and set aside. Beat together the egg yolks and lemon rind. Combine the sugar and cake flour and add to the egg mixture. With the mixer running, stir in the milk. Fold the batter into the stiffly beaten egg whites. Pour the batter into a 2-quart soufflé dish. Place this dish in a pan of warm water and set in the oven. Bake until the layers are separated and the cake layer is lightly browned, about 25 to 30 minutes. Cool and serve with whipped cream.

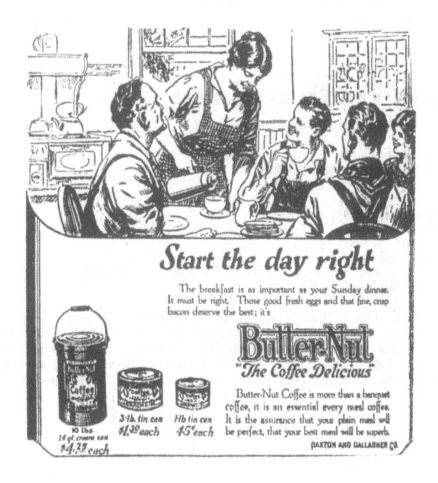

Devil's Food Cake

    1 cup grated baker's chocolate, 4 squares
    1 cup light brown sugar, firmly packed
    1/2 cup milk
    1 cup dark brown sugar, firmly packed
    1/2 cup butter
    3 egg yolks
    1 teaspoon baking soda
    2 cups flour
    1/2 cup milk

Combine the grated chocolate and light brown sugar in a small sauce pan. Add the milk. Simmer over low heat until the chocolate is melted. Set aside to cool slightly.

Preheat the oven to 350 degrees F. Cream the butter and dark brown sugar. Stir in the egg yolks. Add the baking soda and half the flour. Stir in the milk and cooled chocolate mixture. Blend in the remaining cup flour. Pour the batter into a 10 x 13 pan that has been greased and floured. Bake until the cake is firm in the center and just beginning to pull away from the sides, about 50 minutes.

Cocoa Feather Cake

Mrs. John Konken, Chickasaw County, Iowa

    1/2 cup butter
    2 cups brown sugar, firmly packed
    3 eggs
    1/3 cup cocoa
    1 teaspoon cinnamon
    1/2 cup warm water
    2 cups flour
    1/2 cup sour milk
      made by adding 1 tablespoon vinegar to a scant 1/2 cup milk
    1 rounded teaspoon baking soda

Preheat the oven to 350 degrees F. Grease and flour or spray with non-stick spray, a 9- x 13-inch baking pan. Cream the butter and sugar. Add the eggs and beat until the mixture is fluffy. Add the cocoa and cinnamon and then the hot water, mixing well. Stir in 1 cup of the flour with the baking soda. Then mix in the sour milk, followed by the remaining flour. Pour into the prepared pan and bake until the cake is firm in the center and slightly pulled away from the sides, about 1 hour.

Blitz torte

Verna M Saltenberg, Scott County, Iowa

I am sending you this recipe because my family likes it so well and because it is easy to prepare. It makes a light dessert that is different and delightful.

For the cake layer:
1/2 cup butter
1/2 cup sugar
4 egg yolks
1/3 cup milk
1 cup flour
1 teaspoon baking powder
1 teaspoon vanilla

For the meringue layer:
4 egg whites
1 cup sugar
1/2 cup slivered almonds

For the cream filling:
2 tablespoons flour
1 egg
1 1/4 cups boiling milk
1 tablespoon sugar
1 teaspoon vanilla

RKE This recipe looks much more complicated than it is. You make a cake layer and top it with the meringue and just before serving, spread the cream filling between the layers. You end up with a five layer dessert with the ease of a standard cake. Mrs. Saltenberg is right, it is light and delightful. The cream filling must be added just before serving, as it has a tendency to melt the meringue on the bottom layer. Once assembled, it is not a good keeper, but it is so good you'll eat it all up anyway.

Preheat the oven to 300 degrees F. Grease and flour or spray with non-stick spray two 9-inch cake pans. Non-stick pans work well for this recipe.

Crack 4 eggs and separate the yolks and whites. First make the cake batter by creaming the butter and sugar. Add the egg yolks and beat until mixed. Combine the flour and baking powder. Stir half of it into the batter, then the milk and finally the remaining flour. Stir in the vanilla. Divide this thick batter between the 2 pans, spreading it to cover the bottoms.

Now make the meringue topping. In a grease-free bowl with grease-free beaters, whip the egg whites until they begin to stiffen. With the mixer running, add the sugar gradually and continue beating until soft peaks are formed. Spread the meringue over the two cake layers and sprinkle slivered almonds on top.

Bake the layers for 25 minutes or until the meringue is stiff and just beginning to brown. Cool in the pans, but loosen the cake as it cools, by flipping them gently. While the cake is baking, make the cream filling. Bring the milk to a boil in a medium saucepan. Beat the 2 tablespoons of flour into the egg in a heat-proof bowl. Gradually add the boiling milk to the egg flour mixture, stirring constantly. Return this to the saucepan, add the sugar and continue cooking over medium heat, stirring constantly, until the sauce is thick. Stir in the vanilla and set aside to cool. Stir from time to time as it cools to keep a skin from forming on the top. To serve: carefully slip one layer out of the pan and put on a serving plate, spread the cooled filling on it, top with the second layer.

CHAPTER 19

Pies

The Plant for Pie Making
April 13, 1939

The bride was moved by the urge for rhubarb pies which comes to books in the spring. "But why," asked the friend who had dropped in to the very new kitchen, "are you rolling out a crust two feet long?" Blithely the bride responded, "It was the shortest rhubarb I could find."

Tried and True
Pie Crust

Enough for 2 8- or 9-inch pie crusts.

RKE *This is the pie crust recipe I have always used. My mother learned it when she was in 7th grade. This quantity makes enough for a 2 crust 8- or 9-inch pie.*

1 1/2 cups flour
1/2 cup shortening, butter or lard or a mixture
4 – 6 tablespoons ice water

Cut the shortening into the flour. Gently add 4 tablespoons ice water, more if needed, and mix with a fork until well blended and the dough forms a ball. Cover with plastic wrap and set aside in a cool place to rest for 15 minutes. Roll out on a lightly floured surface.

October 6, 1899

Green Tomato Pie

Enough green tomatoes to make 4 cups when sliced thin
3 tablespoons sugar
1/8 teaspoon nutmeg
2 tablespoons flour
1 tablespoon butter
2 tablespoons vinegar
1 teaspoon water
Pastry for a 9-inch two crust pie.

Preheat the oven to 425 degrees F. Peel and cut the green tomatoes into thin circular slices. Arrange them in the pie crust. Mix the sugar, nutmeg and flour and sprinkle over the tomatoes. Dot with the butter. Combine the vinegar and water and gently pour over the tomatoes. Cover with top crust, cut a few slits to allow steam to escape. Place in the oven and bake for 15 minutes. Lower the heat to 350 degrees F. and continue baking until the crust is golden and the filling is tender, about 35 more minutes.

July 18, 1918
Things we have forgotten

It is not so much the information we get — many of them simply emphasize what we already know — but the reminder that home-keeping and house-keeping problems are of vital importance and are worth the best we have to offer. Any problem of the home which is successfully solved by the house-keeper is of vital importance and should be preserved in an accessible form for posterity.
"Mother has forgotten more than I know," a teacher of domestic science laughingly said. But isn't it too bad that mother should have allowed this kind of information to be lost?

Centennial Pie

Esther Thomas

R&E If you like molasses, this is the pie for you. A small slice is plenty, especially if you serve it with whipped or ice cream.

Topping:
1/2 cup flour
1/4 cup sugar
1/4 cup butter

For the Filling:
1/2 cup molasses
1/2 cup water
1/4 teaspoon baking soda
Cinnamon to sprinkle
1 8-inch pie shell

Preheat the oven to 350 degrees F. Make the topping first by mixing together the flour and sugar. Cut in the butter with a pastry cutter or fork until the mixture resembles corn meal. Set this mixture aside. Combine the molasses, water and baking soda. Pour this into the unbaked pie shell. Sprinkle the topping evenly over the molasses layer and dust the pie with cinnamon. Bake until the filling is firm in the center, about 30 minutes.

Molasses Pie

For special occasions, it never fails to please.

R&E Here's another Molasses Pie. If you like walnuts, this one would be especially nice on a chilly winter evening.

3 eggs
1 cup molasses
1 cup milk
1 tablespoon melted butter
1 cup walnut meats (Pecans would be good also)
Unbaked 9-inch pie shell

Preheat oven to 425 degrees F. Prick the pie crust all over with a fork or fill with pie weights. Place in oven and bake for 10 minutes. Remove from oven and lower temperature to 325 degrees F. While the pie shell is baking, prepare the filling. Beat the eggs until light, stir in the molasses, milk and melted butter and mix well. Stir in the nuts. Pour the filling into the partially baked pie shell, and return to the 325 degree F. oven. Bake until the filling becomes firm, about 25 minutes.

Montgomery Pie

Mrs. W.K.M.

R\E *The original recipe indicated this was the quantity for two pies, but it nicely fills a modern 9-inch pie plate.*

Topping:
3/4 cup sugar
1 egg
6 tablespoons very soft butter
1/2 cup buttermilk
1/2 teaspoon baking soda

Filling:
Juice and rind of one lemon
1/2 cup sugar
1/4 cup molasses
1/2 cup water
1 9–inch unbaked pie shell.

Preheat oven to 350 degrees F. Make the topping first and set aside. Cream the butter and sugar. Stir in the egg and mix well. Add the buttermilk and baking soda. Make the filling by mixing the lemon rind and juice with the sugar and adding the molasses and water. Pour the molasses filling in the pie shell. Drop the topping evenly over the top by tablespoons. Bake until the pie is firm in the center, about 35 minutes.

Montgomery Pie

R\E *Another version of the Montgomery Pie. This one has a cake-like filling in the pie crust.*

1 cup sugar
2 tablespoons butter
2 eggs separated
2 tablespoons flour
1 cup milk
1 lemon, juice and rind
2 egg whites
8-inch unbaked pie crust

Preheat oven to 425 degrees F. Cream the sugar and butter. Stir in the egg yolks, and flour. Add the milk and lemon juice and rind. Beat the egg whites until stiff in a clean, grease-free bowl. Fold the batter into the egg whites. Pour this into the pie crust. Bake for 15 minutes at 425 degrees F. then lower the temperature to 350 degrees F. and bake until the filling is set.

Lemon Pie

R\E *This lemon pie makes its own meringue-like topping.*

2 eggs, separated
1 cup sugar
3 tablespoons flour
Juice and rind of one lemon
1 cup milk
1 9-inch unbaked pie shell

Preheat oven to 350 degrees F. Beat the egg whites until stiff in a perfectly clean, grease-free bowl and set aside. Combine the sugar and flour. Stir in the lemon juice and rind and the egg yolks. Stir in the milk until the mixture is smooth. Pour a little of the lemon mixture into the egg whites and fold in gently. When it is thoroughly mixed, add the remaining lemon mixture and fold until completely blended. Bake until the filling is set, about 40 minutes.

Prize Winning Lemon Pie

1 cup sugar
2 tablespoons butter
4 egg yolks (reserve the whites)
Juice and rind of 3 lemons
2 tablespoons flour
4 tablespoons cream
1 9-inch unbaked pie shell

Preheat the oven to 425 degrees F. Cream the butter, sugar and egg yolks. Stir in the lemon juice and rind. Blend in the flour and cream and pour into the pie shell. Bake for 15 minutes at 425 degrees F. then lower the heat to 350 degrees F. and bake until the filling is set, about 30 minutes. Allow the pie to cool slightly and cover with meringue.

For the meringue:
4 reserved egg whites
8 tablespoons sifted powdered sugar

Lower the oven heat to 325 degrees F. Beat the egg whites until foamy. Continue beating while adding the sugar a tablespoon at a time. Beat until the whites form stiff peaks. Spread this meringue over the pie and return to the oven for 20 minutes, until the meringue is set and lightly browned.

Butterscotch Pie

1 cup brown sugar, firmly packed
1 1/2 tablespoons flour
1 1/2 cups hot water
2 egg yolks, well beaten
1 tablespoon butter
1 teaspoon vanilla
1 8-inch baked pie crust

Combine the brown sugar and flour in a 2-quart sauce pan. Stir in the hot water mixing until the dry ingredients are dissolved. Begin heating over medium heat. Add a little of the hot mixture to the egg yolks to bring them up to heat, then stir them into the pan. Cook, stirring frequently especially once the mixture begins to thicken, until the mixture is very thick. Cool slightly. Stir in the butter and vanilla. Pour into baked pie shell. You may cover this with a meringue or whipped cream. Store in the refrigerator.

Sour Cream Raisin Pie

1 cup raisins
1 cup sugar
3/4 cup commercial sour cream
1/4 cup sweet cream
1 egg
1 tablespoon flour
1/2 teaspoon cinnamon
1/2 teaspoon allspice
1 8-inch baked pie shell

Combine the raisins and sugar in the food processor and pulse until the raisins are chopped. Or you may chop them by hand. Combine in a 2-quart sauce pan with the sour cream, sweet cream, egg and flour. Mix well. Heat over low heat until the mixture is thickened. Stir in the spices and pour into the pie shell. Set aside to cool and firm for several hours. Serve with whipped cream or a meringue topping.

Cottage Cheese Pie

4 tablespoons cream
1 1/2 cups cottage cheese (24-ounce package)
1/2 cup sugar
2 eggs
1 tablespoon lemon juice and the rind from the lemon
1/2 cup crushed pineapple (from an 8-ounce can, drained)
9-inch pie crust with fluted edge, unbaked
1/2 cup currants, optional

Preheat the oven to 350 degrees F. Combine the cream and cottage cheese in a blender or food processor and process until very smooth. Combine with the rest of the ingredients and mix well. The original recipe included the 1/2 cup currants. I prefer the pie without them — at least in the summer. Pour filling into unbaked pie crust and bake until it is firm in the center, about 45 minutes. Cool and then chill. Serve with whipped cream.

February 15, 1936

Not so long ago a famous American cook said, "The history of a great democracy, and a great American dish, is inextricably bound together. American statesmen invented democracy: American cooks invented pie. Both have had their ups and downs. Both have been mishandled by poor craftsmen, and improved upon by genius. And both stand today at the top of their own class — at least so stands pie."

Holiday Pie

1 1/2 cups whole berry cranberry sauce
1 cup seeded chopped dates
1/3 cup broken nutmeats
2 tablespoons sugar
1 tablespoon flour
1 tablespoon butter
Crust for a 2 crust 8-inch pie

Preheat the oven to 425 degrees F. Pour the cranberry sauce into the bottom crust. Arrange the dates and nuts over the top. Sprinkle with sugar and flour and dot with butter. Make a lattice crust on the top and bake until the crust is golden and the filling is bubbly, about 20 minutes.

February 14, 1931

Date Pie

For special occasions I like to surprise the children with date pie. This makes a very delicious dessert.

1 box pitted dates, 8 ounce
1 cup sugar
1 cup water
3 tablespoons flour
1 tablespoon cold water, or more
Juice of 1/2 lemon
1 tablespoon butter
1 8-inch baked pie shell

Combine the dates, sugar and water in a saucepan or microwaveable bowl. Cook over medium heat, or at half power until the dates are very soft and can be beaten into a smooth pulp. Mix the flour with about 1 tablespoon of cold water to make a paste. Stir this paste into the date pulp. Add the lemon juice and butter and cook over very low heat until the mixture is very thick. Pour into the baked pie shell, chill and serve with whipped cream

February 15, 1930

The teacher asked her class to explain the word
"bachelor" and was very much amused when a little
girl answered: "A bachelor is a very happy man."
"Where did you learn that?" asked the teacher.
"Father told me."

Caramel Date Pie

1 cup milk, divided
1/2 cup diced dates
3 tablespoons cornstarch
2 eggs
1/4 cup brown sugar, firmly packed
1 8-inch baked pie shell

In a double boiler, scald 3/4 cup of the milk and dates together. Mix the cornstarch with the remaining milk and add to the date mixture. Cook until thickened, stirring frequently. Mix the eggs, brown sugar and vanilla. Add to the date mixture and cook for one more minute after that addition. Pour the mixture into a cooled, baked pie shell. Chill and serve with whipped cream.

Apple Cream Pie

For the pie filling:
3/4 cup brown sugar, firmly packed
2 tablespoons flour
1 cup sour cream
1 egg, lightly beaten
1/2 teaspoon vanilla
2 cups chopped apples (2 – 4 apples)
1 9-inch deep dish pie shell, unbaked

For the crumble topping:
1/3 cup sugar
1/3 cup flour
1 teaspoon cinnamon
1/4 cup butter

Preheat oven to 425 degrees F. Make the pie filling: Combine the brown sugar, flour, sour cream, egg and vanilla. Mix well. Peel and chop the apples into 1/4-inch dice and fold into the filling. Pour into the pie shell. Bake 15 minutes and lower heat to 325 degrees F. Cook 35 to 45 minutes longer, or until the filling is almost done. Test by inserting a knife into the center of the pie. The filling should just barely stick to the knife. Then top with the crumble topping and return to the oven for 10 more minutes.

Make the crumble topping while the pie is baking. Combine the sugar, flour and cinnamon and cut in the butter with a pastry cutter or in the food processor until the mixture looks like oatmeal.

Acknowledgements

This book is the work of countless named and
unknown writers. Where the identity of a columnist or recipe
author is known, I've identified the writer, but many of these
pieces from 50 years of *Wallaces' Farmer* are presented without
an author's name. I have been delighted to work with this
material over the past two years.

Many thanks to the *Wallaces Farmer* family for cheerful
help with this project — Frank Holdmeyer, JoAnn Alumbaugh,
Rod Swboda all provided quick and thoughtful answers to
hurried questions. This project would not be possible without
the support of Sara Wyant at Farm Progress along with
Rosemary Schimek and Dottie Rovner.

Thanks also to Kent Newman of the Wallace House
Foundation (www.wallace.org) and Diane Weiland of the
Henry A. Wallace Country Life Center
(www.henryawallacecenter.com), who provided insights into
the Wallace family. Visit their websites if you would like more
information about this remarkable American family.
Virginia Wadsley, who is researching a
book on the contributions of the Wallace family women,
generously shared a copy of Josephine Wallace's
cookbook and other information.

Al Casciato has worked his incomparable magic,
designing pages of impact, beauty and clarity. Destiny Justic
Scott edited my manuscript with tact and skill and improved
it. I can not thank you both enough.

Thanks to all the friends and family — son John, daughter
Liz and her family John, Justin and Jack for helping me test all
these recipes. Finally a heartfelt thank you to my husband
John for continuing encouragement and cheerful sampling,
even for "just one more recipe" featuring cabbage.

Index

Ordering Cookbooks

Our American Farm Heritage Cookbook series currently includes two great books that are a cooking asset for your kitchen and make thoughtful gifts for any cookbook collector, history buff, antique collector, or anyone interested in expanding their recipe selection. These cookbooks give you unlimited inspiration to plan menus or prepare special treats with authentic historical flare.

Each book presents stories and recipes excerpted from the pages of our magazines to give you historical vignettes of authentic culture and perspectives of the times.

 A Prairie Kitchen presents recipes and interesting items originally published from 1841 to 1900 and gives you insight into the foods, flavors, charm and grit of pre-modern prairie farm life. Laminated full color cover, 7" x 10" softbound, 180 pages.

 Hearts & Homes blends recipes, poems and colorful stories selected from *Wallaces Farmer* magazine editions published 1895 to 1939. Step into the past and experience the tastes, charm and wisdom of this era's heartland farm life. Laminated full color cover, 7" x 10" softbound, 244 pages.

Order cookbooks from the publisher—please contact us for pricing (bulk discounts available).

By Mail:
Farm Progress Companies
191 South Gary avenue
Carol Steam, IL 60188

By Telephone:
(800) 441-1410
or
(630) 690-5600

By E-Mail:
sales@farmprogress.com

Additional cookbook information may be obtained from our Web site (search keyword "cookbook"):
www.FarmProgress.com

Printed in the USA
CPSIA information can be obtained
at www.ICGtesting.com
JSHW052016140824
68134JS00027B/2495